DEATH DOES NOT EXIST

ALSO BY STÉPHANE ALLIX

The Test: Incredible Proof of the Afterlife
When I Was Someone Else: The Incredible True Story of Past Life Connection

IN FRENCH

La petite cuillère de Schéhérazade
Carnets afghans, with Natacha Calestrémé
Afghanistan, aux sources de la drogue
Afghanistan, visions d'un partisan
Extraterrestres: l'enquête
La mort n'est pas une terre étrangère
Après . . . Quand l'au-delà nous fait signe
Entre ombre et lumière, Itinéraire d'un reporter
Nos âmes oubliées
Un fantôme sur le divan
La Montagne magique
La Preuve

DEATH DOES NOT EXIST

WHAT SCIENCE AND SPIRITUALITY CAN TEACH US ABOUT THE AFTERLIFE

STÉPHANE ALLIX

TRANSLATED FROM THE FRENCH BY GRETCHEN SCHMID

HARPERONE
An Imprint of HarperCollins*Publishers*

HarperCollins books may be purchased for educational, business, or sales promotional use. For information, please email the Special Markets Department at SPsales@harpercollins.com.

hc.com

Originally published as *La mort n'existe pas* in France in 2023 by HarperCollins France.

First HarperOne hardcover published in 2026.

Library of Congress Cataloging-in-Publication Data has been applied for.

ISBN 978-0-06-342804-1

Printed in the United States of America

26 27 28 29 30 LBC 5 4 3 2 1

To life

Dying is absolutely safe.

RAM DASS

Contents

1

Luna

You're standing silently in front of the pale wood coffin. I can see so much confusion in your questioning eyes, dearest daughter of mine. How could a three-and-a-half-year-old understand anything about death? You can sense the suffering all around you: the subtle distress, faces frozen in shock, eyes glazed over, bodies hesitant and clumsy in their movements. Every now and then, one of us talks to you. We want to reassure you with a tender, awkward gesture or a few words spoken in a familiar voice, but in those familiar voices, you can sense an inflection or emotion that's unfamiliar, incomprehensible, almost threatening in its foreignness.

You're alone and impassive among a group of adults whose intentions, for the first time in your life, you can't quite seem to make out. It's about as reassuring as a sack of unexploded grenades. Not daring to open your mouth, you observe these adults with their invisible wounds and suppressed tsunamis of emotion.

Death has just entered your life.

Our attempts at reassurance are completely at odds with the atmosphere around you: strange and heavy, a concentrate of present tense, a bottomless pit from which no one has managed to escape. All the levity is gone; no one's playing anymore.

You don't understand. How could you? What is there to understand? Your uncle is dead. Killed in an accident several days ago. You'll never see him again. He's abruptly gone from your life, but right now, you aren't able to comprehend what that means. Have you guessed that the man you knew—the one who was playing with you just several weeks back—is here, forever locked away in this box, never to move again? To a child, death isn't real. The tall, strong, eccentric guy who taught you to climb trees, who asked you strange questions that burned with a fundamental urgency, the man who spun you around in the air and made you burst out laughing—*you'll never see him again.* You don't know it yet, because right now, in these early, innocent years of your life, you live entirely in the moment. But in the decades to come, you'll forget his face, his gestures, his laugh, his expressions. I know this to be true because much later, you'll confess to me how profoundly sad this makes you feel.

Crouching on the ground, I wave you over. You sit down and lean against me, and I pull you close. My dearest daughter, I don't want to hide any part of today from you. I must seem so serious, so lost. Overcome with emotion.

In short sentences, I tell everyone here about your uncle's—my brother's—last moments. I talk about the sun that flooded the sky that morning with heat and light. My words probably come as a surprise to you. You've never seen me like this. There's a strange vibration in my voice. Underneath the assuredness I'm trying to project is fragility, inexpressible sadness, and muffled guilt.

My life has changed forever. I'm thirty-two years old. One week ago, at dawn on an April morning, while you were still asleep far away in Paris, I was with Thomas and a few others on a road in Afghanistan. There was an accident, and Thomas was killed right before my eyes, along with three other young men.

That morning, as I knelt on the scorched earth with your uncle's blood on my hands, the path of our lives took a definitive and singular turn.

The body of a dead person is unsettling. When we look right at it—let alone touch it—we can see that there's something off, something missing. The skin immediately takes on a surreal color, as though in just the first few minutes it goes from living to *artificial*. The wide-open eyes suddenly lose their brightness as dust settles onto them, while the limbs become floppy, ceasing to put up any resistance to manipulation. There's an absence, a void, and yet the body still *looks* like the person we knew. But *they're no longer there.*

So where are they?

In 2001, the death of my brother Thomas led me to this question. How could I have been prepared for it? I wasn't. Who could be? I was with him in central Asia. I took care of his body, brought him back to France so that he could be buried. The shock was enormous. We were close. We shared the same mad impatience to understand the world, and to wander around the parts of central Asia still suffused with memories of sacred times. We'd already traveled together to that place where death took us so brutally by surprise. That moment was a major turning point in my existence; it completely transformed my career as a journalist. And your life, too, Luna.

Where did Thomas go?

2

What I Want to Tell You

That's when I began to ask question after question about death. I felt compelled to use my experience and tools as an investigative journalist to attempt to understand, from a scientific point of view, everything we know about that moment so laden with fear and mystery. In my quest to unravel the mysteries of consciousness, I delved into neuroscience, among other disciplines, and interviewed many researchers around the world as well as people with firsthand accounts to share, particularly people who had had a near-death experience.

In 2013, my father—your grandfather—took his last breath. This only intensified my desire to find answers. I tried out mediums. I studied all sorts of experiences that took place at the border of life and death, and those that took place after the death of a loved one. Slowly, I became convinced that the hypothesis that life continued, in some form, after death was a rational one, corroborated by both science and countless firsthand accounts.

And yet there was always something missing. The ultimate piece of evidence. The one that would dispel any lingering doubts. The one that would explain why, despite the evidence that I'd gathered, there was still disagreement about the subject. Why were science and spirituality still so much in conflict with each other? Why did they seem to be two irreconcilable orientations?

Every so often over the course of my investigation, I found myself plagued by a sort of interior conflict. The scientific method often led to several different hypotheses, and scientists' opinions diverged—sometimes quite radically—as to which interpretation of a set of data was correct. Doubt is an essential part of scientific inquiry. All scientists can do is formulate hypotheses. In fact, this is precisely the point of the scientific method: to propose a hypothesis that might explain a phenomenon and then try to verify it.

By its very nature, science is always evolving; it will never provide us with ironclad answers. Science is a school of doubt. Furthermore, its tendency is to place value only on knowledge acquired analytically, and to consider only that which is reproducible. And yet the reality to which science gives us access is a relative one, for reasons I will come back to later in the book.

Today, this is a universally agreed-upon assessment. Whether they're physicists, biologists, neuroscientists, or something else entirely, scientists understand that a complete understanding of our reality is still, for the most part, out of reach.

In this regard, the nature of consciousness remains one of the most bewildering unresolved questions for researchers. The brain is an enigma. Contrary to what one might think, the entire field of neuroscience is still in its infancy. The tools and methods currently available to neuroscientists are relatively limited, especially when it comes to observing, in real time and with precision, what is happening in our brains. I quickly came to realize that we tend to far overestimate the discipline's explanatory abilities.

And yet I was still looking for answers. Was there *really* an afterlife? Luna, I quickly came to understand that if I wanted to gain access to a wider vision of the world and its subtleties, and to have even a chance of drawing back the curtain on the mysteries of consciousness and understanding where your uncle had gone, I was going to need to explore several different paths. When tackling such a complex and sensitive subject, no one discipline will suffice on its own: you have to combine different approaches.

But were there ways of exploring the nature of consciousness besides science? Like any good Westerner, and especially one from France, the country of Descartes and Voltaire, I was convinced that there weren't. I couldn't conceive of anything better than the scientific method, experimentation, replicability, and the study of matter in order to *objectively* understand the reality in which we lived.

However, consciousness can be approached from many other disciplines beyond neuroscience. Philosophy and psychoanalysis, for example, offered interesting perspectives on the question of death—more subjective, of course, but nonetheless valuable and complementary sources of reflection. But what radically changed the course of my investigation was meeting psychologists, doctors, anthropologists, and specialists in shamanism. Some of them had studied and had personal experience with spiritual practices that have been around for thousands of years, and were able to perceive what they described as other levels of reality.

For decades, many Western researchers have found themselves deeply moved by shamanic ceremonies. This piqued my curiosity. I wanted to go deeper, to try out the approach that was becoming more and more intriguing to scientists; I trusted my intuition.

Every shaman in the world, no matter their particular tradition, claims to be able to enter into contact with the "spirit world." Was that just a belief, or could there be some truth to it? It was with the goal of answering this question that I decided I had to attempt what could potentially prove to be one of the most important experiences of my life. Could I, too, *see* the spiritual dimension that mystics of all stripes have been saying for millennia that they're able to access? Would it be possible for me to see what happens when someone dies, or even *afterward*?

Perhaps somewhat naively, at the time, I took the idea of shamanism at face value. I thought that if I were able to visualize the spirit of someone who had died—your uncle—it would dispel for good the doubts that I'd been harboring about the existence of an afterlife.

Like Thomas the Apostle, as a journalist, I'm unable to shake off the habit of disbelief. I have to see it to believe it. That's what led me to the Amazon.

In 2006, when I took my first trip to the rainforest, you were still a child. Despite the extreme confusion of my first shamanic experiences, I could sense the invaluable potential of the ceremony. Little by little, shamanism opened my eyes to a different way of seeing the world. I came to understand that it was possible to explore reality *differently*.

To learn *differently*.

I began a slow process of initiation, despite my fears of the unknown, its pitfalls and discomfort. To temporarily extricate myself from the countless automatic reflexes that usually govern our lives, I had to embrace vulnerability and letting go.

I learned to make my mind an ally rather than a handicap, and to develop my intuition without losing myself in an imaginary world. This took nearly fifteen years. Fifteen long years, during which I led two parallel lives. As a journalist, I spent most of my time observing, dissecting, and analyzing the extensive body of scientific research on the nature of consciousness, though I was by then aware of the limits of our interpretative frameworks. In my other life, I was on an unsettlingly subjective spiritual journey. These two approaches seem quite different on the surface, but they turned out to be incredibly complementary. It was a time of patient learning, both through reasoning and through extrasensory perception.

Over the course of this quest, Luna, I began to see dimensions of reality that had previously been invisible to me. The intensity and clarity of these experiences were themselves a form of evidence. In the vast reality that had suddenly become perceptible to me, death seemed to have been erased. As though it had never really existed, had never been anything more than a stubborn veil, a porous boundary, a mental illusion.

Today, you're twenty-five years old. The silent little girl I'd pulled to my chest that day in April 2001 has become a radiant woman, despite the sudden and early appearance of death in your life.

There are so many things I want to share with you. At the time, I didn't know what I know now. Now, as the years pass, I sometimes think of the day when it will be my turn to breathe my final breath. I no longer think about it with unease or even apprehension. Instead, it's with a profound sense of serenity, and some curiosity, though no impatience. I know how you must feel whenever I bring it up; I've wanted to talk to you about it so many times these past few years. I understand it's strange to speak about, but what I'm going to tell you will change everything.

I'm going to die. Oh, not right away—don't worry! I'm not eager to make death come faster. In fact, increasingly I feel the opposite, now that I understand how wonderful life is. We still have time, so much time together, but the time will come, and it will be unexpected. That's a certainty.

In light of this, I'd like to tell you now what I've learned over the course of my investigations and my travels, so that when the time does come, you will see things the way I see them, after all these years of looking for answers. I want you to know that I'm convinced that on the day of my death, I will simply stop being visible to you—but my existence will continue elsewhere.

Death does not exist, Luna.

When we die, we don't stop living. We change worlds.

I will try to explain to you how I have arrived at this conclusion. It's not a belief, but rather the logical culmination of a long journey. To understand, you will need to call upon your reason, just as I did—I'm still a journalist at heart—but not exclusively, because when it comes to death, many things are beyond our analytical capabilities. *Knowing* isn't enough. You have to learn to listen to the voice in your heart as much as the voice of your reason. That took time for me—a lot of time, and many different experiences, experiments, and trips to the Amazon.

Your grandfather was devastated by the death of his son. Now, he has joined him. Whenever he spoke of Thomas's death, he would quote Baudelaire, saying that death flings us beyond *the immense wall of fog*, though when Baudelaire wrote those words it wasn't in the context of death. That was what your grandfather was like, remember? He read voraciously and remembered all these sentences from Tolstoy, Flaubert, Stendhal, Gogol, and all the other authors he spoke to—his imaginary friends. As soon as he quoted the music of their words, it was impossible to miss the tears appearing in his eyes and his voice beginning to wobble. Your grandfather was an emotional, cultured, good man. I'll tell you about his last weeks, because they were profoundly enlightening. And his last breath, just a wisp, an incredible moment of love.

Death does seem to hide itself in the fog of our fears, an

unfathomable mystery. And it's true that it spares no one—and yet most people prefer not to think about it until it suddenly storms into our lives. Just like when Thomas died, plunging your grandfather and me and our whole family into bewildering uncertainty.

We run toward death without understanding, like sleepwalkers, and then are surprised to find it makes us anxious. So we fill our days with fleeting pleasures in order to tolerate the spiritual disconnection. The dissonance leads us to feel as though something both essential and unreachable is missing from our existence, and we are powerless to fix it. The extinguished sun. Our forgotten souls.

But life isn't an irreversible slide into guaranteed obliteration. It's not limited to the decades we spend on this beautiful, violent, crazy planet. And death isn't the end of life. Rediscovering this is essential. And it's within our grasp.

It's possible to shed some light on the mystery. When I find myself on my deathbed, if circumstances allow it and I'm able to look it right in the face, the right words will be hard to find—you'll be overcome with emotion, and I'll be letting go. So it's better to say them now. Better to say it all now, especially because at that point, it will be a little too late to speak; at that threshold, silence is so precious. As you place your hand on my body, you will need to keep your movements slow and gentle, and your heart peaceful.

I'm going to explain to you everything I know about that moment: what will be happening inside me, what my soul will be seeing, what will happen to me *after*, and what you can do to help me, if you feel you have the courage. I'm sure that this will allow you to calmly accept the inevitable. And maybe you will be able to feel the love that will take over whichever room we happen to find ourselves in. It will be like a light, something that can be physically perceived.

The moment of death lays bare the most extreme emotions. It's a paradoxical time, one of both inconsolable heartbreak and a form of grace; a door is opening between two worlds.

After my death, I will still be here: sometimes near you, sometimes *elsewhere*, but always connected to you. The love that we share now will remain just as strong—and maybe it will even get stronger; you'll understand why I say this in the pages to come. Love is what connects the two worlds. I'll teach you how to feel that; it's much stronger than absence. Opening ourselves up to it soothes and dispels our confusion.

When I fade away from this world, I will still be alive. Don't doubt it. Don't doubt that the love that we feel for each other is eternal and will allow our souls to remain in conversation.

Beginning this conversation with you about death will have an effect that is even more essential than preparing you for my own, which I hope takes place as late as possible. It will allow you to rediscover an inner path. I've experienced it myself.

Yes, death inspires fear. You've told me. The subject makes you anxious. You're far from being the only one, my dear; it's not at all surprising that you would feel that way. But you've also told me that it's not a fear you refuse to face. You don't want to give in to it. I'm impressed by your clearheadedness. I admire the courage you've proved that you possess by being willing to look your fears and shadows right in the face, and I can confirm that it's by embracing your vulnerability that you'll find happiness and fulfillment. Vulnerability is not weakness. It's the first step toward awakening. It requires a lot of courage and humility to probe the truth of our being. But isn't that the most essential task of our existence?

Death can become familiar to us. It's possible to allay our fears about it and reveal its secrets. At that point it is no longer our enemy, but rather a mirror reflecting our lives. Death unveils the most precious thing that we possess, a dimension of our being: our pure consciousness, which, if we learn to reconnect with it, is a priceless internal resource.

I've come to understand that we are all guided, but we do not know how to listen. Making death our friend, and the object of daily meditation, will profoundly soothe and transform the way we see the ups and downs of our existence. It allows us to constantly feel the immortal flame that burns in the depths of our hearts, the inexhaustible and wise source of inspiration that we all harbor within us. Even now, in this very moment. Knowing ourselves is the beginning of wisdom. The sooner we undertake the inner exploration that allows us to rediscover our souls, the more enlightened and inspired our existences will be.

It took me over a decade to find the right words. They didn't all come from where I expected them to. That's *another* story I want to tell you.

3

How I Began to Investigate Death

After your uncle died, I, like everyone else, was completely bereft. For me, the "afterlife" was limited to the religious and philosophical domains—that is to say, a matter of belief, and something that was effectively impossible to explore in a rational, scientific way. And then I heard about near-death experiences, or NDEs.

You know what those are, right? They're the stories of people who, after an accident, for example, report that while the paramedics were trying to resuscitate them, they were actually observing their bodies from above, thinking that they were witnessing their own death.

Would Thomas have told us a story like this if he had lived?

I began to read up on the subject. Very quickly, the most crucial thing in my eyes was discovering that a significant number of scientists were also interested in the phenomenon.

It was like an electroshock for me. Several of these researchers were alluding to near-death experiences *without* the de facto assumption that they were just unfounded beliefs or hallucinations.

Usually, in the world we live in, whenever someone talks about an unusual experience that's wrongly deemed "supernatural," we tend to think that they're reading too much into it, or they're mistaken, or they're emotionally fragile, or they're lying, or they've dreamed it or hallucinated it, or even that they're suffering from some kind of psychological disorder. This being the case, I was dumbstruck to find that so many scientists thought none of these "explanations" were necessarily correct. While many people refuse to listen seriously to these accounts—because, if they were true, they would upend the skeptics' theoretical frameworks entirely—for others, the challenge only reinforces their motivation to explore them further.

Near-death experiences are a psychological and sociological reality, and studies on them have revealed many surprising results. They are *anomalies*, in the scientific sense of the term: examples of a phenomenon that has been observed in real life, but which deviates from known models and for which there is no conventional explanation.

NDEs came into the public consciousness in the mid-1970s in the United States, after a young doctor and philosopher named Raymond Moody—now a leading authority in the field—published *Life After Life*, a seminal collection of several strange accounts from people who had had a brush with death. They reported remembering the time during which they were unconscious, sometimes even in a coma.

It was the similarities between all these stories that was striking: the sensation of leaving one's body; the perspective of observing the scene from above, sometimes with precise details that would have been impossible for an unconscious person to know; the visions of loved ones who had already died, or spiritual entities; the perception of a bright light or a being of light; a profound feeling of well-being and of being bathed in love; and for some, the impression that they were seeing their entire life flash before their eyes, experiencing something that was both ecstatic and difficult to describe, entering another reality.

Was all of this actually real?

The publication of *Life After Life* gave more people the opportunity to speak openly about their own experiences, revealing just how widespread this previously invisible phenomenon was. In the weeks that followed, Moody began to receive an avalanche of letters from people all over the country sharing their own accounts of such an experience. Not having anticipated such a reaction, he asked his supervisor, Dr. Bruce Greyson, a professor of psychiatric medicine at the University of Virginia, for help. What Moody didn't know was that Greyson had also been profoundly shaken by the words of one of his patients several years before. Greyson was unnerved to find that the young woman's inexplicable story was far from being the only one of its kind.[1]

A single account doesn't lend itself particularly well to a science-based approach, but the considerable number of them that were suddenly in play completely changed the game.

Today, after more than forty-five years of research led by multiple teams, including Greyson's, the data that has been collected about NDEs is priceless. However, the explanation for them remains a scientific mystery. These spiritual occurrences challenge the way we see perceive reality, and change the lives of those who have undergone them.

From a scientific perspective, what is most disturbing is that they upend all our current models. Many of these NDEs take place during a period when brain function is gradually lessening; in fact, the intensity of the experience seems to have an inverse relationship with brain activity. How is it that *hundreds of thousands* of both adults and children (studies indicate that between 12 and 18 percent of people in cardiac arrest experience an NDE) who have been in life-threatening situations in which their brain function was seriously impaired—or even at a complete standstill!—can report afterward that not only were they conscious during the entire episode, but also that those states of consciousness were unusually rich and intense? They describe experiencing unparalleled lucidity, a kind of ultra-consciousness in which everything became clearer, and they could sense a reality that was *more real than real life*.

It's a little bit like if you removed your laptop's battery and destroyed all its circuits, and then it started running faster than ever. It makes no sense. How could the brain allow for an experience of expanded consciousness at the very moment when its functioning is severely impaired? It should be exactly the opposite.

These experiences raise a question with astonishing implications: is our consciousness dependent on our brain? In other words, when our brain is no longer functioning, do we remain alive? Do NDEs describe what happens . . . at the moment of death?

At a conference I attended in Liège, Belgium, I met two researchers who each argued in support of a different answer to this question: Belgian neurologist Steven Laureys and Dutch cardiologist Pim van Lommel.

Steven Laureys is the research director of the FNRS (Belgium's National Fund for Scientific Research), head of the GIGA Consciousness research team at the University of Liège, and the founder of the Coma Science Group in Liège, which he led until 2020. Affable and energetic, he's around my age. Dr. Laureys is one of Europe's leading neuroscience researchers. The Coma Science Group has developed international expertise in comas and unresponsive wakefulness syndrome, the condition that used to be rather indelicately referred to as a "vegetative state."

He and his team have also studied different states of consciousness, which is what led him to his particular interest in NDEs through the lens of neuroscience.

He's not exactly cagey about his stance on the matter, which is that everything happens in the brain: "The hypothesis that my team is testing is that all of these near-death experiences have an organic substrate. That during a coma, there's a cascade of changes to the neurotransmitters in certain regions of the brain. It's simply a question of modified brain activity," he writes in one of his books on consciousness.[2] The implication: that NDEs do not prove that consciousness survives death.

On the other hand, there are equally well-known and respected researchers, such as Dr. Pim van Lommel, who claim that NDEs demonstrate that consciousness does not come from the brain and that it therefore must live on after death, since NDEs occur when the brain activity seems to be at a standstill.

Cardiologist and medical expert Dr. van Lommel is the author of the most significant clinical study to date on NDEs, which was published in the prestigious medical journal *The Lancet*. He's one of the leading experts on the subject, along with Bruce Greyson and several others. His study made major waves in the international medical community because it demonstrated that it is apparently quite possible to remain conscious even when all brain functions have ceased. Titled "Near-death experience in survivors of cardiac arrest," the study was groundbreaking in both its scale—344 cardiac arrest survivors were interviewed in a dozen different hospitals—and its duration: the interviews took place five and then eight years after the events took place. Sixty-two people, who made up 18 percent of the study's participants, reported having had a near-death experience.[3]

After the conference, I met with Steven Laureys in the sprawling university hospital complex in southern Liège that houses the

Coma Science Group, where he worked. As I entered the hospital, I had to make my way through a busy crowd of patients, families, and caregivers on their lunch break. The cafeterias were bustling with activity. I found the elevators I needed in a hallway and headed up to the fifth floor of the GIGA tower, where the CSG premises are located.

When I arrived, the atmosphere that prevailed was one of absolute calm.

Steven Laureys's office was a large, light-filled room overflowing with books, articles, files, and . . . a resin model of a brain, the exact replica—to scale—of his own brain. Warmly, as though we were already friends, the smiling father of five invited me to sit at a large conference table. We'd first met several years before on the set of a French national public television show and had been in touch every so often since then, though we had never sat down and had a frank discussion. How could a neurologist study a phenomenon such as NDEs, which are, by their very nature, impossible to reproduce? I began questioning him.

"What does your research involve?"

"What I'm trying to do is use scientific methodology—with curiosity, and without dogma or preconceptions—to compare what I think I understand with what I'm able to measure. Obviously, I'm a neurologist, so I work on the brain to test hypotheses. I can't ignore the fact that if we change the structure or functioning of the brain, for example with anesthesia or hallucinogens, we change our thoughts, perceptions, and emotions. Consciousness is complicated."

"It's the biggest mystery there is."

"Yes, and until we understand consciousness, it's going to be hard to explain near-death experiences. The fact remains that they are a physiological reality deserving of more study. I wish more of my colleagues took an interest in them so that we could stop with the binary of 'I believe in them, I don't believe in them.' On one hand, you have the people who claim that NDEs are proof that the soul exists outside of the body, but who don't go any further. I'm a bit more curious; I need a theory with predictive power. On the other hand, you have those who immediately disregard them as untrue. Neither of these attitudes serves us well. The problem is that we don't really know when such an experience is happening, and we can't reproduce it in a lab."

The man sitting across from me had first become known for his work on comas and disorders of consciousness—patients who fail to regain consciousness after a traumatic accident—as well as unresponsive wakefulness syndrome and locked-in syndrome, the latter referring to patients who are paralyzed but still conscious.

GIGA Consciousness is a team of around fifty people, not counting external collaborators. Most of them are psychologists, doctors, and engineers, but some are physical therapists and physicists. The teams are working to better understand the different types of brain activity that take place in varying states of consciousness: comas, hypnosis, meditation, and trances, as well as, indirectly, those who have had a near-death experience.

In the first stage of GIGA Consciousness's NDE research, Dr. Laureys's team collected nearly two thousand firsthand accounts, a significant sample size for a subject like this. Participants were volunteers who came forward following a call for testimonies, meaning that this first stage was, by nature, retrospective and limited. All the same, it yielded some very rich, and sometimes even surprising, insights.

After that, Dr. Laureys's teams challenged themselves to attempt to "reproduce" in the lab several types of experiences that are phenomenologically similar to NDEs in order to see what happens in the brain during these altered states of consciousness.

For several years now, the GIGA Consciousness teams have been trying a number of techniques to induce these states of consciousness—for example, using hypnosis on people who had experienced an NDE and asking them to remember their experiences. While it was clear that the subjects weren't reliving their NDEs under hypnosis, they did report perceptions and sensations similar to those they had originally experienced. During the experiment, their brain activity was monitored by electroencephalogram (EEG), a device that measures the electrical activity of the cortex—the outer part of the brain and the epicenter of its most sophisticated neurological functions.

Dr. Laureys's teams also tried using virtual reality to make people "relive" via simulation an out-of-body experience, testing the technique both on near-death experiencers and a control group and recording the brain activity of each. In addition, the researchers tested other induction methods, such as syncope—small, fleeting losses of consciousness—as scientific literature had revealed a potential link between hallucinations that occurred during syncope and NDEs.

On a more unusual note, they collaborated with shaman Corine Sombrun, who is capable of entering a trance state at will. Her participation enabled them to see the impact of this very specific state of consciousness on brain function.

GIGA Consciousness also works with the Centre for Psychedelic Research at Imperial College, London, to explore the effects on brain imaging of psychedelic substances that induce powerful, transcendent experiences, some aspects of which bear strong similarities to NDEs. I'll come back to this at length later.

The goal of this whole body of research is to observe, under laboratory conditions, experiences that have certain phenomenological similarities with NDEs and to see the associated patterns of neural activity. Each study has brought to light a correlation between the neurophysiological states of the test subjects and their accounts of what they experienced. The researchers collected important new data. However, while these other states of altered consciousness may resemble NDEs, they might be, neurologically speaking, quite different—especially because one of the most striking characteristics of NDEs is that they often happen when the brain seems to be no longer functioning at all.

It was with this objection that I continued my conversation with Dr. Laureys.

4

Brain Death and Clinical Death

"You observe correlations between altered states of consciousness and the associated patterns of brain activity," I said to Dr. Laureys, "but NDEs sometimes occur when the brain is in great distress, or even when its activity has ceased entirely, don't they?"

He seemed taken aback. "When its activity has ceased entirely? No."

"What do you mean, no?"

"People act as though it's been proven that during NDEs, the brain is inactive, or even in a state of death, with no function whatsoever. But that's not the case. No one comes back from brain death."

Already we'd reached the heart of the debate: is the brain still active during these experiences or not? For Dr. Laureys, as a matter of principle, it *must* be active, because his work begins from the assumption that all conscious experience is associated with visible activity in the brain. This is what he has always learned and observed as a neurologist. That's why all his research is aimed at better understanding the brain activity of people experiencing something that *resembles* an NDE, because NDEs are assumed to be caused by "changes to the brain's functioning." This hypothesis is supposed to be the "rational" one, but it seemed highly debatable to me based on the facts, so I was impatient to hear Dr. Laureys's arguments.

Also, no one claims that it's possible to come back from brain death. Death is a gradual process of deterioration. When the heart stops, it brings to a halt the oxygenation of organs and cells, but not all of these degrade at the same rate. Oxygen and glucose are the vital source of brain activity, and when there's a reduction in that supply, the brain will cease functioning within a few seconds. This is "clinical death," a state that can be temporary and, most importantly, reversible. However, after several minutes without a supply of energy, the neurons will begin to die off. This is "brain death."

After brain death, several organs can still be transplanted, because they're still *alive*—heart, lungs, liver, kidneys—but the person won't be able to come back: their brain is now irreparably dead. No one in a state of brain death has ever come back to life.

However, many near-death experiencers were in a state of clinical death, which precedes brain death and which can last several minutes. Their brains were in standby mode; the neurons hadn't all died, but nonetheless, they didn't seem to be active. This was the period of time that interested me. I rephrased my question to Dr. Laureys.

"No one says that people who have experienced NDEs were in a state of brain death, but some of them were in a state of clinical death. And in clinical death, the brain switches itself off very quickly, right? Several studies on cardiac arrest[1] indicate that after ten to twenty seconds at most, there's no more blood pressure and no more blood flow . . . so one would assume that there can't be any activity in the brain."

"You're correct that there's no more blood pressure—that's a mechanical function. If the pump stops, there will be no more flow to the brain. In real life, however, the heart just doesn't suddenly stop. It often goes into fibrillation, which means it starts beating very fast and irregularly and is no longer very efficient. But during resuscitation, we don't know exactly what's going on. So, yes, obviously, there are often moments where we can observe a significant drop in blood supply. And of course, the brain is very fragile. On the other hand, it's also stronger than we can imagine, so sometimes, with current resuscitation techniques and hypothermia, we can manage to preserve brain activity.

"The studies I'm talking about show that there actually isn't any irreversible damage to the brain in the first few minutes, but that just a few seconds after cardiac arrest, the brain stops receiving any blood supply whatsoever.

"In cardiac arrest, many things happen that are difficult to observe. Yes, the brain will show signs of distress, then slowing down and gradually flatlining. But I wouldn't say with any certainty, 'After however many seconds, there's no more activity.' In reality, there's a lot more variability than that."

I understood his argument, but wanted to push him further. "But research shows that the exact time between cardiac arrest and the cessation of all brain activity is ten to twenty seconds at most. I didn't invent that."

"You want my opinion, I'm giving you my opinion. The question that you're asking is worthy of a doctoral thesis. For me, there are two interpretations. You could say that the brain is inactive, and that that's proof that consciousness must lie elsewhere. But you could also say that the brain is stronger than we think and that, even if it's in distress, there's still a little bit of output, a little bit of brain activity. For now, I'm remaining cautious."

Several critical care specialists I interviewed shared Dr. Laureys's reservations, pointing out the difficulty of ascertaining the vital signs of a patient undergoing resuscitation. The fact remains that once the oxygen supply to the brain is cut off, neurons pause their activity so as to retain as much energy as possible.

"Yes, that's true," Dr. Laureys confirmed when I mentioned this.

"They won't die for several more minutes," I continued. "And in this interval between the suspension of oxygen to the brain and the moment of brain death, there's no more activity."

"We don't know that. We diagnose brain death only after a few minutes of cerebral anoxia (oxygen deprivation in the brain). And a 'flat' EEG is not enough to diagnose brain death."[2]

"But what could be fueling brain activity when the blood that delivers the oxygen that's crucial for brain function isn't flowing?"

Once again, he dodged the question. "This is really a scientific debate that merits more study. It's been said that when some people have a near-death experience, their brains are no longer working. Maybe. But maybe not. It's possible—and this is what I think—that much less brain activity is needed for perception and thought than what we've historically believed. It's an avenue worth exploring."

This is Dr. Laureys's argument: since the brain isn't irreversibly dead, we don't know what could be going on in it, even during cardiac arrest. The hypothesis that a kind of "residual activity" causes these NDEs cannot be ruled out. I had already discussed this with several researchers, and I told him so.

"Yet many NDE specialists, such as the psychiatrist Bruce Greyson, for example, find it hard to imagine how residual activity in the brain could cause a conscious experience. Even putting aside cardiac arrest, many NDEs take place at a time when the brain is in great distress. How could such a rich experience be associated with brain activity that is greatly reduced from normal?"

"That's exactly the question we're studying," Dr. Laureys replied. "I think it's worth considering. I think that we really know very little about what happens during the experience. Personally, I'd be thrilled to discover that consciousness is outside the brain! I'd win the Nobel Prize for sure. But you have to try to do this while thinking about your own convictions critically."

"It seems to me that's what Greyson does. And like other scientists who are skeptical of the neuronal origins of NDEs, he works with and relies on reports supported by medical records, and there are hundreds of them![3] These researchers explain that, while consciousness is correlated with the simultaneous activity of many different brain regions, 'residual activity' cannot produce a conscious experience. Dr. Bruce Greyson admitted to me that he doesn't believe it would cause an NDE."

Dr. Laureys laughed. "It's a belief, then."

I didn't back down. "He didn't put it in those words. It's his research that has led him to consider this the most likely hypothesis. The idea that residual activity that's so subtle it's not even detectable could be the cause of these hyperreal narratives and lucid thoughts contradicts all the neuroscientific models of brain function."

"I don't think that we can say that until we've understood the neural correlates of consciousness. And Greyson hasn't done any experiments with EEGs, let alone high-density (256-electrode) EEGs, as my team and I have."

"What if there are no neural correlates of consciousness? What if consciousness doesn't come from the brain?"

"If there aren't any? I'd be very happy if I found out there was something else. But I still have sensory consciousness—what I see and hear and perceive right now—and for the moment, observation shows me that if I shut down activity in the consciousness brain network, I won't have any more perceptions. By definition, consciousness is subjective. I have no problem saying that we don't understand consciousness. I've been called a materialist and a reductionist, but, well—reducing a big problem to smaller ones is the scientific approach."

"Do you consider yourself a materialist?"

"What do you mean by that?"

"That everything comes from matter."

Dr. Laureys took a few seconds to think before answering me. "We know quite well that not everything comes from matter. Since Einstein, we've known that matter and energy are connected. But I'm still a neurologist, and a scientist. I study the brain, and I continue to think that's useful—even if no one can explain how something material, like a brain, which I do believe plays a major role, can shape our thoughts, perceptions, and emotions."

"The big question."

"Yes. The subject of our research unit in Liège and in Canada!"

"Actually, many researchers hypothesize that NDEs might be the glitch that will enable us to model a broader conception of consciousness. For example, by distinguishing one level of consciousness that is entirely linked to brain activity from another that's independent. Is that a path you'd be curious to explore?"

Dr. Laureys smiled. "I'm not a philosopher, nor am I a priest. My approach is scientific, down-to-earth, pragmatic. I want to understand. How could we test the hypothesis you're suggesting? You can tell me that consciousness is 'cosmic,' and that we're all connected . . . Okay, but I'm not going to be happy with a poetic explanation. Maybe it's a kind of energy? A wave? Whatever it is, I need it to be defined. Then we'd be able to test out a real scientific hypothesis with explanatory and predictive value."

The afternoon was drawing to a close, the light coming in from the big windows in Dr. Laureys's office beginning to fade. We'd been talking for over an hour, and it was time for him to leave; he had to take one of his kids to camp. He suggested I come with him so that I could get closer to my hotel, as the university hospital is far from the city center.

After we picked up his son and said hello to his wife, Vanessa Charland, a neuropsychologist and mindfulness meditation instructor, Dr. Laureys dropped me off in downtown Liège. I walked along the banks of the Meuse River as night fell.

I was a little skeptical after our interview. I appreciated the friendliness of our exchange, and understand Dr. Laureys's position, which is that of a researcher designing experiments to better grasp what is happening to the brain in altered states of consciousness; he's a neurologist! But I was disturbed by how determined he was to stick to the idea that residual brain activity during resuscitation can produce a state of consciousness as intense as an NDE, even though I knew that for him it's not an "explanation for NDEs" but rather a working hypothesis. As a scientist, he didn't want to dismiss it without having tested it. That's the essence of the scientific method.

However, it seemed to me that this hypothesis about residual activity—which has never been observed, and which supposedly takes place despite physiological changes and a cortex that is apparently not functioning—required turning a blind eye to some of the essential aspects of an NDE. So many incredible things happen during these experiences that make the hypothesis impossible. I'll come back to this point soon and explain further what those things are; they force us to reexamine our assumptions about the nature of consciousness.

But first it might be useful for us to look a little more closely into what neuroscientists know about consciousness, and what they don't know. Like the question of its origins.

By the way, Luna, when I say "consciousness"—what does that mean to you?

5

What Do We Know About Consciousness?

Dearest daughter, how do you know that you're alive? How is it that you're able to observe your own existence—to think, to feel, to love? Because you're conscious that you're you? Of course, but how are we conscious? Why do we have an inner experience? Is it a process or a state? Is it an ability developed by our neurons while we're in the womb, for example, or is it a permanent state, overlooking our biological development from afar?

The term "consciousness" is used to refer to your subjective experience, by nature hard to grasp: the flow of thoughts and feelings that you feel when you're awake.

But where does consciousness come from?

The brain? That's the theory that seems most logical. Why? Because neuroscientists have observed neural processes that underpin our subjective experiences of consciousness.

For example, electrochemical activity detected in a particular area of the brain might be associated with a particular function of consciousness: language, memory, perception, wakefulness, etc. And then there's the fact that even minor malfunctioning of our brain apparently alters our consciousness.

We have a considerable amount of evidence attesting to this relationship. Brain damage can lead to a loss of consciousness. Strokes can put people into comas. Seizures cause a temporary loss of consciousness that's always accompanied by specific changes visible on an EEG. There's no doubt that there's a link between our conscious experience and our brain. But does a link between two elements always imply a causal relationship?

No. What we've observed are *correlations* between neural activity and states of consciousness. But to say that activity detected in any given zone of the brain that's associated with a particular state of consciousness is its *cause* is speculation. Neuroscience can prove only that neural activity and mental states are related. This point is essential.

In reality, the question of the origin of consciousness is a mystery for the scientific community. This major scientific and philosophical enigma—how can the brain, a biological structure composed of 86 billion neurons, within which an even greater number of interactions take place, produce an inner experience?—has been dubbed *the hard problem of consciousness*. And no one has the answer.

In a special issue published for its one hundred and twenty-fifth anniversary, *Science* magazine called it the second most important unresolved scientific question today.[1] The commonly accepted hypothesis that consciousness emerges from brain activity is disputed among neuroscientists, and its opponents include eminent researchers at the most prestigious institutions in the world. Christof Koch, for example, a leading American researcher in the field, explains in his book *Consciousness*, "Subjectivity is too radically different from anything physical for it to be an emergent phenomenon."[2]

What he means by this—and his analysis is shared by other

well-known scientists as well as philosophers[3]—is that our inner experience, our personal subjectivity, is so radically different from the physical elements that make up our material reality that it would be impossible to explain how that inner experience could magically emerge from a set of neurons, no matter their quantity.

By no means is it self-evident that something as immaterial as consciousness could spring forth from matter.

In fact, the idea is beyond comprehension.

Philosopher Bernardo Kastrup agrees wholeheartedly, writing, "The emergent properties of a complex system must be deducible from the properties of the lower-level components of the system."[4] In other words, something made up of purely material elements cannot produce something immaterial, such as the sensation of existing. Referring to the role of the brain, he continues, "How and why that structure, function, and behavior are accompanied by *inner experience* is deeply problematic for materialism. Your personal computer also has structure, function, and behavior. However, its internal calculations do not seem to be accompanied by any inner experience at all."[5]

It's true: a calculator has no emotions.

At least until proven otherwise, even the most advanced of computers doesn't have any inner experience. Artificial intelligence may imitate consciousness, but it's not conscious; it's just . . . intelligent. It can carry out extremely fast calculations; it's capable of learning, and of developing some sort of functional autotomy; but it cannot be moved to tears in front of a landscape, a flower, or an Odilon Redon painting.

No, a computer doesn't have any inner experience, even if there are a few billionaires seeking physical immortality whose ambition is to change this, and even if this is the premise of some poignant speculative fiction, like that movie we watched together, Luna—*Her*, with Joaquin Phoenix.

But in reality, the extreme complexity of a computer—like that of a neural network—doesn't automatically result in conscious experience. Imagining the brain as a kind of supercomputer might help illustrate certain aspects of how it works, but it's not a useful analogy when it comes to explaining how we subjectively experience the colors, tastes, smells, sights, or sounds of the world around us. Nor is it capable of explaining the psychological phenomena I'll be exploring in the rest of this book, including near-death experiences.

So why is the theory that consciousness comes from brain activity so widely supported by the majority of scientists, intellectuals, and the general public, when it's not based on any scientific demonstration and when it actually poses fundamental problems?

It's based on a kind of unconscious certainty that pervades our society: that everything can be explained in physical terms, and everything can be understood once we've identified the cause-and-effect relationships that drive our material reality.

This way of thinking is called materialism. The materialist view is that humans are extremely complex biological machines. Everything we are and do should therefore, *in theory*, be explicable in terms of physics, chemistry, and biology. Our identity, our emotions, our memories, and our very beings cannot exist outside of matter. Therefore, our consciousness can be nothing other than a *production* of our brain activity.

This theoretical model seems solid, and is still the one that, on the surface, seems best adapted for understanding our daily reality. But all the same, it's a hypothetical model, and one that's increasingly thrown off balance by NDEs, among other things.

The materialist view operates like a pair of distortion goggles. Without realizing it, we're looking at and interpreting the world through a filter. Scientists more than anyone.

Scientists need theories in order to interpret the results of their research. Even the most methodical scientific experiments are *always* interpreted subjectively, according to a theoretical model. From the beginning, scientists have developed models for understanding the world based on the knowledge that's available to them. They use these models to analyze reality and interpret the phenomena they observe within it. But knowledge evolves, and new discoveries regularly come along to contradict the earlier knowledge on which previous models were based.

Over the years, we have experienced several scientific revolutions that have forced us to change our models and our theories. We use the word "paradigm" to refer to these models.

If you look at the history of science over the past few centuries, you'll see how fleeting scientific "truths" are. Our understanding of reality has always been dependent on the knowledge we've had at the time, which is by definition incomplete. So why would now be any different? Why would our current paradigm—the materialist paradigm—be definitive and final, when none of the previous ones were?

Given that it's based not on certainties but on hypotheses that are, from a logical standpoint, unlikely to be permanent, we can say that materialism is a metaphysical stance rather than a scientific one. Adhering to it without challenging it is a form of belief.

And that's exactly what we're doing, even though—as Dr. Laureys rightly pointed out to me—the materialist paradigm ceases to function as soon as we venture into *extremes*. Newtonian physics, for example, works for the macroscopic world in which we live, but it can't explain phenomena in the extremely small subatomic world. At that level, matter no longer behaves like matter. Other laws of physics prevail.

Have you considered the implications of this paradox, Luna? For about a century now, we've been using two physical theories to describe our world, according to the scale at which we observe it: quantum physics for the microscopic, and the theory of general relativity for the macroscopic.

Two completely opposite models. For one reality.

You have to admit that this proves that our models are incomplete, and that materialism is increasingly unsuitable for describing the astonishing depths of reality. The theory of relativity explains everything in physical terms—causes and effects between material components—while quantum physics smashes to bits the very concept of a material reality. I'm not one of those people who uses quantum physics at every opportunity to justify anything and everything—quantum physicists are the first to say that if you think you've understood quantum physics, you haven't understood anything!—but there is one fact that is universally acknowledged: it completely upends our conception of matter.

Quantum physics also bears witness to the fact that we've been engaged in a profound paradigm shift for decades now. The consequences of this revolution can be seen in many different scientific fields. Physics, of course, but also neuroscience, biology, astrophysics, etc. All the foundations of our worldview that have been passed down for three centuries are undergoing a massive change. It's a truly exciting time for science.

Still, paradigm shifts are a long process. Especially now. And if the materialist paradigm is proving particularly resistant to change, it's first and foremost due to the difficulty of modeling the theories that could lead to the next paradigm. But there are also more irrational reasons.

In the Western world, we've grown up with this materialist way of thinking. It's so ingrained in us that we're no longer aware of its influence on our worldview, nor is the entire scientific community. These unconscious psychological and cultural dynamics have little to do with scientific logic, and for most of us, they hold us back from challenging our preconceived ideas—a process that would be essential for the development of a new model.

Despite the fact that it's no longer infallible, the materialist view still influences the way we approach a problem and influences our decisions on what can be accepted as a fact. This is true for researchers, too. And yet the scientific method is supposedly based on a completely opposite process: it is careful observation and analysis of the facts—even and especially those that run counter to our theories—that is supposed to lead us to new models. In science, facts should always take precedence over theories, and we should always be willing to modify accepted knowledge as new data emerges.

Let's get back to consciousness. Anomalies such as NDEs are the new data that's forcing us to reexamine our certainties. NDEs are disconcertingly complex in that they're inexplicable from a strictly materialist viewpoint.

Here's just one example: how can we explain the fact that many people report having had the impression of being outside their physical bodies during an NDE, a perception that's backed up by the details they were able to report? No brain mechanism can allow a person who's in a coma or in the midst of being resuscitated or undergoing open-heart surgery to be able to describe everything that's happening in the operating room. Much less the room next door! And yet such cases exist, and they've been studied, analyzed, and verified.

One study by Dr. Janice Holden of the University of North

Texas examined the accuracy of out-of-body perceptions during an NDE. The subjects of the study, about a hundred people, were able to report precise observations from their NDEs that were later corroborated. For example, one person described what had occurred in the operating room while they were in cardiac arrest, and the surgeon confirmed in an interview that the description was perfectly accurate.

Of these one hundred cases, 92 percent were completely accurate and 6 percent were partially accurate. Only one case was inaccurate.[6]

Conventional explanations chalk near-death experiences up to a form of hallucination—a cognitive illusion brought on by a state of shock, or a lack of oxygen in the brain, or the drugs administered during hospitalization or surgery. Another explanation is that these experiences are a psychological defense mechanism evoked when facing the threat of death. Each of these hypotheses might "explain" an element of NDEs, but never the entire picture. Moreover, none of them explain why a person's personality can be so profoundly transformed by an NDE. Bruce Greyson told me, "We know what happens to people who have hallucinations from lack of oxygen and from drugs; they don't transform their lives the way near-death experiences do. And certainly people who have hallucinations don't have accurate out-of-body perceptions. It seems like something else is going on here. Those materialist explanations do not explain the near-death experience. . . . I don't have a better explanation, and that's probably why it's hard to get near-death experiences accepted in some fields—because we don't have a good theoretical explanation for them. It certainly fits the facts to say that something in you leaves your body, and actually perceives and thinks and feels from an out-of-body perspective. But what that is, I don't know.

I mean, there are religious terms for it, but we don't have scientific vocabulary for it yet.[7]

This is the heart of the problem.

There's a visual I like from the philosopher Karl R. Popper: to prove that not all crows are black, you only have to find one single white crow. I'm not a neurologist, but I am a journalist, and for years now, I've been analyzing studies and scientific articles as well as interviewing witnesses and researchers, some of whom are among the world's leading NDE specialists. Luna, I think I've seen more than one white crow.

6

Impossible Experiences

The room was packed. Several hundred people had turned up to attend this conference in Liège on "Grief and the Invisible Dimensions of Consciousness," organized by clinical psychologist Evelyne Josse and transpersonal therapist Martine Struzik. I'd already run into Steven Laureys, who would give a talk later on.

On stage, Dutch cardiologist Dr. Pim van Lommel had begun his lecture. In a warm, confident voice, the tall, elegant, altogether Dutch man was giving a talk on the "continuity of consciousness"—its permanence even beyond death. Pausing regularly to allow the interpreter to catch up, he meticulously detailed his arguments, which were based on his research on near-death experiences. He mentioned a story from a coronary care unit nurse that he'd heard during the pilot phase of the study that he published in *The Lancet* in 2001.[1] I remembered having been struck by the story when reading his book, *Consciousness Beyond Life*, which included it.[2]

Dr. van Lommel explained to the room that the file had been reviewed by his research team, who had also asked the nurse to tell her story just as she'd experienced it, as objectively as possible. He began to read her story.

During the night shift the ambulance crew brings in a forty-four-year-old cyanotic [purplish-blue skin discoloration] comatose man. About an hour earlier he had been found in a public park by passers-by, who had initiated heart massage. After admission to the coronary care unit, he receives artificial respiration with a balloon and a mask as well as heart massage and defibrillation. When I want to change the respiration method, when I want to intubate the patient, the patient turns out to have dentures in his mouth. Before intubating him, I remove the upper set of dentures and put it on the crash cart. Meanwhile we continue extensive resuscitation. After approximately ninety minutes, the patient has sufficient heart rhythm and blood pressure, but he's still ventilated and intubated, and he remains comatose. In this state he is transferred to the intensive care unit for further respiration. After more than a week in coma the patient returns to the coronary care unit, and I see him when I distribute the medication. As soon as he sees me he says, "Oh, yes, but you, you know where my dentures are." I'm flabbergasted. Then he tells me, "Yes, you were there when they brought me into the hospital, and you took the dentures out of my mouth and put them on that cart; it had all these bottles on it, and there was a sliding drawer underneath, and you put my teeth there." I was all the more amazed because I remembered this happening when the man was in a deep coma and undergoing resuscitation. After further questioning, it turned out that the patient had seen himself lying in bed and that he had watched from above how nursing staff and doctors had been busy resuscitating him. He was also able to give an accurate and detailed description of the small room where he had been resuscitated and of the appearance of those present. While watching the scene, he had been terrified that we were going to stop resuscitating and that he would

> die. And it's true that we had been extremely negative about the patient's prognosis due to his very poor condition when admitted. The patient tells me that he had been making desperate but unsuccessful attempts at letting us know that he was still alive and that we should continue resuscitating. He's deeply impressed by his experience and says he's no longer afraid of death.

As I mentioned earlier, hundreds of reports of NDEs during a cardiac arrest just like this one have been collected and studied.[3] Discrediting them without further study makes no sense.

I'm emphasizing this point, Luna, because if the brain is implicated in some way, and there is an explanation for NDEs that is solely neurological, that explanation *must* apply to the experiences that occur in this particular set of circumstances, when the heart is in great distress and brain function is compromised. That's why I'm now going to explore specifically the NDEs that take place during cardiac arrest; they're the ones that are most difficult to attribute to a biological cause.

As Steven Laureys himself confirmed, the brain is the organ that uses the most energy to function in proportion to its weight. That means that the blood supply to our brain is significant.[4]

However, numerous studies have shown that during cardiac arrest, the heart actually stops beating, or else it enters into ventricular fibrillation; meanwhile, blood flow and oxygen circulation in the brain rapidly plummet to near-zero. Signs of this slowdown in activity are visible within six to ten seconds after cardiac arrest begins. Within ten to twenty seconds, activity comes to a complete stop, which quickly leads to the three major signs of clinical death: absence of cardiac output, absence of breathing, and absence of brain stem reflexes.[5]

Neuroscientists say that consciousness is most likely the

product of simultaneous activity in many different areas of the brain. How, then, can we imagine that a miniscule amount of persistent brain activity—not even measurable due to the limits of current technology, and therefore hypothetical—could be the root of an experience described as "more real than real"?

After Pim van Lommel finished his talk, I joined him at the front of the stage. Our reunion that morning was warm. We hadn't seen each other for years, but time seemed to have passed him by—he had the same white hair, the same energy, the same enthusiasm as the last time I'd seen him. There was a break in the schedule, and while the audience trickled out of the room, I suggested that we find a quieter place where I could record our conversation.

Dr. van Lommel's first encounter with NDEs, at the age of twenty-six, was a funny one. It was 1969, the early era of cardiopulmonary resuscitation. Before 1968 and the widespread introduction of modern CPR techniques, everyone who went into cardiac arrest died.

The young doctor was part of the Netherlands's third cardiac intensive care unit. One day, his team was attempting to resuscitate a patient; after four minutes, the patient regained consciousness. While the doctors were thrilled to have succeeded, they were taken aback to hear that the man was strongly displeased about having been saved.

When they questioned him, he spoke about a tunnel, a light, music, and beautiful landscapes that he'd seen during the period of time when they were fighting to restart his heart.

At the time, Dr. van Lommel knew absolutely nothing about NDEs and didn't know what to think of this story. He tucked it away into a corner of his mind until nearly two decades later, in 1986, when he stumbled upon a book called *Return from Tomorrow* by a man named George Ritchie.[6] In the book, Ritchie, an American psychiatrist, recounts the story of an NDE that happened to him in 1943, when, as a young medical student, he "died" for nine minutes due to complications from mistreated pneumonia.

Dr. van Lommel was so struck by this book that he began to ask his patients who had survived cardiac arrest whether they remembered anything from their period of "unconsciousness," as much out of curiosity as out of medical interest. To his great surprise, out of about fifty patients over the course of two years, twelve reported having experienced something similar to an NDE.

This awakened his scientific curiosity and marked the start of his desire to study the phenomenon more rigorously. The result was the study I mentioned earlier, the results of which were published in *The Lancet* in December 2001: the most important prospective study ever carried out using strict scientific methodology.

We were able to find a quieter place for our conversation. I took out my notes, started the recorder, and began to question him.

"On what basis do so many scientists assume that near-death experiences are caused by residual brain activity?"

"Most skeptics don't know anything about near-death experiences. They think they're nonsense, but when you ask them if they've read any articles or books on the subject, they say they haven't."

Dr. van Lommel's response was scathing, but I pushed forward with my line of questioning. "Neuroscientists have only very crude tools to figure out what's happening in the brain. They can't be as precise as they'd like to be when it comes to understanding how the brain works. Several critical care specialists I've talked to have said that, given our current knowledge, it's impossible to rule out the hypothesis that residual, undetectable brain activity is the root cause of NDEs."

"That's what they're hoping for. It's the last explanation they can offer. Most neuroscientists still believe that consciousness is a product of brain function. But when you go into cardiac arrest, consciousness disappears within a few seconds, and blood flow to the brain drops to zero within one second."

"One second?" I echoed.

"One second. In one second, there's no more blood supply to the brain. Very quickly, patients stop showing any motor cortex reflexes. No more swallowing reflex, no more pupillary response. This is true for all cardiac arrest patients, which means that there are no longer any brain stem reflexes. No more breathing. And when we measure cortical activity with an EEG, it's flat. After ten to twenty seconds there isn't the slightest bit of activity. The clinical results of several studies on induced cardiac arrest in monitored patients show that there's no more brain activity—not in the cortex, not in the brain stem, not in any of the deeper structures of the brain. In the most efficient cardiac intensive care units, resuscitation takes about 60 to 120 seconds on average; that's the minimum, but generally, it takes more time before the blood pressure and heart rhythm are restored. So the 562 survivors of cardiac arrest in the four prospective NDE studies had zero activity."[7]

Dr. van Lommel explained to me that, when our consciousness is active, as it was at that very moment when we were chatting, all the neural centers of our cortex are working together. That's referred to as a "global neuronal workspace." He continued:

"According to neuroscientists, it's the coordinated activity in this global neuronal workspace that enables awakened consciousness. Yet during cardiac arrest there's no more activity. What we've observed with near-death experiences is the paradoxical occurrence of amplified consciousness without any brain activity, whereas it would seem that we should be observing no subjective experience at all in these patients, since the parts of their brains that are supposedly necessary for conscious experiences are no longer functioning."

"But the argument I hear most often," I interjected, "is that, given how limited our understanding of how the brain works is, it's impossible to say that cardiac arrest systematically leads to the shutdown of all brain activity, and since the neurons are still alive . . ."

"It's a common argument, but it's misleading. The question is not whether there's brain activity of any kind, but whether there's measurable brain activity of the specific kind that's considered necessary for conscious experience by modern neuroscientists—namely, visible and coordinated activity in numerous neuronal centers. The global neuronal workspace."

It is, in fact, often pointed out that in many firsthand accounts of NDEs following cardiac arrest, we don't have EEG proof that the people were actually in cardiac arrest at that time. During cardiac arrest, the priority isn't to perform an electroencephalogram, it's to save the person's life. The studies that Dr. van Lommel was mentioning, with which I was familiar and which I had mentioned during my conversation with Steven Laureys, had been conducted on patients in whom cardiac arrest was induced as part of the process of inserting an implantable cardioverter-defibrillator.

In these controlled conditions, it's reported that the EEG is flat within twenty seconds of cardiac arrest.[8]

Without this objective measurement—which is impossible to carry out, and which more importantly is useless in the context of resuscitation—is it possible to prove that brain activity has stopped based on other clinical signs?

7

Death in Real Time

The answer is yes: it is possible to prove brain activity has stopped through the absence of "brain stem reflexes."

Checking these reflexes right away is something we've all seen in TV shows like *ER*, when the doctor shines a light in the eyes of a patient who has turned up unconscious. Normally, in bright light, the pupil will constrict—except when the brain stem, which controls those motor reflexes, is no longer active.

The absence of pupillary light reflex is therefore evidence that activity in the deepest areas of the brain, the last to be affected, has stopped. So is the absence of swallowing reflex in a person who's being intubated. These clinical signs show that everything above the brain stem, including all the parts of the cortex associated with consciousness, have ceased to function.

Since Dr. van Lommel had held in his hands the medical file of the "lost denture man," I asked him how cardiac arrest had been diagnosed in that particular case.

"His electrocardiogram (ECG) showed ventricular fibrillation," he answered. "When he arrived in the emergency room he was cold and blue. He had no motor reflexes, no brain stem reflexes, and dilated pupils. That proves that his brain was inactive during that time. And yet he was able to describe everything he'd observed from above during his coma."

Ventricular fibrillation is an abnormal heart rhythm characterized by rapid, random, and ineffective contraction of the heart's ventricles, or lower chambers. Disordered electrical activity causes the heart to quiver instead of pumping blood normally, which cuts off the oxygen supply to the brain. Although this isn't the definition of cardiac arrest, it's functionally equivalent. Ventricular fibrillation causes a loss of consciousness within seconds. If not promptly treated, it leads to irreversible brain damage after about five minutes and death shortly after that.

Dr. van Lommel continued his explanation of the denture case. "It took about an hour and a half of cardiopulmonary resuscitation to restore the patient's circulation and blood pressure. He was young, forty-four years old, which is why the team worked so hard to bring him back."

"One might argue that his brain can't have been deprived of oxygen for more than five minutes in a row," I pointed out, "since he had no brain damage afterwards. It can't have been an hour and a half of anoxia! During resuscitation, he underwent chest compressions and he was put on a ventilator to prevent brain damage, so his brain was intermittently receiving blood . . ."

"Yes, of course," Dr. van Lommel replied, "but during resuscitation, they weren't restoring 100 percent of blood pressure. Maybe 30 percent or 40 percent."

"That's not nothing!"

"In our study we had a recording of every patient's electrocardiogram, showing their heart's electrical activity. The ECGs of patients in cardiac arrest always revealed an arrythmia that's generally fatal (ventricular fibrillation) or asystole (flatlining). For the resuscitations that took place outside the hospital, we received the ECG performed by the paramedics. All the patients in our study experienced both a complete stoppage in brain function and an expansion of consciousness with accurate perceptions, at the same time. We'd carefully recorded all the medical information: duration of cardiac arrest, duration of period of unconsciousness, how many times the patient had to be resuscitated, and what drugs in which doses had been administered to the patient before, during, and after resuscitation. As I said earlier in my talk: we must therefore come to the surprising conclusion that, in our study, during cardiac arrest, all the reported elements of an NDE were experienced during a temporary functional loss of all cortical and brain stem functions."

One of my friends, Cédric Meckler, is a former military doctor and a neuroscience researcher. I always find it fascinating to talk to him about consciousness; his scientific rigor is truly impressive. He's helped me a lot, particularly in my research on cardiac arrest. After corroborating what he's told me with what I've learned from other critical care specialists, I now have a clearer and more precise understanding of all the variables involved in cardiac arrest and resuscitation.

During cardiac arrest, circulation stops immediately in what's known as circulatory arrest or "no flow." Although there's no more cardiac output, a tiny bit of blood might still enter the brain. That blood is desaturated; its oxygen levels are insufficient, though some oxygen might remain, bound to the hemoglobin in the red blood cells. There are therefore still some energy reserves in the blood even though it isn't flowing.

Also worth noting is that oxygen desaturation following cardiac arrest is progressive, and doesn't affect all the parts of the brain at the same rate. Some can remain functional longer than others. And a brain cell doesn't go from normal activity to zero all at once. The body enacts protective measures, prioritizing where the available oxygen should go. It's possible that the remaining available blood flow will be redirected to the brain stem because once the brain stem is impacted, it's all over. But it's the body that "decides" on these priorities.

We have to distinguish between oxygenation at the organ level and oxygenation at the cell level. At this point, cells still have a tiny bit of oxygen in reserve. When the heart stops pumping and hemoglobin stops delivering oxygen to the brain, the cells go into standby mode, switching to other metabolic pathways that consume very little oxygen.

The brain cells aren't dead, because once resuscitation is complete, they resume normal activity. It's possible that a redistribution takes place in the parts of the brain that must be "favored" at all costs so that they can "resume normal activity" afterward. Some areas can continue to operate at a minimum, and others cannot.

But this is a cellular survival mechanism. The neurons go into standby, running on energy-saver mode thanks to the mitochondria, a cell's energy powerhouses. The electrical activity of the cells is basically nonexistent. The tiny bit of energy they do use isn't wasted; it's used only to preserve their integrity.

All the doctors I've asked about this agree that on the face of it, it seems unlikely that conscious experience could occur at this time, since the conscious activity usually observed in the cortex requires a significant amount of oxygen.

The fact that cell integrity remains intact until more than five minutes after the onset of cardiac arrest may suggest that other survival mechanisms are at work. If neurons don't irreversibly die when a patient is coming back from an NDE—and they don't, because if they did, there would be aftereffects, if the patient survived—then it follows that they were never totally extinguished, only paused. The neurons retained their polarization, and a survival mechanism kicked in to enable another form of consciousness.

To imagine that this survival mechanism is the biological "cause" of NDEs is to imagine that consciousness might not be dependent on the global neuronal workspace, as most neuroscientists believe, but instead on a much more subtle kind of cellular activity. The global neuronal workspace activity would merely be an observable correlation.

But in reality, this conjecture is based on nothing more than the desire to find a neurological explanation for NDEs. This desire—however rational it might seem—calls into question all the established, known, and observed models of brain function that neuroscientists have come up with so far.

An article recently published in *Annals of Neurology* revealed that researchers had observed surprising and powerful brain activity several minutes after cardiac arrest.

In the study, which was covered in French media,[1] researchers monitored nine patients admitted to the intensive care unit for extremely severe brain damage—three brain aneurysms, one stroke, and five head injuries, one of which was from a bullet. The patients' injuries were so devastating they were deemed incurable, their families signing a do-not-resuscitate (DNR) order. But before taking them off life support, the neurologists placed electrodes on their brains so that they could measure and record brain activity through electrocorticography (EcoG). Like electroencephalography (EEG), EcoG measures variations in electrical potential caused by neuronal activity; however, unlike with EEG, the electrodes are placed directly on the brain, rather than on the skull, enabling the recording of very low frequencies that can't pass through bone.

Through this study, the team of researchers, led by Professor Jens Dreier from the Center for Stroke Research at Berlin's Charité Universitätsmedizin—the largest university hospital in Europe—were able to establish a precise chronology of what takes place between cardiorespiratory arrest and the definitive shutdown of the central nervous system.[2]

They could watch death in real time.

After a period ranging from two to five minutes, the neurons began to explode—they *depolarized.* This irreversible cellular death was accompanied by a kind of surge: one final variation in the cell's electric potential that caused a chain reaction, spreading through the brain in a "wave of terminal depolarization" that moved through the brain at a speed of three millimeters per second.[3]

Some have hoped that this unexpected display of brain fireworks might be a new "explanation" of NDEs. Yet this phenomenon destroys neurons for good. It marks the beginning of brain death, which takes place gradually, starting at the back of the brain and continuing toward the front. Although the wave of terminal polarization does provoke sudden intense activity, it's irreversible. No one has ever come back from brain death.[4] This depolarization has nothing to do with NDEs.

These are very technical points, but they illustrate the futility of the mostly speculative efforts to find "possible biological explanations" for NDEs. These explanations—which aren't really explanations at all—are a way to avoid tackling the heart of the issue: our materialist theoretical model is obsolete.

Stubbornly persisting in seeking the origin of NDEs only in the brain puts the focus on the details rather than the phenomenon as a whole. NDEs are rich, complex, and profoundly mysterious. If we really want to give ourselves a chance to grasp what they have to teach us about the nature of consciousness, we also have to consider the aspects of the experience that don't fit neatly into our models.

Starting with the firsthand accounts, as the majority of NDE researchers have done, and considering them carefully and without preconceived ideas, we can see that all the "neurological explanations" sidestep several common aspects of NDEs that remain inexplicable, even with a brain that's functioning perfectly: veridical out-of-body experiences, in which experiences acquire verifiable information they couldn't have otherwise acquired; extrasensory perceptions; encounters with people who have already died; etc.

By widening our field of research, we can see clearly that NDEs are inexplicable from a strictly neuronal point of view.

"NDEs are caused by the brain" and "NDEs cannot be caused by the brain" are therefore not two equally plausible hypotheses.

The first one, which tends to be defended by the part of the scientific community unfamiliar with NDE research, is what we might call a "hypothesis based on principle." It postulates that as a matter of principle, all conscious experience must have a neuronal cause, even though the neuronal cause for NDEs has not yet been discovered. In the context of NDEs during cardiac arrest, this hypothesis involves contradictory assumptions and ultimately rests on one argument, which is really more like a stubborn bias: "It *has to be* from the brain!"

The other hypothesis is currently under development. It's based on a vast body of data from different scientific fields and countless firsthand accounts that have been collected, analyzed, and dissected by doctors, psychiatrists, psychologists, and neuroscientists who are studying the NDE phenomenon in all its complexity. This second hypothesis views consciousness as independent from matter.

It seems that NDEs are most likely linked to a temporary, spontaneous, and accidental connection with a fundamental dimension of our consciousness, and that this is completely independent of our brain activity.

8

Continuity of Consciousness

I'm getting to the point, Luna. For Dr. Bruce Greyson, as well as for most of the researchers I've been able to meet, the fact that the out-of-body perceptions of a near-death experiencer can be corroborated by the accounts of their medical teams is an extremely convincing argument in favor of the objectivity of those perceptions.[1]

Dr. Greyson told me about one witness account he'd investigated:

> One fellow that I know had emergency coronary artery bypass surgery. During the procedure, he claims to have left his body and observed it from above. He later drew a picture of the heart, marking where the infarction was. He'd had no way of knowing that. But the most surprising thing to him was that he said the cardiac surgeon was flapping his arms like a chicken during the procedure. He demonstrated to me what he meant. He didn't know why the surgeon had been doing that. Later on, when he recovered, he asked the surgeon, and the surgeon got very flustered and said, "Who told you about that?" The fellow said, "Nobody told me about it. I was watching it. I died, and I left my body, and I saw you do it."

> The surgeon got upset, and said, "Well, you're alive now, so I must have done something right." Since I'd been a doctor for thirty years, and I've never seen any surgeon do that, I asked the surgeon about it when I interviewed him. What he said was that he had let his residents start the operation and he had come into the operating room later. His hands were sterile, because he'd washed them, and he didn't want to risk contaminating them while he was watching. So he put them against his chest, where he knew they wouldn't touch anything. When he wanted to show the interns where to cut, he would make motions with his elbows. He was Japanese and had been trained to do it this way in Japan. He said he had never seen anyone else in the United States do it this way, but it was how he had been trained. That's an example of someone who claimed to have left their body, and saw something that was linked to a certain time during the procedure when we know he was unconscious—he'd already had his chest cut open. It was something he couldn't have known about. The other doctors in the hospital didn't even know that this surgeon had this habit.[2]

NDEs require us to adapt our methods of scientific investigation. If we stick exclusively to conventional methodologies, cramming NDEs into the same little boxes we always use, we're excluding essential data, such as the accounts that Dr. Greyson was telling me about in our interview.

"I remember the story of a man who, during his NDE due to cardiac arrest, sensed not only the presence of his deceased grandparents, but also that of a man he didn't know. Ten years later, his dying mother confessed to him that he was the product of an extramarital affair; she had hidden from him the identity of his real father, who was Jewish and who had been deported during World War II. She showed him a photo, and the near-death experiencer recognized in it the man he'd seen ten years earlier while he was in cardiac arrest. The man was actually his biological father! This type of account shows us that we're not talking about hallucinations or dreams—these perceptions can be verified and confirmed in factual reality."

NDEs sometimes contain other objectifiable elements that are even more disconcerting, such as encounters with people who have died without the experiencer having known about their death. Dr. van Lommel offers up one such case in his book:

> At the age of sixteen I had a serious motorcycle accident. I was in a coma for nearly three weeks. During that coma I had an extremely powerful experience. . . . and then I came to a kind of iron fence. Behind it stood Mr. Van der G., the father of my parents' best friend. He told me that I couldn't go back any further. I had to go back because my time hadn't come yet. . . . When I told my parents after waking up, they said to me that Mr. Van der G. had died and been buried during my coma. I couldn't have known that he was dead.[3]

These types of experiences are referred to as "Peak in Darien" experiences, in reference to John Keats's poem "On First Looking into Chapman's Homer." The poem describes the amazement of Spanish conquistador Hernán Cortés upon climbing a mountain in Darien, in what is now Panama, and seeing the Pacific Ocean for the first time, when what he'd expected to see was a continent spreading out before him. Keats's metaphor is used here to illustrate the awe we feel in front of something completely unexpected—such as the surprising apparition, during an NDE, of a person whom we don't know is dead.

Dr. Greyson narrowed in on these experiences in particular for one of his studies.[4] In a recent conversation, he explained to me how important it is to pay close attention to these "Peak in Darien" NDEs: "If you encounter your beloved grandmother during an NDE, one can always argue that it was your desire to see your grandmother that led you to imagine her. But if you see your sister, whom you believe to be in perfect health, and she says to you, 'I died in a car accident ten minutes ago,' and then you return from your NDE and someone calls your family to tell them that your sister had just died ten minutes before, how could you possibly explain that if you believe that consciousness originates in the brain?"

How indeed *can* you "explain" such encounters?

For Dr. Greyson, and for many other researchers with whom I've had the opportunity to discuss this subject, accounts like this—when they're corroborated and verified—are one of the strongest pieces of evidence that point to our consciousness surviving the death of our brains. This is also Dr. van Lommel's firm conviction. When I asked him whether he believes in an afterlife, he answered: "I don't use the term 'afterlife.' Life refers to a biological phenomenon in a physical world. When your body is dead, there is no longer a physiological vessel, but consciousness is still there. That's why I say 'continuity of consciousness.'"

"What convinced you of the continuity of consciousness? Was it a specific event?"

"No, it was a slow process. At first I had scientific curiosity: the stories I was hearing were 'impossible,' and then I read up on NDEs and met lots of patients. When you meet so many people and hear so many of their stories, the idea starts to take hold. I was a materialist scientist. As a student, I'd been torn between physics and medicine, and then once I was a doctor I decided to specialize in cardiology, because there's a lot of physics in the field. I'm very grounded. Very critical. It took me years to accept that what I had learned about the brain—that it created consciousness—was wrong."

I smiled, recognizing myself in his description. "So what is the relationship between the brain and consciousness?"

"We know that the brains of patients in cardiac arrest are not functioning. We can see that under the influence of psilocybin or LSD or ayahuasca, several areas of the brain are less active and yet consciousness increases. Heightened consciousness while the brain is less functional: the brain is a filter, an interface."

Later I'll come back to the groundbreaking contributions of psychedelic research, which is profoundly changing the field of neuroscience. For now, I was asking Dr. van Lommel how he thinks about consciousness in light of his work.

"I compare consciousness to the 'cloud,' the virtual storage space for an infinite amount of data. You need an interface to receive what's there. But the interface doesn't produce it. Your computer and your phone don't produce websites. In the same way, you need a functioning brain to 'receive' consciousness—in fact, a *very small part* of nonlocal consciousness. During a near-death experience, the filtering threshold changes so that suddenly you can receive a lot more nonlocal information."

The term that Dr. van Lommel was using, "nonlocal," is borrowed from quantum physics. It refers to the profoundly unsettling nature of atoms that, at the microscopic level, do not obey laws of causality. They transcend space-time, and are neither its building blocks nor its prisoners. This point is essential. If consciousness has a nonlocal dimension, the implications are staggering. I asked him to elaborate.

"I believe that consciousness is a primordial and fundamental component of our universe. We have a body, but we are not that body. We *don't have* a consciousness, but we *are* that consciousness. This implies that our ego—the accessible part of our consciousness—is not who we are. A higher part of our consciousness is interconnected with everything: the past, the present, and the future. I call this the nonlocal dimension of consciousness."

"So in that case, what does death represent?"

"From this perspective, death is merely the end of your physical aspcct—nothing morc. My opinion is that there is neither a beginning nor an end to consciousness; birth, death, and life are therefore only changes in its state, not the end. Our true consciousness is nonlocal, and ordinary consciousness is just one aspect among others."

Dr. van Lommel's words are seriously astonishing, Luna, don't you agree? And yet I've come to realize that his isn't a fringe, isolated opinion; it's a conclusion that more and more scientists are coming to. Studying NDEs, and particularly the extrasensory perceptions that accompany them, suggests that nonlocality does seem to be a fundamental property of consciousness.

We use the word "consciousness" to refer to several very different kinds of interior experience. Let me clarify: you're used to your "waking consciousness," the one you experience *by default*, which is profoundly dependent on your brain function. We could also refer to this as "brain consciousness."

But NDE research shows that this is only the tip of the iceberg.

This "brain consciousness" is merely the limited manifestation we're used to in our daily lives. Yet during an NDE, as brain activity diminishes significantly or even ceases altogether, a more fundamental dimension is revealed, characterized by unlimited extrasensory capacities—this is what we mean by "nonlocal."

Something in us is capable, under certain circumstances, of transcending space and time.

This tells us that these two dimensions of consciousness have radically opposing relationships with the brain. The first dimension comes from brain activity and can be observed directly by neuroscientists. The second dimension, the fundamental one, is clearly inhibited by brain activity and can be seen only by accident, when our brain activity is altered or even paused completely—such as during an NDE, or a shamanic experience, a topic I'll return to later.

If nonlocality is a property of this fundamental dimension of our consciousness, it means that it has neither beginning nor end. That means that fundamental consciousness lies outside time and space; it lies beyond death.

This is what religions refer to as "the soul." NDEs highlight its reality.

The reality of a nonlocal dimension of consciousness, the only one able to explain NDEs in their entirety, is what philosophers and spiritual teachers are talking about when they refer to humans as being of a spiritual nature.

I can guess the question on the tip of your tongue, dear Luna: if consciousness is nonlocal, if we're a soul incarnated in a body through space and time, what happens to us when the body dies? Do we hold on to the personality that's so familiar to us? Do we stay *us*? You've told me that this is a question that bothers you. I know that you're afraid that your current identity will disappear once you pass to the other side, even if life does continue after death.

You asked me one day why—if your fundamental consciousness is immortal—you don't have any memory of who you were before you were born. It was an astute question, and led me to the next phase of my investigation. I'll come back to it.

But before I do that, I want to tell you about other inexplicable phenomena during which consciousness seems to break free from brain activity and reveal its nonlocality. It's not just NDEs; there are many other types of experiences, particularly those on the threshold of life and death, that call our certainties into question. It's not surprising that palliative care workers so often witness these anomalies.

Dr. Greyson drew my attention to one such phenomenon, which, in his view, destabilizes the materialist model even more than near-death experiences do.

9

The Unnerving Phenomenon of "Terminal Lucidity"

When sixty-year-old Serge was admitted to the palliative care unit of the Mons-Hainaut regional hospital in western Belgium, he had only a few weeks left to live. He had a glioblastoma multiforme (GBM), a grade-4 brain tumor, that had been discovered four months earlier and was now terminal. At this stage of the cancer's development, further treatment was futile; two days earlier the doctors had decided to stop radiation and refer Serge to palliative care. Palliative care refers to everything that can be done when there's nothing left to be done: physical and psychological care right up until the end for the patient and their loved ones. A palliative care unit is a special place where two worlds meet—the world of the living and the world *after.*

The head of the palliative care unit—a nurse named Laeticia Légat, who had been there for eight years—was the one to welcome Serge. Several years later, when I interviewed her, she told me all about it.

"He arrived in a car with his children. He walked like someone who'd been drinking. He was struggling with his balance and had to be supported so that he didn't fall. He was conscious, but very confused and disoriented. He answered our questions, but only with a yes or a no; he was unable to form full sentences. He was extremely weak."

"Was that because of his tumor?"

"Yes. His children admitted to us that they weren't sure if he even recognized them. He was also suffering from partial paralysis, probably due to a brain compression, either from the tumor or from cerebral edema caused by the tumor."

"What was he like in the hospital?"

"His condition deteriorated rapidly. He became more and more confused and he stopped eating and drinking, to the point where we had to administer fluids intravenously. He could barely stand up and would collapse without assistance. After a week, he was sleeping most of the time, and we had no more contact with him. There was nothing unusual about his situation: most of the time, this type of deterioration is irreversible. That's why it had such a profound effect on me when, after sleeping deeply for more than a week, he woke up in a condition much improved from when he had arrived. For three days, he was awake. It was completely inexplicable to me. Then he fell back into sleep and died four days later."

"Was it only his psychological condition that improved, or did his motor abilities improve, too?"

"Both, because he was able to eat and drink on his own. He started talking again, forming complete sentences and expressing his wishes. He even went outside with his children, whom he was able to recognize again. During the surge, he could enjoy time with his family—of course, it was only for three days, but he was perfectly aware and lucid in a way that he hadn't been since before his admission."

"The surge?"

"Yes, that's the term we use. You see it sometimes: a period of time when the patient seems better, a brief surge for a day, sometimes a little longer. Maybe they haven't eaten for weeks but suddenly they're able to eat a meal. Generally, the next day or the day after that, they die."

She was talking about it as though it were a common phenomenon, which intrigued me.

"Is this something you see often?" I asked.

"Yes. It happens all the time."

"So why did this man's case make such an impression on you?"

"Because for him, the surge was unusually drastic, to the point where we noted it in his medical records: 'Without any obvious rational explanation, the patient is conscious again and able to communicate with his family.'"

"What did you mean by that?"

"It made no sense that the man could suddenly wake up from a deep sleep when his physical condition was relentlessly deteriorating. We hadn't made any changes to his medication, nor had we stopped any treatment that might have induced deep sleep. Why did he wake up for three days in a neurological state that was indisputably better? We didn't understand."

"What did the doctors say?"

"They had no explanation."

"Why was it so extraordinary? Why wasn't it possible for him to feel better for a few days?"

"Because the man was totally different during those three days. In a much better state than when he was admitted. The type of glioblastoma he was suffering from frequently progresses rapidly. He was displaying neurological signs specific to intracranial hypertension, which had severely altered his behavior, to the point where for a whole week he was barely awake at all. And then, totally inexplicably, he woke up, he was feeling better, he was walking, he could recognize his loved ones, and he died four days later. Out of my whole career, it's the situation that has had the greatest impact on me."

This "surge"-like phenomenon has a more official name: "paradoxical lucidity," or "terminal lucidity" for the cases—and most of them do fall into this category—that precede the moment of death by several days or even hours. The German biologist Michael Nahm has devoted several studies to the subject[1]; for some of them, he collaborated with Dr. Greyson.[2] He defines terminal lucidity as "the reemergence of normal or unusually enhanced mental abilities" shortly before death.[3]

As I mentioned earlier, Dr. Greyson confided during our meeting that to him, terminal lucidity is the most impressive demonstration of the idea that the brain does not create consciousness.

Why?

When people with advanced Alzheimer's or another type of dementia that causes severe damage to the brain suddenly become completely lucid again, recognizing the people around them and speaking in a coherent way that they've been unable to do for a long time, it's neurologically inexplicable. Their brains are too damaged for this under normal circumstances. "We have no explanation as to how this could happen," Dr. Greyson admitted.

Yet in many cases, this complete mental clarity can appear suddenly and unexpectedly, shortly before death, in people with obvious brain damage—due to a stroke, a tumor, or advanced Alzheimer's—who had previously been in a vegetative, nonresponsive state.

In one of their articles, Nahm and Greyson noted that in 84 percent of cases, terminal lucidity seems to occur in the last week before death, and in 43 percent of cases it occurs on the last day.[4] What's more, it's a more frequent phenomenon than we might expect.

Christelle, an American therapist who has specialized in end-of-life support for many years, told me that for her, terminal lucidity was a familiar phenomenon. She has frequently observed these strange, fleeting interludes in people suffering from dementia or Alzheimer's—where it seems like they're *coming back*, after having just minutes before been *not there.*

I don't know if you remember, Luna, but this happened to your great-grandmother. We went to see her together at the hospital and found her completely *gone*. The next day, however, she was entirely lucid again; she recognized us, and we were able to talk to her normally.

More generally, I've frequently heard about this "surge" phenomenon during visits to palliative care units in Europe and the US and in interviews with end-of-life caregivers and doctors. In one study carried out in the UK, seven out of ten caregivers in a retirement home said that over the previous five years, they'd witnessed patients with dementia become lucid several days before they died.[5]

Dr. Philippe Poulain, head of the palliative care department at the Ormeau Clinic in Tarbes, in southwestern France, told me that he estimated that 10 percent of people experience this type of phenomenon at the end of their life. He was personally aware of cases involving people affected by severe brain disease. For him, terminal lucidity is also accompanied by an improvement in the patient's physical state.

How can a brain that's so irreparably damaged it hasn't allowed a person to interact normally for years ever regain these capacities? The question is particularly perplexing for people with Alzheimer's.

Alzheimer's disease is a neurogenerative disorder characterized by the progressive degeneration of neurons in brain regions that control abilities like memory, language, reasoning, and attention. It causes irreversible damage to the central nervous system, largely due to the abnormal accumulation of a protein called beta-amyloid, which clumps together into "senile plaques" in the spaces between neurons. Little by little, the lesions multiply, eventually spreading into the upper regions of the brain.

It's usually at this stage that patients begin to show behavioral changes, leading to a diagnosis. Meanwhile, the irreversible damage is well underway. At first, they forget small things; then they forget the people they know, and then their own pasts. Finally, they begin to lose even their self-awareness.

As of now, no one has found a way to dissolve the beta-amyloid protein without dissolving the rest of the neurons.

In one of his articles, Nahm presents several case reports of people with Alzheimer's who experienced terminal lucidity. "The first case concerned an elderly woman who suffered from the illness for fifteen years and was cared for by her daughter," he writes. The woman was unresponsive for years and showed no sign of recognizing her daughter or anybody else. However, a few minutes before she died, she started a normal conversation with her daughter, an experience for which the daughter was unprepared and which left her utterly confused."[6]

In another, Nahm and Greyson present the case of a ninety-two-year-old woman who had been diagnosed with Alzheimer's nine years earlier and who no longer recognized any of her immediate family members, including her son. Twenty-four hours before she died, she regained consciousness and recognized everyone; she was perfectly lucid about her condition, her age, and where she was, despite having lost all her memories years earlier.[7]

We know that several forms of dementia, including Alzheimer's, are widely associated with the irreversible degeneration of the cerebral cortex and hippocampus, leading to confusion, disorientation, and memory loss, among other symptoms. Given that terminal lucidity comes on very suddenly, it's unlikely that neuronal regeneration is its cause—especially because it precedes death by several days, hours, or sometimes even minutes.

As Nahm puts it, how can we explain a period of dramatic behavioral recovery when the functional consequences of neurodegeneration are thought to be irreversible?[8] How could this be possible? It's not.

And this brings us to one of the most daring hypotheses put forward by leading researchers about the relationship between matter and consciousness.

10

Ghosts in the Hospital

Greyson's opinion is that when our brains are sufficiently damaged, they loosen their grip on the fundamental dimension of our consciousness. In the case of paradoxical lucidity, that would mean that a person's consciousness is temporarily able to operate the body (speech, motor skills, etc.) without use of their brain, as the cerebral areas that generally control these functions have been completely destroyed.

American neuroscientist Julia Mossbridge agrees wholeheartedly: "As a person is dying, perhaps she disengages from the damaged brain so as to give her access, once again, to those memories. But then, how is she able to speak?"[1] We've seen with NDEs that consciousness doesn't disappear when the brain is compromised, but with terminal lucidity, it's the body that's able to function again after years of irreversible neurodegeneration. Mossbridge concludes that in these situations, "the mind could directly manipulate the body without the mediation of the brain."[2]

Without the mediation of the brain? It sounds like science fiction, and yet I've heard this idea expressed many times, including by Dr. Eben Alexander, a famous Harvard-trained American neurosurgeon who experienced an NDE that completely transformed his worldview.

This experience, which he wrote about in his book *Proof of Heaven*, which became an international bestseller,[3] was a revelation to the stubborn materialist. We discussed terminal lucidity after a talk I'd given to researchers at the Division of Perceptual Studies at the University of Virginia, which he'd attended.

"I know of one patient whose metastatic cancer had taken over more than half his brain," he told me, "a man who hadn't spoken a sentence for months. Just before dying, he came back to life and spoke to a loved one. I heard about another case from a neuroscientist friend of mine who heads up one of the top neurosurgery training programs in the world. His father was suffering from progressive dementia and hadn't been speaking for weeks. And yet when my friend went to his bedside, his father came back to life and began talking, even saying that the soul of his own mother—my friend's grandmother—was in the room. Despite his very rational background and worldview, and even though he hadn't seen his grandmother himself, my friend was totally convinced of the reality of this experience, given what he knew of his father and the way this had occurred. This type of thing doesn't happen as a result of the brain making it up. His father's brain had been out of commission for weeks."

"So how do you explain it?"

"For me, this demonstrates the presence of a soul. When the soul leaves, the body is an empty shell. During terminal lucidity, the soul returns to the body in order to express something. It doesn't need the brain for that."

"But how is it able to manifest itself in a body whose brain is so damaged?"

"It's the mind that creates reality. The reality you observe is the manifestation of the soul—a projection. It uses the body and the brain as a projector of reality."

What Eben was suggesting was that our mortal biological selves are merely ephemeral material projections of a fundamental nonlocal consciousness that's capable, in the case of terminal lucidity, of exerting an influence on matter. It's as if our bodies, and all of material reality, are just images projected on a screen, while the nonlocal consciousness is the projector. The lifegiving force that animates all of material reality, including bodies, is not found on the screen, in matter; it's found in the projector—the fundamental consciousness. It's a crazy concept. And yet over two millennia ago, Plato had already suggested something similar with his allegory of the cave. Moreover, for more than a century now, this idea has become an acceptable scientific hypothesis, especially following the epistemological upheavals provoked by the discovery of the theory of quantum physics.

Max Planck, one of the founders of quantum mechanics, declared in an interview published in *The Observer* in 1931 that he considered consciousness as fundamental and matter to be derivative from consciousness.[4] For Erwin Schrödinger, another of the founders who was awarded the Nobel Prize in 1933, consciousness is the true bedrock of all matter. It's the foundation of the universe. And numerically, consciousness is one.

Matter as a derivative of consciousness.

In other words: according to this hypothesis, the physical world is an emergent phenomenon of consciousness, which could be a form of subtle energy, or a field underlying the visible universe—a bit like the image of a gravitational field—or perhaps something else entirely that remains undiscovered.

This fundamental consciousness permeates every layer of the physical world. And that physical world is ultimately nothing but a spatial and temporal projection.

It's like how the moon we see on the ground after a rain shower is not the moon itself, but merely a reflection. Our brains—and, by extension, our bodies—as well as the entire material world are, in fact, consciousness in a material configuration. Slivers of fundamental consciousness, frozen in time and space.

The most startling part of this hypothesis is the idea that our mortal biological selves are nothing but material and ephemeral incarnations of a fundamental, nonlocal, immortal consciousness. I'll come back to this later.

Many spiritual teachings agree on this point: consciousness is the source of material reality and has the power to act upon it. This point of view is supported by mind-body approaches and techniques, such as meditation. By allowing us to reconnect directly with fundamental consciousness, a regular meditation practice modifies matter—to be precise, our brain circuitry—as recent neuroscientific research has shown. Meditation grants our bodies access to the *source code* of our fundamental consciousness, so to speak, and in doing so, allows our consciousness to *reinform* our metabolism. This is even more pronounced in integrative medicine, where we harness the power of the mind to act on the physical body.

Many fields of medicine and science illustrate this reality, which has incidentally been known to spiritual teachers since the dawn of time: consciousness acts upon the body.

Returning to the discussion about the end of life: a story from Sylvie Ouellet, a Canadian friend of mine who witnessed a case of terminal lucidity, echoes this theory.

"My grandmother had devastating Alzheimer's," she explained to me. "It made her unable to speak for years. She stayed alive for years, in a state that wasn't unlike that of a baby. Her brain was irreparably damaged. But in the last moments before her death, she suddenly opened her eyes, smiled, and said to my father, 'Oh, it's beautiful.'"

"This was a few minutes before she died?"

"Yes. She passed away just two minutes later, in a state of incredible joy and serenity."

Sylvie has a medium's sensitivity to energy and is a spiritual and psychological instructor, so she spoke about this experience in spiritual terms rather than medical or scientific ones. It was a perspective that provided a whole other dimension to the question of consciousness.

"It was as though we were witnessing the reintegration of her consciousness into her damaged body," she continued. "I don't believe that consciousness is fully in the body at such an advanced stage of illness. But once it decides to use the body as a vehicle to transmit one last message before death, it's able to do it without being constrained by the effects of the disease."

We tend to try to explain any phenomenon using our point of reference, which is matter; that's what scientists do. But Sylvie was noting the same thing: all spiritual teachings describe matter as an *effect*. The cause is elsewhere, in what is immaterial. The fundamental consciousness. Yet it's still capable of manifesting outside the physical body if it decides to. This is what terminal lucidity cases seem to illustrate.

"So brain diseases like Alzheimer's or age-related cerebral atrophy don't imprison a person's consciousness?" I asked.

"My interpretation is that it's the personality that's directly affected; it's put to sleep by the limitations caused by the disease. But the soul, the consciousness, is not. Only its expression is. The constraints imposed on consciousness are already enormous in a body that's functioning normally; they're even greater in a body whose brain has been damaged. But sometimes, consciousness can overcome these constraints to express itself one last time through the body, like with terminal lucidity."

During terminal lucidity, the consciousness seems to be able to free itself from the constraints of the body. Can it go so far as to do away with the body altogether?

That's what other, even more unsettling phenomena that have been witnessed by doctors and end-of-life caregivers would suggest.

In September 2019, I met Dr. Marie-Jeanne Jacob, chief of medicine in the palliative care unit at the regional hospital in western Belgium where Laeticia is head nurse.

At a conference, Dr. Jacob alluded publicly to her experience working with patients who are dying. "The confidence and respect established over time with a patient means that they are willing to share what they're thinking and feeling as they reach the end. Patient after patient will describe in detail a person who's sitting in the room with them. Sometimes that person has already died—often their father or mother. It's a presence, a breath, a *walker* in the department. What these perceptions have in common is that it's difficult to define them. Maybe we don't yet have words to describe it? Or maybe, in our medical approach to death, there isn't room for these subjective observations, even though they're a part of our day-to-day lives? But these particular observations—which we mention in professional contexts with a smile, if not a sneer—aren't ever the focus of workshops or conferences. They still belong in the *paranormal* category, where we lump together anything that's unconventional. As you can tell, we think that these patients are telling the truth, and that their visions are probably real, but they're difficult to grasp."

Dr. Jacob's team talks very freely about this subject, which Laeticia confirmed. "Colleagues have sometimes seen shadows, wandering figures in the hallways," she told me. "One nurse sensed a hand on her shoulder when she was washing the body of a dead person. And when you listen to the patients, they're often saying the same thing. For example, in our department, in one particular room, several patients have seen a little white dog."

"What do you mean?"

"Our rooms are numbered one to six. In room five, very often, dying patients see a little white dog. I should clarify that we don't have a dog in the department."

"No matter which patient?"

"Yes. They tell us, 'Get the dog out of here,' or 'What is that dog doing in my room?' But there is no dog! And this always takes place in the same room."

"And the patients haven't spoken to each other?"

"No, they've never even seen each other. Since I've been here, at least six patients have talked about this dog. Every time it's in room five. Another time, a woman asked me why there was a man sitting near her bed. I didn't see anyone, so I asked her to describe him to me. Her description was exactly that of the patient who had occupied the room before her."

"Really?"

"She told me that he had a little mustache and an IV drip, and described how he was dressed. Just like the previous patient, who had died, and whom she'd never met. It's very common for patients at the end of their lives to describe people who are present in the room."

"Why couldn't it be a symptom of dementia specific to the end of life?"

"Because it happens over and over. And because it happens at the very end of a person's life. If it was a kind of confusion or hallucination, or a side effect of medication, the person would be talking about it all the time, but it really only happens at the end. As for the little dog, how could you attribute it to dementia when several people have seen the exact same thing?"

In the quiet of our hospital wards, in hospice care, and in the homes of people who have reached the end of their lives, these phenomena occur frequently, bearing witness to the fact that the moment is more like a metamorphosis—a passage between two worlds—than it is a plunge into nothingness:

Visions at the threshold of death, when people say they can see deceased relatives or friends, or religious figures, and that they're able to communicate with them;

The feeling that some experience at the moment of a close friend or family's death, as though they can sense the dying person's presence, or even see it, even though they're far away from their bedside—as though the dying person has come to warn them that they're passing on;

Auditory or physical phenomena, such as noises, music, moving doors, falling objects, strange electrical noises, and clocks stopping at or just after the time of a loved one's death;

Clouds of mist, shapes, light, or radiance emanating from the dying person;

And that mysterious lucidity, that heightened consciousness, just before passing on . . .

These phenomena, arguments in favor of a nonlocal consciousness, aren't confined within hospital walls or perceptible only to caregivers. Accounts of them come from everywhere, especially from those who are in mourning or about to be. And when we study each case more closely, the conventional explanation that it's a hallucination brought on by pain or grief can usually be dismissed quite quickly.

Luna, did I tell you that after your grandfather's death, I found out completely by chance that some members of our family had spontaneously communicated with someone who had died?

11

An Unexpected Visit

It was the end of summer, the end of September, and the air was beginning to cool down. The banks of the Seine were bathed in sunshine. With great emotion, I was exploring the large property where your grandfather spent many vacations during the first years of his life.

This was before the war, in the early 1930s. "Boisette" was like a dream for him. The vast estate had been purchased by my great-great-uncle in 1904.

For my father, Boisette meant freedom and wild adventure, which made a nice change from the Parisian apartment where he usually lived with his parents, Lise and Louis, whom you never met. It was a grand, imposing building with vast, tree-filled grounds that bordered the river and two cousins, Catherine and Bernadette, who provided a temporary reprieve from the solitude he usually faced as an only child.

Many of the oldest photos I have of him were taken here. In one of them, he's four years old, dressed in shorts and a leather jacket. He's sitting on the steps below the terrace, to the right of his mother, and they're looking at each other—him with intensity, her with gentle love.

More than ninety years had gone by since this photo was

taken. It was disconcerting to find myself there, in a place where the years seemed to overlap. The enormous tree to the left of the house, the pathway leading to the riverbank a couple hundred yards below, the air I was breathing: it felt like I could almost see the little boy come running up from the other end of the property, his shoes covered in mud.

My father's cousin Catherine was still living here when she died a little over a year before my visit. She was a very old woman, ninety-five years old. The last occupant from this bygone age. The property had just been sold. Catherine's daughters, my cousins Sonia and Olga, suggested I come see it before it no longer belonged to our family. I'd never been.

Olga was the one to welcome me.

The house had already been emptied. All that remained were intangible memories. The words seemed to echo in the big bare rooms. Olga gave me a tour, showing me the frescoes on the living room walls before we headed up to the second floor. The squeaking stairs, one bedroom after another, all empty—and yet I still expected to see my father as a dreamy-eyed little boy come running out of one, or his father, Louis, with his architectural plans under his arm, or Lise coming around the bend of the hallway. But it's not our expectations and desires that bring forth ghosts. If they come, it's for other reasons, reasons of their own.

Back on the first floor, we went out onto the terrace, and I told my cousin that I wanted to be alone in the park, in the silence interrupted only by the rustling of leaves.

"Take your time," she told me, and returned inside to take care of the last few boxes.

One summer, when he was very young, your grandfather built a raft and set off recklessly down the river, dragging along Catherine's younger sister, Bernadette, who was one year younger than him. A devilish urge for adventure had come over him, I'm sure. Already he was experiencing a geographer's thirst for landscape and exploration.

I searched for the memory of the raft in the lapping of the waves. It must be there? Perhaps it was hidden underneath the leaves of the trees leaning over the water? I didn't want to tear myself away. I stood there for a while, gazing at the opposite bank, before finally deciding to head back to the house, where my cousin had promised me a cup of coffee.

Her mother's death had been heart-wrenching for Olga. Catherine died in this very house, in the living room, in which they'd set up a home hospital bed. Her condition had begun to deteriorate sometime in May, and she died on July 4, just after 8 p.m.

Olga and her sister, Sonia, were alerted immediately and came from Paris in less than an hour. Catherine's body was still in the bed, forevermore motionless. The two sisters decided to watch over her, refusing to allow their mother to be taken to a cold and anonymous mortuary. Night fell, and time ceased to feel real. What is there to do in moments like these? You want to stay close to your loved one, perhaps pray for them, and allow the reality of an irremediable absence to sink in. Neither Olga nor Sonia had any thought of sleeping, and around 2 a.m., they went to the kitchen that adjoined the living room to make some herbal tea.

Olga described the scene to me in detail, knowing that she could trust me with the strange story of what she and her sister experienced that night in July.

"We were both here, in the kitchen. I was getting bowls from this cupboard while Sonia was filling the kettle. She was about to put it on the stove when both of us spontaneously turned around at the same time. It was like when you have the sensation that there's someone watching you—I don't know how to describe it any better than that. We both felt that there was something behind us, so we turned around, and we saw Mom."

"Your mom? Catherine?"

"Yes, even though her body was in her bed in the living room. She was in the kitchen, facing us from several feet away."

"What exactly did you see?"

"A very bright white human form. We could distinctly see her silhouette and the oval shape of her face, even if we couldn't make out her features. Sonia and I both reacted in the same way—we wondered if we'd gone crazy. We both could see her. There could be no doubt as to her presence. I don't know how to explain it. She appeared to us at the same time."

"Did you speak to each other?"

"Sonia and me? Yes, we said, 'Are you seeing what I'm seeing?' 'Yes!' 'Me too!'"

"Was it a flash?"

"Oh no, it lasted for what seemed to me like two minutes, even though that's hard to say exactly. But it was a long time."

"Two minutes! That really is long. And during that time . . ."

"We looked at her, and we looked at each other. At one point, Mom started moving in a way that looked like dancing, so I asked Sonia, 'Do you see what she's doing?' And she answered, 'Yes, she's dancing the Charleston.' 'That's exactly what I'm seeing, too,' I said. Mom was moving her arms, her legs, showing us how joyful she was. She radiated joy. The joy of being free. That's what I sensed. She hadn't been able to move for a long time—she'd been paralyzed by the pain and weakness of her aging body. It seemed like she was draped in white veils. It wasn't an old woman I was seeing, it was almost a young woman, twenty-five years old. She was made of white light—an angel without wings."

"Wow."

"Yes, glowing with that beautiful white light."

It was hard for me to imagine the sight; it seemed so extraordinary. Eagerly, I kept asking more questions. "What happened then?"

"All of a sudden, we couldn't see her anymore."

"She disappeared?"

"I don't know . . . All of a sudden I wasn't seeing her."

"Did you talk to Sonia after that?"

"We looked at each other, saying, 'Can you believe it?' It was extraordinary. For both of us, it was so obvious that it was Mom."

"You didn't have any doubts about what you'd just seen?"

"Not a single one. Especially because it was so unexpected. I could never have dreamed of experiencing that. But no, there was no doubting it. Plus, we both saw it! We were stunned to realize that we had the same vision."

On my way back home, I called Sonia, who confirmed every detail of her sister's story. "It was a luminous silhouette. You couldn't exactly see her features, but there was no question that it was Mom. Her silhouette was very recognizable. There was a lot of light and a lot of joy coming from that face. You could almost see her smile, even though her features weren't defined. How happy she was to be free! There's no other word for it . . . being free. Inexpressible joy radiated from her luminous form. It's hard to describe it, it's just an experience . . . I don't know if Olga told you, but she started to do a few steps of the Charleston. She'd loved dancing when she was younger. It was such a wonderful gift she gave us. As though she had come just to show us how happy she was to have finally crossed over to the other side."

Luna, you told me a little while ago that some of your friends who have lost a loved one have confided in you that they've experienced something similar. Perceptions that were subtle and strange. I'm not surprised. Studies show that between 40 and 50 percent of grieving people report these types of experiences. They're called "after-death communications," or ADCs. The Swiss researcher Evelyn Elsaesser conducted the largest international study to date on the subject.[1] Her team collected and analyzed more than a thousand firsthand accounts.

Her research highlights and corroborates the conclusions that many psychiatrists have drawn from the countless stories they've heard from their patients: ADCs have nothing in common with hallucinatory phenomena or compensatory mechanisms linked to grief. As the psychiatrist Christophe Fauré pointed out to me, if they did, then every grieving person would experience an ADC, but that's not the case. "If it were a protective mechanism against the pain of grief, it would occur almost systematically. The human mind does have protective mechanisms; they're pretty much universal, and there aren't all that many of them. And most importantly, we know what they are, we can observe them, and they're activated as soon as they're needed. However, not everyone has an ADC. So why should they occur only at certain times and in certain people?"[2]

When we study these various forms of ADCs seriously, it appears that they cannot be explained in psychological terms. They occur without the communicator having wanted it or sought it out. Signs, messages, apparitions . . . these aren't rare and highly suspect occurrences. They're a daily reality for hundreds of thousands of people every year.

The phenomenon is both commonplace and earth-shattering. So many families are affected. Ours is no exception, as shown by my cousins' story.

They had told me about it because they felt confident that I would be receptive to hearing it. And that's often the problem:

when these experiences occur, few people dare talk about them out of fear of the reactions they'll get from those around them. They fear others will think them gullible, or carried away by their suffering, even though the authenticity of the experience, however impossible it seemed, makes it so that they have no doubt in its veracity.

The vast majority of ADCs occur in the hours, days, or weeks following a death. It's as though the deceased person's desire to reassure their loved ones is an irrepressible priority for them.

The stories vary. Sometimes the deceased literally appears, as for Olga and Sonia. Or sometimes they make their presence known in other ways, murmuring a word or a phrase, or touching the person's arm.

I know that you read the book that I wrote about this a few years ago, in which I collected a number of accounts of ADCs, each one more moving than the last.[3] A mother who saw her son appear very clearly in the silence of the night, fifteen days after his death; Stéphanie, whom you know, seeing her partner standing in the kitchen in the middle of the day, a month after his fatal accident; a wife sensing her husband lying down next to her in bed the night before his funeral. A hand on a shoulder, a breath of wind when all the windows are shut, a scent wafting through the air, a few words heard when no one is there, etc.

These experiences are always spontaneous. They're surprising and destabilizing. They're calming, too, profoundly so, and in this way they can be powerful resources in the grieving process—that is, if they're treated with respect and openness by those around us. Listening is the key. Listening without judgment.

After your uncle Thomas died, I didn't have any contact with him, though I would have loved to. However, at the scene of the accident, something did occur that I found troubling. I could feel in myself a kind of astonishment and confusion that didn't belong to me. How can I explain it? I was in a state of shock, obviously, but I felt like I was immersed in a cloud of confusion that had nothing to do with my own state, and which seemed to pervade the whole scene. It was so striking at the time that I even spoke to Thomas to *explain to him* what had just happened, as though I was obeying an unconscious need.

You know how sometimes you'll find yourself next to someone who's experiencing something very heavy, and even if they don't show it, you can sense that they're not okay? It's like the emotions are seeping out of them and you're able to pick up on it.

At the time of Thomas's death, that's exactly what happened for me.

I wasn't then capable of putting it into words—or even believing that it was possible!—but it was this: I could feel Thomas's immense confusion. And so without thinking, I spoke to him: looking down at his body, I told him that he had just died. I didn't make it a big speech; I was so overwhelmed. I simply said to him, "You're dead. You've just died. I'm going to take care of you."

I believe that was when everything changed for me, that something clicked in the depths of my unconscious. It took me years to realize it, but without knowing it, it was Thomas I was sensing at that moment. He was there, *still alive*, in the air around me, while I was on my knees in front of his lifeless body, holding his abandoned hand. His liberated soul mingled with my own.

My patient and methodical scientific investigation—everything I've just shared with you—allowed me to realize that this was within the realm of possibility. But how could I be sure?

How could I overcome the limitations inherent to the scientific approach when trying to understand a phenomenon that is by definition subjective? Would it be possible to reproduce that moment? To establish contact with Thomas?

It was at this point in my investigation, as I was wondering what kind of experience would be enough to convince me that communication with him was possible, that I discovered shamanism.

Do you remember? You were nine years old when, in 2006, I took off for the Amazon for the first time with a truly crazy expectation: to see your uncle. I think it's time now to tell you the whole story of my journey. It's difficult to describe, and without it I would never have found essential answers to the questions that wouldn't stop tormenting me.

12

Beginning My Journey with Amazonian Shamans

All around the world—from Mongolia to the Amazon, from the Himalayas to the Hawaiian archipelago, from Australia to southern Africa, and in a thousand other lands—shamanic traditions are still practiced, though their origins have been lost to the sands of time.

"Shaman" is a generic term that comes from the Tungusic languages, spoken to this day in Eastern Siberia and Manchuria. Its definition has expanded to refer to all those who have acted as intermediaries between humans and the spirit world since the dawn of humanity.

Different groups around the world have their own qualifier to describe a shaman's local function in the community: healer, medicine man, soul guide, etc. What all these "shamans" have in common is that they're the bearers of esoteric knowledge—esoteric in the Greek etymological sense, coming from the term *esôteros*, meaning "from within." This knowledge isn't passed down from other people; it's received directly and subtly through an initiation into the endless wisdom of the spirit world.

All shamanic traditions consider these *spirits* to be an integral part of our reality. Though they are invisible to us, the spirits of plants, animals, the deceased, and other beings act upon our material dimension, interacting with us without our knowledge. They reveal themselves to those who are capable of perceiving them, whether spontaneously or through various mind-body practices or psychoactive substances. Could "spirits" be another kind of reflection—furtive and immaterial, but unfathomably prolific—of the fundamental consciousness that pervades the living world?

Shamans explain that they can connect with the spiritual realm by means of visionary states. In doing so, they can heal and seek help or knowledge. The Asháninka people of the Amazon refer to spirits as *the hidden ones.* I like this phrase, because if something is *hidden*, we can find it.

My experience in the Amazon was awe-inspiring. At the time, I had spent the majority of my professional life crisscrossing the steppes, mountains, and scorching plains of the Indian subcontinent, the Horn of Africa, the Himalayas, and central Asia. I'd never experienced the colossal organism—dark green, humid, and magnificently alive—that is a tropical rainforest.

Before Thomas's death, I'd sometimes had disconcerting experiences during my reporting trips, but I didn't pay a lot of attention to them; I was an investigative journalist devoted to "serious" subjects like the war in Afghanistan, regional social and political crises, and the heroin trafficking routes between the Golden Crescent and Europe.[1]

Now I know how important shamanism is to the regions I'd spent so much time in. I hadn't crossed paths with a single shaman in central Asia, perhaps because in post-Soviet states, eighty years of crushing domination had forced practitioners into hiding. And, of course, I hadn't been looking for any.

During those years, my life couldn't have been further from any subject related to spirituality. Even when I was reporting on the "Tibet question," even when interviewing the Dalai Lama in November 1989, I showed only a polite interest in Buddhism. I was too busy trying to decipher the intricacies of the geopolitical situation between India and China.

Your uncle's death changed everything, causing the big existential questions that had tormented me when I was a teenager to bubble up again. Suddenly, nothing seemed more essential than trying to answer them. Everything else became secondary.

After his funeral, I was incapable of simply returning to my life as a journalist as though nothing had happened. It was impossible to go off on a reporting trip to this or that conflict zone and leave gaping open the cosmic void that Thomas's brutal accident had created.

Let's just say that my hopes were excessively high when, in July 2006, I got off the plane at the Iquitos airport in the heart of the Peruvian Amazon. It was hot and humid, and the scent of the surrounding vegetation mingled with that of diesel fuel. I knew quite well that this attempt to "see my brother in the land of the dead," to take the shamanic worldview at face value, might seem delusional, or naive at the very least.

But then again, why not?

Why should we automatically assume that these practices are baseless beliefs, when so many studies have detailed the profound coherence of the indigenous cosmologies they come from? When shamans the world over, no matter their cultural origins, say exactly the same thing about the existence of a spirit world that we might be able to access?

It seems more rewarding to think that the field of possibilities is much wider than I've been taught. I'm happy that we share this. At some points in life, Luna, it's better not to ask yourself too many questions, or else you'll stay frozen right where you are. Sometimes you have to take the plunge and throw yourself into the unknown even if you don't have all the information yet. The answers don't come from hesitation, they come from action—from taking risks, and from learning from the mistakes we make along the way.

And so even if my knowledge of shamanism was admittedly patchy before I took off for South America, and even if I was chasing a dream, I *felt* that I had to explore it, no matter how extravagant it was. I had to see for myself.

For the most part, Amazonian shamans are *curanderos*, which translates to "healers." They use a psychoactive decoction called "ayahuasca" that contains dimethyltryptamine (DMT), a psychotropic substance that naturally occurs in many plants. *Ayahuasca* is a Quechua word meaning "vine of the dead." Ingesting it induces powerful visionary states and allows one to enter into contact with the spirit world. The beverage is the foundation of a *medicina*, a sacred medicine based on an alliance between plant spirits and humankind.

I find the term "entheogen" better suited for these trance-inducing natural substances than "psychedelic." They've been used for millennia for spiritual or shamanic purposes.

Many plants and mushrooms have these psychoactive characteristics. "Entheogen" is a neologism created at the end of the 1970s from the Greek words *entheos*, or "inspired by the divine," and *genesthai*, "birth." An entheogen is therefore a substance that enables a spiritual or ecstatic experience. An encounter with the soul.

The beverage known as "ayahuasca" is actually made up of two different plants: the ayahuasca vine, or liana (*Banisteriopsis caapi*), and leaves from the chacruna (*Psychotria viridis*), which contain the psychoactive substance DMT. Consumed on their own, chacruna leaves don't have any effect, because the DMT is inhibited by enzymes in our digestive system.

How did shamans in ancient times find out how to circumvent this inhibitory effect by combining chacruna with another plant—the ayahuasca vine, which contains MAOIs, or monoamine oxidase inhibitors—that prevents DMT from breaking down in the intestine? It's the combination of these two plants that gives the decoction its immense psychoactive power. One of them on its own would have no effect.

If you ask contemporary shamans this question, they respond quite naturally that the spirits were the ones to teach them the recipe for the sacred beverage.

It's a perplexing answer. Trial and error is statistically extremely improbable—there are literally tens of thousands of different plant species in the Amazon. It might be reassuring to our supposedly rational minds to think that they did it by chance, but logically, this answer doesn't hold up very well.

The origin of ayahuasca is its first mystery.

When I began this Amazonian adventure, I had never taken a single drug in my life. As a journalist reporting on the cultivating of poppies, from which opium is extracted, and the trafficking of heroin, made from poppies, I'd observed their devastating effects—both from trafficking and consumption. Before you were born, Luna, I spent several years as an Afghanistan and central Asia correspondent for an NGO that focused on the geopolitics of drugs. There I discovered just how much damage heroin can do to society; it would never have occurred to me to touch it myself.

In France, ayahuasca is considered an illegal drug subject to the same restrictions in terms of both possession and usage as cocaine and heroin. But it's not at all the same thing.

In the Amazon, ayahuasca is viewed quite differently.

In Peru, as in several other South American countries, it's considered by the authorities to be part of the country's cultural heritage, and its consumption is not only legal but central to age-old traditions.

As I began to take an interest in Amazonian shamanism, I soon noticed that the term "drug" is used to refer to substances with a wide range of effects and levels of dangerousness. This conflation of things that are nothing alike, and the legislation that goes along with it, isn't based on health, medical, or cultural data; it's based on wildly uninformed political considerations and judgments.

For example, with ayahuasca, there's no risk of overdosing unless you drink something like several liters of the beverage, which is physically impossible. Moreover, research shows that it's not addictive. Just the opposite, in fact: ayahuasca can be used therapeutically in treating drug addicts, heroin addicts especially.[2] However, it does require a supportive framework, because its effects can be very destabilizing and should only be experienced with intention and under specific circumstances. It can also provoke nausea and even vomiting. Taking ayahuasca is no small thing.

All the same, it's markedly different from heroin, cocaine, fentanyl, and their derivatives, which are addictive substances that cause reduced cognitive and social abilities and are extremely harmful for your health.

They are the exact opposite of psychedelics that are consumed in a structured, guided way.

Ayahuasca is at the heart of an ancestral practice based on a symbiotic relationship with nature. Shamans use it to treat the physical and mental illnesses of those in their care. For millennia, this sacred beverage has been a priceless asset for humans adapting to one of the most inhospitable environments on the planet.

Ayahuasca, and in general many psychoactive substances, are at the heart of practices intended to foster sacred experiences, connections to both an internal and external reality.

I remember it as though it were yesterday: my "first time" was nearly my last, even though I was guided by a shaman who had been recommended to me and who had introduced many visitors to Peru to these ayahuasca ceremonies. I'd planned a four-week-long trip, which gave me the chance to try it several times. I landed in Lima and, after one night in a hotel, headed for the heart of the Amazon rainforest, full of hope and expectation.

Night had fallen, and I was sitting in a maloca, one of the round huts where these ceremonies traditionally take place. I was impatient, but all the same felt a certain kind of apprehension. That day, I was wearing a blue scarf that had belonged to Thomas. A little bit of him with me, just a few hours away from what I hoped would be our reunion.

13

Ayahuasca

Two candles were burning in the middle of the maloca, projecting dancing shapes onto the walls. To my left was the shaman. Next to his mattress was a jumble of objects, bags, and plastic bottles. Several of them contained a dark, opaque liquid: ayahuasca.

The forest around us had been plunged into darkness, and millions of nocturnal insects and amphibians produced a stridulating hum.

I'd been reminded constantly that ayahuasca can cause vomiting, so I made sure to keep my plastic basin close at hand, along with my flashlight and notebook.

With slow movements, the shaman examined the different bottles around him, searching for the one for the ceremony. I looked at him quietly. He was calm, seeming almost sleepy. His voice was gentle, and he joked around a little. Squinting in the candlelight, he wiped off a tiny glass, lifted it to eye level, and poured in a little bit of ayahuasca before putting the bottle down. He wrapped his hands around the glass, brought it to his lips, and blew on the liquid with long, staccato whistles. After several minutes he called my name.

"Estephan . . ."

I sat down facing him and took the glass that he was holding out to me, filled with a thick brown liquid.

"Quiero ver a mi hermano muerto."

It's the only sentence in Spanish I've learned by heart: "I want to see my dead brother." I said it without knowing whether I was supposed to be speaking right then.

He looked at me intently, his eyes soft.

"Sí . . ."

There was benevolence in the smile that stole onto his face. I raised the glass and swallowed the ayahuasca, surprised to find that it wasn't as unpleasant as I'd been told. It was pungent, tasting of earth and macerated plants. A big gulp. I salivated and swallowed several times to soften the astringent taste lingering in my mouth.

Here we go. I could barely contain my emotions. After blowing on his own glass for a long time, the shaman took a drink from it, then got up and extinguished the candles, plunging the maloca into darkness. I had no idea what was going to happen next, or how long it would take for the substance to take effect.

I widened my eyes and waited restlessly for something to appear. The moon cast a bluish glow through the mosquito nets. A light breeze was stirring the branches of the trees, their shadows drawing pale shapes inside the maloca. I was on high alert, feverishly turning my head toward every movement I could detect around me.

The minutes passed.

Half an hour passed.

No visions. No matter how hard I looked, I couldn't see anything changing. However, I was starting to feel more and more nauseated; my stomach was twisting, and I felt very weak.

I was resisting a growing urge to vomit. I realized that I was absolutely exhausted, to the point where I decided to lie down. But that only worsened my nausea. I was sweating; I couldn't find the right position; every movement was uncomfortable. I curled up in the fetal position, but then I lost control and had to straighten up quickly to vomit violently into the basin that I managed to grab just in time.

It provided temporary relief.

Then I felt sick again. Physically destroyed, as though my insides were knotted up and my muscles had been run over. My head spun when I lay down, but it was worse when I tried to sit up: pain throughout my whole body. I started to tremble. My movements were clumsy and unsure; I adjusted the cushion against the wall of the maloca—maybe I would feel a little better propped up?—but no, I couldn't escape the nausea that was coming over me. I felt like there was something in my stomach that needed to get out. A black, viscous mass in my guts.

I lost all sense of time.

The experience was punishing. It was too hard.

I could hear a jerky whistling sound, very faint at first. I'd lost my bearings and couldn't identify its source. It got louder, then turned into a song, a sort of lively melody. Was it the shaman? Or was it something else? I was no longer sure whether my eyes were open or closed, as though that no longer affected my perceptions one way or another.

The song spurred my thoughts; it was spinning in my head, dancing, crushing me. I wanted it to stop, wanted this terrible physical discomfort to cease. I wanted to sleep. I couldn't take it anymore. Nothing I could do provided any relief. I was overcome by my flesh, my guts; my body hurt, so bad. *Stop! Have mercy . . .* Was there anyone who could stop this?

Let's get it over with!

"Estephan?"

Was the shaman calling to me?

I dragged myself over to him, painfully.

"What . . . ?"

He didn't answer, but instead began to sing again. I couldn't stand up straight; my kidneys hurt; my arms were wrapped tightly around my painful stomach. An immense weariness came over me, demoralizing me.

This was going on too long. I was getting annoyed. Never mind Thomas. I wanted this to stop. *Finish your song and let me sleep. I've had enough now. My head is spinning, and I'm in too much pain.* During the rare moments of respite, I tried to calm down and express my gratitude to ayahuasca for cleansing me. Wasn't that what they'd told me? That ayahuasca had this purgative role? I hadn't realized the extent of the violence this implied. To be on the safe side, I thanked the plant mentally for what it was doing to me. But I didn't actually care about being cleansed at all. That wasn't what I'd come for; I'd come to see my brother. If that wasn't going to be possible, no big deal, we could just end things right there. Anger spread throughout my body like hot liquid.

His singing was getting on my nerves!

Finish your song and let me go to bed.

I didn't understand anything. I was nothing but anger. Anger with myself, mostly. Anger at being this sick, for no payoff. My body was wrecked, I couldn't stop vomiting, my skull hurt, I was exhausted. I was such an idiot.

Leave me alone . . . just leave me the hell alone.

At the end of the song, I crawled to my mattress and gathered what little strength I had left so that I could fight my way out of the maddening malaise. Lying on my side, motionless and trembling, I waited for the effects to begin to fade away. Would it ever stop? Eyes closed, exasperated by the unpleasant physical sensations, emptied of all energy, my body limp and abandoned, with nothing but spasms of bile coming out and burning my throat, I had no choice but to wait. It must have been several hours before I was able to fall asleep.

When I opened my eyes, surprised to be feeling a little better, dawn's rays were peeking through the openings in the maloca.

The day passed like a mirage. The nausea was still there. I was bewildered. What had I done wrong? Why had it been so difficult physically?

When I saw the shaman a little later, he assured me that my reaction was normal. He explained briefly that I first had to get out whatever was inside of me, and only after that would I see images from my past and my brother. But what did it mean to "get out whatever was inside of me"? I would have to start all over.

14

Learning to "See"

That first horrible night, doubled over with cramps, I'd sworn never to try again. But the next night, curiosity won out over apprehension, and I drank ayahuasca once more. And then once more the next night. And again the next night. . . . It was four weeks of near-daily initiation.

After several ceremonies, I became more familiar with the first effect: distortions in my perspective when it came to the sounds and noises of the forest. As the ayahuasca spread throughout my body, the humming of the insects around me transformed into a kind of surreal shimmering, as though millions of little crystals were clinking against each other. My senses mingled and overlapped.

Alongside that effect, the experience remained physically demanding. I no longer had control over my own body, and that sensation was terrifying. In general, my nights were hard. Nearly unbearable. I was intermittently overwhelmed by images and visions that were difficult to describe; plus, I was still vomiting, quite a lot.

The shaman said that I was afraid of something inside me. He didn't know what it was. And I didn't understand what he meant by that.

Under the influence of ayahuasca, everything in my field of vision—the floor of the maloca, the walls—moved, transforming into a teeming organic mass. *Things* were crawling on all the surfaces of the hut, right before my eyes, like a muddle of shapeless insects. I also saw more and more snakes. They appeared in the form of a tangled mound of hundreds of undulating reptiles; when I tried to hold on to the vision, I was sucked right into it and grew even more disoriented. At times, the panic was unspeakable; at other times, the visions were staggeringly beautiful.

However, every morning after a ceremony, I found that I couldn't understand what had been so frightening to me hours before. Even though I went through periods of time that felt almost unbearable, afterward, I couldn't seem to figure out what had provoked them. The terrors weren't connected to what I was seeing, but to what I was feeling physically.

I continued to cling to the possibility of seeing Thomas. Every evening, drinking the ayahuasca, I repeated the same request: that I be shown death, and that I encounter my brother.

As the weeks and ceremonies went by, I sometimes had the sensation that there were other presences around me during moments of relative calm. It kept my hopes alive. I thought I could perceive shadows, characters, and luminous shapes that seemed like tall, slender human bodies. And I continued to have very powerful but confusing visions: dark organic forms, snakes that merged with vines, landscapes of vibrant vegetation. Both sublime and disturbing. My perception of myself grew muddled—sometimes I felt like I was outside my body, but it was never clear.

The psychoactive effects of ayahuasca are extremely intense both physically and psychologically, and they're a far cry from the simple visionary experiences I was originally expecting. Ayahuasca seizes your body, grinds it down, and shakes it; meanwhile, your perceptions shift chaotically. It's very hard to get used to it.

In general, I didn't understand anything. I was subjected to a synesthetic avalanche in which, superimposed on top of what I could see in real life—the maloca, dancing shadows from the moonlight—was a fabulous world of moving forms, and I was unable to tell whether my eyes were shut. Even when I tried to make a conscious effort to open or close them, it didn't change what I was *seeing*.

I had a feeling that ayahuasca was revealing a field of perception that lay on top of my usual vision and hearing. Like so many researchers, writers, and explorers before me, I realized confusedly that what was happening was probably related to what's been described as opening the *doors of perception*. We owe this phrase—which the writer Aldous Huxley used to describe his own experimentation with entheogens[1]—to the poet William Blake: "If the doors of perception were cleansed every thing would appear to man as it is, infinite."[2]

But if that's what that was, I was overwhelmed by the infinite, and incapable of integrating the mass of new perceptions it represented. It was too radically different.

I felt like someone born blind and suddenly offered the chance to see for a few brief moments. It was so "new" that it was almost insurmountable.

Luna, imagine that you don't know what light is, nor forms, space, or colors. And then suddenly you can see—but how could you possibly understand what you're seeing? You have no visual reference for it. You're overwhelmed by cognitive stimuli you were completely unprepared for, stimuli that have no connection to anything your brain is already familiar with. That's exactly what I was experiencing.

While we're talking about visual perception, I should clarify a few things to help you understand why my experiences were so confusing.

In day-to-day life, it's not our eyes that "see," it's our brains. Our neural circuits create visual images of the world we're looking at based on acquired models. The brain interprets the stimuli captured by the retina and, from a reduced proportion of these sensory signals, *guesses* the rest based on its past experiences. When we "see," the images that appear in our head are actually mental reconstructions.

As one of the world's leading brain specialists, the German neurophysiologist Wolf Singer, professor emeritus at the Max Planck Institute for Brain Research in Frankfurt, puts it:

> Perception is actually not as holistic as it appears to be. We scan complex scenes serially, and actually much of what we seem to perceive we are in fact reconstructing from memory. Which of the many signals actually reach the level of conscious awareness is determined by a host of factors, both conscious and unconscious.[3]

In other words, the brain is constantly interpreting based on what it's previously learned. It takes several elements and uses them to produce a vision of the whole in our mind, in an imaginative process akin to *hallucination*; literally, our brains deceive us.

Our perception of the world isn't a literal transcription of reality; it's a mental reinterpretation.

This goes for visual perception as well as all other types of cognitive perception. Everything is filtered and analyzed. We don't consciously determine how this sorting process takes place. It's a function of how our sensory organs have developed and how our brain is structured. Therefore, the way we perceive the world is linked to the way we've learned to experience it. On the basis of this acquired experience, the brain concentrates on the sensory signals it deems essential and uses them to deduce what it expects to see.

During my shamanic ceremonies, I experienced this neurological reality: my brain was overheating. Confronted with an avalanche of perceptions it wasn't used to, it fought to try to make them fit with my unconscious patterns of interpretation, the mental frame of reference it had been building ever since I was born.

And of course that didn't work at all!

Another world may have been appearing for me, but my brain was completely lost and couldn't understand any of it. In a way, this brain automation was preventing me from *seeing* the true nature of the *vision of the mind* opened up by ayahuasca.

There was a battle inside me between a mind determined to use what it knew to try to understand what was going on and a more profound dimension of my consciousness that was gradually unfolding. Each night, I experienced my neurologically human handicap for perceiving otherness. We aren't made to see what we've never learned to see.

We have to learn.

This raises the question of the role of my unconscious during those nights where the ayahuasca threw my usual state of consciousness into upheaval. In my "visions," what belonged to my brain's attempts to reduce ambiguity—to its interpretations of these completely new perceptions—and what belonged to external reality?

At that stage, I was still incapable of measuring the breadth of my unconscious interpretations, except on very rare occasions. For the moment, the invisible world could have been a screen onto which my inner world was projected, and I didn't have enough experience to be able to exercise discernment. What belonged to me? What was outside me?

For example, some nights, faces would come out of the darkness. They leaned over me, watching me. Aztec or Incan faces, shrouded in intricate patterns that didn't stop moving. Coming closer to me, they covered my face with black fabric, and suddenly everything went dark. Then I could begin to perceive shadows again, entities with indistinct forms.

Who were they?

Real presences? Real presences, but ones onto which my brain has projected these particular appearances, because they were available in my bank of mental images? Or pure, irrelevant hallucinations?

Each ceremony lasted for several hours. For me, the ceremonies were a constant struggle to try to understand, to resolve, this essential question. All my efforts seemed to be in vain. Oddly enough, this didn't discourage me.

Under the influence of ayahuasca, reason no longer functions normally. The plant opens up a sensory and subjective space in which analytic thought is a handicap. The more I clung to it, the less clear things were. The more I sought to "understand," the more lost I became. I kept being told that I had to "let go of my mind," except that this leap of faith was nearly impossible on a neurological level, at least for me. Should I drink more? Would increasing the DMT in my system finally quiet down my brain's machinery? I tried a larger dose and became even more unsettled. My analytical capacities were too impaired and unstable. Even the slightest vision created chaos, and I couldn't control the incessant flow of my thoughts.

Are you wondering if I'd given up on your uncle? I hadn't. I'm stubborn. Despite the chaos, I couldn't stop thinking about

Thomas during those nights. When I tried to concentrate on him, expressing the desire to see him again, a maelstrom of undefined sensations and images ensued. What if this longing were interfering with my experience?

But I persevered, because increasingly often, I got the strange feeling that he was there, at the fringes of my reality—that those eyes that appeared to me could be his. That's what motivated me to keep pursuing my quest, which may not have been so far-fetched after all.

One night, the sensation that there were other intelligences around me was so strong that I spoke to one of them directly. I had an intuition that they might be *intermediaries* come to help me. There was no rational basis for this idea, just a feeling at the time that it was obvious. "Go find Thomas for me!" I said to the imperceptible ghost, who might have only been in my head, or might have really been by my side.

But then I fell back into the cognitive whirlpool, as though this request and its attendant expectation were clouding everything up again, making my perceptions unintelligible once more.

The nights passed, and no two were alike. Sometimes, the visions were truly disturbing, while other times they seemed astonishingly real. But Thomas didn't appear. Surprisingly, this didn't discourage me, as I had a feeling that there really was another world, lying just beyond the veil of my mind . . .

When my trip came to an end and I had to return to France, I had only one goal: to get back to the Amazon as soon as possible.

15

He Was Looking at Me Silently . . .

On my second trip to the Amazon, Natacha, your stepmother, came with me. We were working on a story about ayahuasca for *Geo* magazine.[1] Natacha was in charge of the text and I was in charge of the photos, which left me with enough mental space to pursue my attempts to "find your uncle."

During our first ceremony together, there were several times when I had the intuition that there was a veil between me and *invisible presences*—maybe Thomas?—that just wouldn't disappear. Natacha made a thought-provoking suggestion: maybe it was difficult for the dead to *come* to us? Perhaps it was up to me to make the effort to go meet him where he was, in the world of the dead.

So the second night, I told the shamans I had a new request: I wanted to see death, experience death. *I wanted to die.*

During the next few nights, as soon as the ayahuasca kicked in, I found myself gripped by an even more unbearable fear. Vertigo, vomiting, panic. My body was giving in to it. And then one night, suddenly, I could feel that each of my organs—my lungs, my liver, my heart—was completely shutting down. In just a few seconds, all my vital functions were going to stop. I was actually going to die. Like an idiot, in the middle of the jungle, just because I had the genius idea to ask it of the plant. What a moron I was!

An indescribable panic rushed through me.

"I don't want to die, I just want to *see what happens afterward*!" With all my strength I tried to block it, to regain control; I touched my arms, I kneaded my thighs, I sat straight up, eyes wide. It was one of the most terrifying nights I've ever experienced. I couldn't ask to die again. Very, very bad idea.

The next night, the shaman told me that fear was surrounding me in a kind of sphere, and that if I could manage to extricate myself, everything after that would be calm. I had to maintain faith in the ayahuasca no matter what happened, he said. If I "died," it wasn't for real; I wasn't actually going to die, I would just believe that it was happening. Fear, and my desire for control, were barriers to the experience. I had to keep my heart open. I had to ask for love.

Okay, I'll try.

His advice was certainly wise. Away from the maloca, in broad daylight, it all made a lot of sense to me. But the problem was that during the night, I was constantly on the edge of the abyss, and I couldn't master my emotions.

On subsequent nights, I no longer asked to die, merely to "see death," taking refuge behind the idea that shamans and the ayahuasca spirit would be sensitive to this semantic nuance. At the same time, was that really wise? I had been so afraid of feeling my body start to shut down . . .

But I couldn't bring myself to give up.

Beyond those moments of fear, the nights were so powerful, so full of extraordinary visions and sensations that felt so real; the very intensity of what I was experiencing sustained my hope that anything was possible. That spirits existed, that my brother was waiting for me. How could I stop when I might be so close to the goal?

Again, I sensed that there were presences around me. It was an impalpable sensation, and an uncertain one—I didn't literally see them—and yet it was so dense and so obvious in the moment. These presences had come to tell me things that I couldn't quite pick up on. My body and mind were getting in the way.

Then, around the tenth evening, I took a substantial dose. It triggered a very strong effect and I saw Thomas. The "vision" was both incredible and also *banal.*

He was crouching by my feet, as though he were just a guy waiting for something. After the shock subsided, I was overcome by uncertainty. My analytical mind had been jolted awake. *Wait! This can't be real! This can't* actually *be happening?*

I was conscious, I was lucid, I wasn't dreaming. Sitting against the wall of the maloca, I could distinctly see the hut bathed in clear moonlight, the trees outside, my things around me, and the so-familiar silhouette of a man, unmoving, who had been dead for years.

I reasoned with myself: I was the cause of this apparition. It must be some kind of hallucination. I had been waiting for this moment for so long; I had such a strong desire for it; I couldn't believe it. Yet Thomas was there, crouching by my feet, on my right. I could see him distinctly, even though the contours of his body weren't very clear. He was a little bit transparent, like a body-shaped sheath made of light and mist. I looked at him without being able to decide if he was real; to be on the safe side, I told myself that he wasn't.

He was looking at me silently.

When our eyes met, he seemed stunned. Then he moved his arms insistently in my direction, as if he'd been waiting a long time for me to finally see him and he was expressing his joy that I had finally done so.

But it wasn't possible.

It couldn't be real.

He wasn't saying anything, but it seemed to me like his lips were moving. He kept looking at me. His eyes met mine. This lasted for several very long seconds, and then, very subtly, he faded away. The apparition lost its form by degrees, like a fading image. An evaporating mist. And then he was gone. I scanned the now-empty spot where he had just been. There was nothing there anymore. What had just happened? Not a word had been said.

That evening, like the previous ones, Natacha had also taken ayahuasca and spent the ceremony next to me in the maloca. Usually, we were too preoccupied with grappling with our own experiences to speak to each other; we weren't even capable of it. But once the effects of the plant started to wear off, we'd gotten into the habit of sharing a few sentences, attempting to describe what often turned out to be indescribable.

That night, when she leaned toward me, her first words shocked me.

"I think I saw Thomas," she told me.

"What do you mean?"

"At one point during the night, I saw a white shape, and right away I thought it was Thomas."

"Can you describe exactly what you saw?"

"It was just that: a white shape. But it really seemed obvious to me that it was Thomas. It's the first time I've had that feeling since we arrived."

"Where did you see him?"

"He was crouching at your feet, on your right side . . ."

When I told her about my own vision, she was speechless. We realized that we each experienced this at the same time—at the end of the ceremony, when the singing was over—and that we saw "Thomas" in the same spot in the maloca. For me, the silhouette was perfectly recognizable and clear, whereas for her, it was blurrier; but she could feel, deep down, that it was Thomas.

The "coincidence" of our two visions was inexplicable. Ayahuasca ceremonies last for hours. During those hours, Natacha and I had literally *thousands* of different visions, and were overcome by images and sensations. Plus, we had participated in ten ceremonies since our arrival.

Yet this was the one and only time where we saw the same thing, at the same time. And it was Thomas.

But that doesn't necessarily mean it was real, does it? How could we be sure? I wanted certainty; I couldn't bring myself to believe it.

It's crazy, Luna, I know. I'd been waiting for this moment for months, and when it came, I was paralyzed by doubt, so imprisoned in my mental habits that I wasn't even sure I believed it. Do you think that's illogical?

I asked myself this question, too, in all seriousness. Was my hesitation rational? Wasn't there a kind of unconscious self-sabotage in this compulsive tendency to maintain a sense of doubt, no matter what? It's as though it was no longer discernment, but instead a form of denial of reality. Or perhaps, on the contrary, I was right to cling to my demand for objectivity amid the chaos of my nights?

And yet: if this vision of Thomas were created by some sort of unconscious psychological mechanism born of my expectations, why wouldn't it have happened at any other time, when my desire to see him was just as strong? And more importantly, how would that explain Natacha's vision?

When dawn came, the mechanism kicked back into gear: I

had to try again. I had to see him once more, *to be sure.* On the nights that followed, my hope was ten times stronger than before, as was my impatience. But no new "apparitions" revealed themselves for the rest of the trip.

Obviously, in real life, things don't happen like they do in *The Matrix*. You can't just take the red pill to *wake up*. You can't learn a foreign language in a weekend, and the same goes for shamanism. Traveling into the world of the spirits, and beginning to understand their language, requires patient study.

And I had to recognize that, at the end of my second trip to the Amazon, I was only at the beginning. It's not enough to see; you also have to understand what you're seeing.

Shamanism allows us to explore a new territory for which we have to draw our own maps, plunging us into uncharted areas of the psyche. I, a Westerner accustomed to the rigor of the scientific method, was visiting new lands, and my research coupled with my newfound experience confirmed that they were more than imaginary hallucinations. But I was the only one who could gain entry, and the only one capable of evaluating whether they were real. And I hadn't had enough practice yet.

Over a period of eight years, I would travel to the Amazon four times. In total, I would participate in several dozen ayahuasca ceremonies.

Each time, I seemed to understand a little better what I had to do to dispel my confusion and the invasion of doubts: confront my fears, identify their origins, and revise the internal dynamics that influence my life. Basically, I had to *really* get to know myself.

I've explained to you, Luna, how the brain restricts our perceptions, reducing our cognitive space to a small, everyday slice of material reality. The experience I was accumulating, as well as the growing number of discoveries in both neuroscience and psychology, were shedding light on what happens when brain function is modified and the cognitive filtering system begins to lift.

During those moments, anything that makes it through the filter—such as the spirit world—is still partially influenced by residual analytical brain activity, as well as by the crushing presence of the hidden forces of our unconscious. The darkness of this space is what sustains doubt, fear, and confusion.

Ayahuasca, and psychedelics in general, disable the neural patterns that underlie our daily functioning by breaking down our filtering tools, literally exposing our unconscious to the light.

This is deeply distressing for our mental protective strategies—everything our unconscious has seen fit to develop over the course of our lives to help us adapt to the society into which we were born. All our psychic wounds, our fears, our emotional knots, our repressed memories—everything hiding deep down inside of us and forming what Swiss psychoanalyst Carl Gustav Jung called "the shadow" that we try to reject or deny—come out in fits and starts, sometimes violently, insinuating themselves into our visions.

And yet while this mental mishmash feeds our confusions and fears, dictates some of our choices, and contributes to our way of seeing the world and our veiled perceptions of ourselves, it also shapes our personality. Without our realizing it, it contributes to our equilibrium.

Although the ego is sometimes described as a mental prison, one that we need to break out of in order to open ourselves up to the spiritual, it's also indispensable armor for our lives. If we violently deconstruct it, what do we replace it with?

It's for this reason that shamanism and psychedelics are not without psychological risk. If we're fragile, it exacerbates our fragility. If we're depressed, it amplifies our unhappiness. This is why these experiences must absolutely be carried out within a structured, ritual framework, guided by shamans, or trained psychotherapists, if in a place where this type of assisted therapy is legal. Blowing up our unconscious mental protective mechanisms without being accompanied or guided is like stripping completely naked in the middle of a snowstorm.

Even with proper accompaniment, it's been profoundly destabilizing for me.

In short, my journeys with shamans taught me that opening the doors of perception will also open the doors onto all we spend our lives not wanting to know about ourselves. At the same time, they reveal previously imperceptible dimensions of reality.

Seeing invisible worlds also means seeing inside ourselves.

Both the light and our shadows.

It has a profound impact.

I didn't realize it at first, but when I began these experiences with the shamans, I was also embarking on a destabilizing journey of self-introspection. I'd only wanted to see my brother; no one had told me that I was going to also be exploring the depths of my own mind, nor how disturbing that would be. My shamanic experiences were a process of deconstruction. My mental structure became more fragile, laying bare its concealment strategies. Each time, I felt my armor become more porous. I became psychologically less watertight, almost transparent.

My journey with the shamans would slowly take an unexpected direction. Little did I suspect that it would give me the opportunity to discover so many hidden aspects of my inner world.[2]

In the words of spiritual teacher Ram Dass, a former professor of psychology at Harvard: "If we are to learn from our darkness and contain it as a wounded elder bears his scars to heal and strengthen, we must be able to step outside our Egos, as Soul."[3]

This is what I wanted to tell you at the beginning of this book, Luna, when I talked about vulnerability. Being vulnerable isn't about being weak; it's about splitting open our armor to see what's hiding underneath. Giving ourselves the chance to discover what led us to build up this armor also means undertaking a repair process that might potentially allow us to do without it in the future.

Stripping myself bare like this was the only way for me to be able to see your uncle again—if the experience repeated itself—without being tricked by my fears and hesitations, and without confusing my fantasies with reality, or vice versa. I would be able to discern more easily what's *inside* from what's *outside*. Able to identify my inner ghosts, so as not to confuse them with those that inhabit the spirit worlds.

16

The Unconscious and Its Ghosts

What was it that I was afraid of during those nights with the shamans? Where did that indecipherable anguish that kept paralyzing me on the threshold come from?

I noticed it during those highly intense moments, but hadn't that private fear been in the background for my whole life?

We spend our lives building up armor, a protective shell, because it's invaluable for us in our daily lives as social creatures. It helps us maintain balanced cohesion between our personalities and the unconscious forces that drive us. This armor-shell-ego protects us from anything that threatens our mental stability. Those threats could be real, imaginary, or simply exaggerated, thanks to our childhood wounds and the countless demands we've been subjected to without even realizing it—by our education, our conditioning, and the people around us.

This shell-ego becomes a kind of opaque veil that plays into the confusion we feel in our relationships with the world around us, as well as in our relationship to our own inner world of emotions—a confusion that fosters repetitive and neurotic mental patterns. How can we free ourselves without throwing things off balance?

Discovering the essence of our soul and connecting in a lasting way with our most profound self is the goal of many spiritual traditions, which emphasize the importance of getting to know ourselves more deeply.

This is because there are ghosts dwelling in the depths of our unconscious.

They're the ones who are afraid of life. Of the unknown. Of the future.

Our unconscious isn't a passive part of our mind, a kind of storage facility for the unimportant residue of our lives. In fact, it's exactly the opposite.

It's the core of the reactor, a melting pot of emotions, fears, and repressed thoughts that fuel our confusion, impact our actions and decisions, and distort the perception we have of both the world and ourselves. They're the cause of our misinterpretations, our fits of anger, our recurring dissatisfaction, our negative emotions, our tendency to repeat self-sabotaging or failing behaviors, our relationship doubts, our malaise. They are the architects of the personalities that we believe ourselves to have, with all their strengths and weaknesses.

The spiritual traditions I'm referring to encourage us to free ourselves from illusion and distance ourselves from the chains of habit, not for *moral* reasons, but so that we can rediscover the essence of our being. What we don't know about ourselves—our repressed memories, our desires, our fears—interferes with our ability to perceive and discern, and makes us prisoners of our own confusion. Puppets and sleepwalkers.

In all of us, multiple universes, both internal and external, live alongside each other. The psychoanalyst Carl Gustav Jung refers to different mental forces that inhabit us as "archetypes"—unconscious symbolic representations that influence our experience and behavior.

These core archetypes are the driving forces behind our

psychological energy. The "self" symbolizes the totality of our being. It's the force behind our desire for fulfillment and self-actualization.

The "shadow" refers to the parts of our personality that we repress or ignore—the things we don't accept, or that we would prefer to hide from others or ourselves.

The archetypes of the "anima" and the "animus" are derived from archetypes of feminine and masculine and correspond to vital energy. They take the opposite form from our biological sex, acting as a counterbalance.

The "persona" archetype represents the identity that we construct for ourselves as individuals in relation to society. The persona is a mask intended to help us blend into social norms, to make us seem rule-abiding and faultless. It's easy for us to identify with it so much we forget who we are.

In my case, my persona is inextricably linked to my career as a journalist, which I've had ever since the end of my teens. My experiences in the Amazon showed me the extent to which I've become a "journalist" in every part of my life. I approach any question, whether a professional or personal one, in the same way: I'm always trying to "understand," to "be objective," like any good journalist. Impartial, methodical, and analytical in my reasoning.

But this archetypal identity is so inseparable from who I think I am that it unconsciously prevents me from hearing anything that "isn't objective"—that is to say, my perceptions and emotions, all those internal dimensions that are by nature subjective.

My persona certainly makes me a competent journalist, but it also fought so hard to convince me that the apparition of Thomas couldn't be real.

These archetypes are invisible, active forces. An archetype is neither good nor bad as long as it doesn't assume a dominant position in our unconscious, crowding out the others—a bit like my persona has done, in my case. If we're controlled by one sole facet of our personality, it cuts us off from our other inner forces, estranging us further from our soul.

These archetypes manifest themselves in our behaviors and thoughts, without our consciously understanding their source, through a process of transference called "projection."

"Projection" is a term used in psychology to refer to a common human behavior: transposing our inner world and our own feelings and mental forces onto an external person or object. When we "project" onto someone or something, we attribute to them or it certain strengths (that we would like to find in ourselves) or weaknesses (that we have but don't own up to).

Projection prevents us from perceiving others as they actually are. It also blurs our perceptions of ourselves, our environments, and all our life experiences.

And yet we all project. All the time.

We project onto our spouse, our career, our relationships, personalities of all stripes, God, spiritual leaders, meditation, shamanism, etc. What does this mean? It means we're attempting to fill our voids or hide our cracks.

It's in our nature, as imperfect and wounded human beings, to be at least somewhat cut off from parts of ourselves and the vital energy attached to them. Projection plays a compensatory role in the imbalance experienced by our unconscious.

In this way, it's a mechanism that connects to our internal world, but only if we manage to distance ourselves from the external support of projection. It's not the projection itself that's important; it's what it reveals about us. The trap is our tendency to remain fascinated by the external object or person, and to expect that something exterior will fill our interior void.

One example: when we venerate spiritual leaders or saints, we're projecting onto them a little of what is divine in us. This can lead to two radically different situations. In the first one, projection can lead us to imagine that they are the only keepers of this divine spark, forgetting that we, too, are its guardians. In the second, by contrast, projection can serve as a mirror—because true spiritual leaders are mirrors, nothing more. They represent the best in us, projected onto an exterior figure. Like points of reference. Their sole purpose is to help us rediscover the immortal, wise part of ourselves that we all harbor in our hearts.

I know: the difference is subtle, and it's a difficult exercise, all the more so because we're immersed in a world that's exclusively concentrated on material reality, constantly encouraging us to fix our hopes and dreams onto others, the guardians of our expectations of happiness and balance: spouses, therapists, careers, possessions, celebrities, politicians, spiritual leaders, etc. We believe these "external supports" will rebalance us, make us happy, save us, without our having to dig deep inside ourselves.

It's an illusion.

This collective cloak-and-dagger show offers countless eternal mirages to further disconnect us from our inner resources.

Projection is particularly prominent in romantic relationships, where it can cause disturbances. For example, projecting our anima or animus onto our partner enables us to connect with the love we carry within ourselves. Self-love, unconditional love. It's a colossal source of energy. But if, due to unconscious overcompensation, we're cut off from this vital force, we tend to look toward our relationship to fill our inner void, and end up disappointed.

This engenders a feeling of missing something, of dissatisfaction, of frustration. But our partner can't fill this void. That's not their role. If the relationship is already shaky, it will end. But if it's otherwise pleasant, things get complicated. As we get increasingly frustrated with not finding in the other person what we're lacking in ourselves, we begin to think that we might need to look elsewhere, to *find something better*.

We'll jeopardize our relationship in the unconscious and vain hope that going off to seduce another "support," another partner, will finally get rid of this void. This call from our vital force takes on the guise of sexual desire. But the "sexual desire" that drives us to change partners has nothing to do with what's going on unconsciously. The desire that the unconscious is expressing in this context is not intrinsically sexual in nature. It takes on this sexual form because the mechanism is unconscious. By focusing on the sexual aspect, we deny ourselves the possibility of understanding the profound nature of what our unconscious is covertly whispering to us.

What is it whispering?

This desire is an attempt to reawaken the force of the anima or animus, a life force from which we've been cut off. To act on this desire is to miss the point. And odds are that we'll repeat this mistake over and over again, racking up short-lived relationships destined to fail that become less and less satisfying each time. What seems like desire is actually a projection, a sign, not something to be satisfied or curbed.

We go through life largely ignorant of the unconscious forces that influence us, unaware of the profoundly emotional nature of our beliefs, opinions, and certainties.

In the "rational" world in which we live, we satisfy our soul's desire to rediscover its divinity by being drawn to devotional objects, questionable spiritual leaders, exotic practices that exempt us from any soul-searching, or even intoxication from alcohol and other numbing substances, like moths to a flame.

We *consume* as though our hunger is insatiable, but this only deepens our spiritual void. We seek our life force through sexual freedom, not realizing that choosing to fulfill our fantasies instead of listening to our inner voice causes this life force to wither away.

When the outside world becomes a fascinating and all-encompassing object of desire, dreams, pleasure, and expectations to satisfy, it cuts us off from ourselves.

We seek our soul on the outside. We seek love on the outside. We seek God on the outside. But they've been within us the whole time.

In the context of psychotherapy, projection can be an essential means of communication with our unconscious, provided we're aware of it. Dreams and altered states of consciousness can offer a window of observation on these mechanisms at work, in the sense that they amplify the manifestations of our projections. Shamanism is an extraordinary amplifier.

Every time I returned from the Amazon, after a few weeks, I would notice the reappearance of a kind of irritation. It was as though, despite my feeling that I had made progress and despite the intensity of my experience, I had missed something.

The spiritual path doesn't exempt us from working on ourselves. Quite the opposite, in fact.

This is really the essential lesson that I took away from my first trips to the Amazon. They allowed me to understand that I was still *spiritually bypassing*. The psychologist John Welwood defined spiritual bypassing as the unconscious tendency to "use spiritual ideas and practices to sidestep personal, emotional 'unfinished business,' to shore up a shaky sense of self, or to belittle basic needs, feelings, and developmental tasks."[1]

We all have "unfinished business." So what was mine?

Were my journeys in search of my brother serving as a way for me to dig myself out of my sadness at having lost him? I was probably in denial about the fact that I had to process and integrate the emotional wound inflicted by his death; perhaps I was setting off for the rainforest in an attempt to make it disappear. Of course, our "unfinished business" doesn't evaporate into thin air thanks to the magic of denial. To the contrary: it waits wisely in the depths of our unconscious for just the right moment to rise up again.

Was my shamanic quest masking a form of avoidance? Could my unbridled desire to see the world of the dead be hiding my fear of confronting the pain of living while wounded?

These are the questions that arose from my shamanic journeys, but any spiritual practice can lead to a kind of self-avoidance, whether it's monastic life, meditation, or prayer. It's not a question of which specific path we choose, but of how we choose it. If we're searching for a way to flee discomfort, with the goal of reaching an idealized state of serenity, odds are that we're spiritually bypassing. At some point, we'll experience a highly destabilizing backlash: depression, feelings of failure, guilt, spiritual burnout, etc. John Welwood has written about this process in great detail:

> Spiritual teachers often exhort us to be loving and compassionate, or to give up selfishness and aggression, but how can we do this if our habitual tendencies arise out of a whole system of psychological dynamics that we have never clearly seen or faced, much less worked with? People often have to feel,

> acknowledge, and come to terms with their anger before they can arrive at genuine forgiveness or compassion.[2]

I realized that in some ways, using shamanism to access the spiritual world, expecting its strength to exonerate me from having to work on my emotions and weaknesses, was leading to a form of avoidance of what was uncomfortable in my life.

It's like I was imagining that covering up my grief with new experiences would make it go away, which is ultimately a form of magical thinking. Welwood explains that awakening isn't something to be acquired, a bonus add-on for our soul that covers up the faults, confusion, and wounds we've managed to stifle. Quite the opposite: awakening emerges once we've listened to and integrated our flaws, confusion, and wounds so that they no longer have to act like invisible mental viruses.

For clarity to come from awakening, we have to dissolve all the unconscious contents of our mind: all the underlying psychological dynamics and survival strategies that have formed our personality.

We're not fighting our personalities; they're what make us functional and balanced on a social and psychological level. We reassure them, we listen to them, and we care for them; in doing so, we show them that they're not our true nature.

As Welwood says, psychological work helps us to *find ourselves*, whereas spiritual work goes one step further and helps us to *let go of ourselves*. In this way, psychological work and spiritual work are "two sides of one whole dialectic of self-discovery."[3]

Two complementary ways to dissolve our protective resistances and enter the spirit world without being blinded by the confusion of our own inner world.

We have to know ourselves before we can surrender ourselves.

This sentence had never seemed as true to me as when I accompanied my father, a great reader whose erudition had always impressed me, to the threshold of death. A brilliant intellectual, he had impatiently looked to literature and philosophy for answers to his questions about the meaning of life and its inevitable end, but he hadn't known how to begin the process of inner work, nor did he ever imagine that dismantling his armor might be liberating. If he had, it might have eased his mind a little when the time came.

17

The Decline

That's right, Luna, you were there, but I didn't think it was the right moment to talk to you at the time. It was so surreal that I have to admit I didn't know what to make of it myself. We were all together celebrating Christmas. I can visualize us now, in the house. You must have been playing with your cousin. I was in the living room when your grandfather approached me and asked me to come with him to his studio. Surprised by his uncharacteristic formality, I followed him outside to the studio where for years you'd watched him paint and write.

A painter's studio. Total creative chaos: there were canvases everywhere—on the walls, on the floor, piled on top of each other. The works in progress were laid out flat on tables. The smell of solvents and acrylics, and old books, too, some of them arranged on the shelves, others scattered here or there, lying open, exposing their music to the light, alongside scattered pages dense with notes and thoughts he'd written down in his thick handwriting.

We sat down close to the heater. I could see that he was hesitant. After a few seconds, without any preliminaries, as was his wont, he announced: "I won't make it through the year."

Just like that, out of the blue. I could see he was serious, but what was he talking about? I widened my eyes, holding myself back from saying the only bland words that came to my mind. I knew I should let him explain; what did he mean? Why was he throwing something like that at me?

He looked at me with his usual restrained tenderness, took a breath, and continued: "After Thomas's death, when I got sick, you were worried, but I knew then I wasn't dying. Now, I can feel that I am."

When he said this, your grandfather had a hundred and seventy-six days left to live. None of us knew this, except him, apparently. But I couldn't seem to take him seriously. How could I? It was true that he'd gotten thinner, but that was normal; he had just turned eighty-five. That didn't mean he was about to die! How could he possibly know that he wouldn't make it through the year?

I had to say something, but I knew that it was pointless to contradict him. The important part was what he was trying to express, which was beyond words. Why was he telling me this? Did he really think it was true? Was his health actually that bad?

He dodged my overly specific questions, displaying an assurance that was almost calm, as though he *knew*. He wanted to talk about his death and how he'd like us to handle it—as soon as the two of us finished talking, he would call my brother Simon to tell him the same thing.

I could immediately tell how stupid it would be to try to reassure him. He hadn't decided to begin this conversation just so that I could deny it, saying something like "What are you talking about? You're in great shape, you'll outlive us all," though I did wonder whether his statement might just be a little bout of pessimism.

No, I put that thought immediately out of my mind. He was very lucid and focused. I could sense intuitively that he wasn't waiting for me to contradict him. He was full of confidence. He wasn't looking for my pity—that wouldn't be like your grandfather at all. He wanted my undivided attention, and to be alone with me for a little while. There were no traces of emotion in his voice, but there was a sort of seriousness. This conversation was important: he wanted to *prepare me*, to share his wishes; he was anxious about when he would no longer be here.

He said he didn't want intensive medical treatment to prolong his life.

He would prefer to die here, at home, if at all possible.

As for *afterward*, he didn't care. Burial, cremation . . . it made no difference to him.

There: now the important things had been said. The solemnity of the moment eased a little. We smiled at each other awkwardly; what were we supposed to say now? How could we just start talking *normally* again after that?

I was the one who decided not to change the subject. He'd opened a door to something we so rarely spoke about; I didn't want to close it too quickly, as though we were trying to rid ourselves of a burden, sinking back into the comfort of our denial.

I asked him if he was afraid. "Well, it's not exactly a happy thing to think about." Had reading my work enlightened him a little about what happens after death? "Maybe a little," he told me. Well, in that case, I didn't really know what else to say.

It's an unusual thing when your father tells you that he can feel his own death approaching. For me, that's when it happened: December 22, 2012.

The next night, I dreamed about Thomas. I was standing in front of a big river, and I needed to rig up some kind of boat in order to cross it. In the dream, I knew just how to do it: I had to unravel a mat made of woven sticks, pick out the longest ones, crush them a little, and put them back together to make a kind of flimsy canoe.

Thanks to the magic of the dream, I did so and was immediately in the canoe.

I paddled with my hands to the middle of the river and discovered that Thomas was with me.

But as we approached the bank, he fell overboard. I paddled back to where he'd disappeared beneath the surface. Plunging my hands into the dark water, I groped around for him desperately, and managed to find his fingers, which I grabbed onto as best I could.

However, I soon lost my grip, and my boat was swept away by the current. As I drifted away, unable to stop the boat's motion, I turned around, scanning the water, and yelled, "Get out, get out of the water!" Nothing moved under the river's muddy surface. Thomas was down there somewhere, invisible.

I finally managed to turn the boat around, paddling toward where he was submerged. There were no landmarks to guide me, and I couldn't be sure exactly where he was. Lying in the boat on my stomach, with virtually no hope left, I plunged my hand back into the water blindly. A miracle: once again, my hands found his. This time, I held onto him firmly and managed to pull him out of the water. He was exhausted, nearly unconscious. I told him to stay between my legs and hold on to my waist with his arms, and I paddled backward toward the bank. I'd saved him. Then I woke up . . .

Christmas passed and the new year began. I have to confess that, in the weeks following the disarming discussion I had with your grandfather, things returned to normal. What he'd told me was too unreal to really have an impact on my daily life. Admittedly, he wasn't in great shape, but he'd recover. He was far from being at death's door.

However, as the weeks passed, it became clear that his health was slowly starting to decline. The conjecture that once seemed purely hypothetical now seemed plausible. Yes, he could die. He did seem to be heading that way . . .

In mid-March, you and I visited him together. Your uncle Simon was there, too. Over the previous two weeks, your grandfather had been growing weaker. He slept a lot. He'd gotten even thinner. His face was gaunt. But his mind was still all there. His voice was a little raspy, and I could tell that long sentences were tiring for him. He'd stopped drinking wine. Alcohol seemed disgusting to him now, he said, and he had no appetite.

The next week, Natacha and I headed off on another trip. I had been reluctant to go, but Papa had promised me "not to die before I got back." How could he have made such a promise? After we left, he regained a little strength. He underwent some tests to try to understand why his body was growing weaker. His appetite picked up again, and his spirits improved. But this respite was short-lived, and soon he was declining again. Your grandmother told me on the phone that he wanted peace and quiet, and that more and more often, he wanted to be alone. But he no longer had the strength to be.

He had stopped painting.

I was still stunned by our conversation in December. Had he known?

I wanted to be with him right then, but did he need anyone? What did he think about all day?

Night had fallen. It was the Wednesday before Easter. The next day would mark twelve years since Thomas had died on that road in Afghanistan. I couldn't sleep. The sound of insects and frogs filled the night. With the time difference, it couldn't have been far off from the exact time that the accident had taken place. In the south of Kabul, the sun would have already risen, and vehicles would have been driving in the dawn light on that road not far from Maidan Shar.

In the morning, I spoke to your grandfather on the phone.

He told me that he had driven alone to buy wooden sticks for one of his paintings. He was painting again. He was eating a little, but he could feel that he was getting weaker. He told me, "I can't wait for this to be over, one way or another." And I didn't know how to respond. I could tell that he was beginning to let go. He had had enough. He was tired. It made me sad that I didn't know what to say. I could sense that he didn't want to hang up, but nothing came to mind in the way of intelligent remarks.

I thought it was the first time that he had said he wanted it to end, even if he had added "one way or another."

When I returned to France, he was still alive. He had "waited for me," just like he had promised. As soon as the plane touched down, I rushed off to see him. I found him emotional, hypersensitive. He observed the forest and sky around him with the eyes of someone telling himself it would all be gone soon; his face was hollow, his skin a little yellow.

We were both in the kitchen. I asked him if he was afraid of death. "Yes," he answered. "Even if there is a lot of evidence suggesting that consciousness survives physical death, I'm still afraid." And then he changed the subject.

Soon thereafter, your grandmother told me that your grandfather was declining even more, that his organs were no longer functioning well. He didn't want to see anyone and no longer had the strength to stay in his studio. She was exhausted, too. For months, she had been carrying everything alone.

18

The Most Important Man in My Life

At the beginning of June, everything accelerated. Your grandfather was rushed to the hospital when the pain came back. His condition was getting worse. At the hospital, he was given sleeping pills, but they had the opposite effect. Instead of calm nights, he was plagued by terrible nightmares. He seemed to be losing his mind completely. Because he was so agitated, his nurses decided to tie him to his bed, which only added to his distress and confusion. I learned of this in the early hours of the morning when I received a call from my helpless mother. An hour later, I was at the hospital. The sight of him strapped down in his bed was unbearable. He was very confused and disoriented. When he saw me, he asked me to untie him and go with him downstairs, where Simon was waiting . . . in the Rolls-Royce. What Rolls-Royce?

I did as he asked and threw the leather straps on the floor. *You'll never be tied up again, Papa,* I promised him. The nurses and the doctor on duty made no fuss about my spending the night with him. Maman, Simon, and I had just decided to take shifts at his side, never leaving him alone again.

After several hours, the sleeping pills finally wore off, and Papa was lucid again. In the nights that followed, however, he didn't sleep at all. He lay there unmoving, exhausted. He asked several times to get up, and I helped him, carrying his thin body that he had entrusted to me. Something had changed. Why had he become so agitated in his sleep? What was this confusion, this inner turmoil? And how could I help him?

We didn't speak much. Everything that wasn't essential had become unimportant. I would have loved to be able to pass on to him all I felt I had learned. "If you're afraid, know that there's nothing to be afraid of! Nothing! You can be sure of it."

"How do you know?"

"I can feel it in every cell of my body. I don't know how to explain it to you, but I'm positive."

". . ."

"Do you want to tell me anything?"

"About what?"

"About what you're going through . . ."

"I suspect that Plato didn't say everything . . ."

He had asked your grandmother for only one book: volume one of a leather-bound, annotated collection of Plato's complete works. He'd feverishly read and reread it for decades, especially *The Apology of Socrates*, in which Plato recounts the trial that led to Socrates's death sentence, and the passage in *Phaedo* that describes his death.

"What do you mean?"

"I'm talking about Socrates's death as narrated by Plato. I suspect Plato didn't say everything. Maybe Socrates was given an opiate in addition to the poison hemlock. I don't understand how he could be so calm otherwise. He drank the poison and asked his slave to help him walk around the room until it took effect. When his legs grew weak, he lay down and continued to discuss philosophy. Can you believe that? How could it be possible?"

"How could what be possible?"
"Being so calm, for goodness' sake!"
"In the face of death?"
"Yes . . ."

Simon, Maman, and I continued to take turns being on night watch. Papa kept getting weaker and weaker. Death was there now. It might be impossible to predict the exact day, but it was becoming more and more inevitable. Papa told us that he'd like to "go" at home, in the sun, surrounded by the three of us. We would do everything we could to make it possible for him to return home, but for the moment, his condition required too much care. Was that care really necessary, though? Wasn't it time to stop trying? What was the point? He was dying. No one knew how to make that decision. It's so hard to find the words in circumstances like these.

At dawn one morning, at the end of one of my night watches, I could sense that he was agitated—he kept shifting around in his bed, once again unable to fall asleep—so I got up from my cot and put my hand on his. He murmured: "Death didn't want me last night."

"Do you have something to say? Something weighing on your heart, something you need to get out?"

"No . . ."

"You know the decision to leave is yours, right?"

"Yes . . . to die in peace . . . in peace . . ."

On Thursday, June 13, he seemed to be in much better spirits than the previous days. In retrospect, this was the "surge" frequently observed by end-of-life caretakers. It seemed like it would be possible to take him home early the next week. I returned to Paris; Simon was taking that night's shift, and Maman would take the next night.

So why did I come back?

Why did I find myself with the irrepressible need to make the trip again on Friday evening? I found him alone in his room; Maman would arrive after dinner. I sat down in the armchair. He was sitting up in bed, awake and present. Our conversation was limited, with long stretches of silence; we talked a little about literature. His dinner tray arrived, but he barely touched it. He was looking out the window at the fading daylight.

Just before 8 p.m., knowing that Maman would be arriving at any minute, I asked him if it was okay for me to head back to Paris. He was fine—a little confused, but fine. Yes, I could go, he told me. When I left the room, he followed me with his eyes and then turned to look back out the window before I had crossed the threshold.

I took three steps down the hallway, but something was holding me back. I reasoned with myself, took another few steps in the direction of the exit as though in slow motion, then suddenly turned around and retraced my steps back to his bedroom. Hearing me enter, he turned toward me.

"Are you sure I can go?" I asked him.

"Yes."

Seeing my hesitation, he looked at me intently, his voice soft. "Yes, it's fine. Go ahead."

"Okay, well. Goodbye, then."

"Goodbye, my Steph."

His eyes met mine directly, as though he were searching for something. The seconds seemed to last forever. Then, once again, he turned slowly toward the window. The sky that's beginning to turn pink, the rooftops of the town, the church spire. The darkness slowly setting in.

And I returned to Paris.

That was the last time I spoke to my father. Our last minutes together, just the two of us.

The next day, Saturday, June 15, late in the afternoon, he fell into unconsciousness after having shared precious words—his last ones—with my mother, the love of his life.

When night fell, I was back alongside Simon and Maman at the bedside of a body that was declining irreversibly. His eyes, still and open, were no longer seeing our world; they were probably seeing *the other one*, on and off. His breathing was regular. But he still seemed like he was resisting. His arms moved from time to time, as though he wanted to express something. We talked to him, urging him to let go.

There we were. Closer than we'd ever been to my father's death. All four of us were on the threshold, but only one of us would cross over. The night passed like this, and then a new day began. The last one. I headed off to sleep for a few hours, then came back early in the afternoon, when I was alone in the bedroom. Maman and Simon had gone to take their turn to rest.

Two hours passed, and then your grandfather's breathing got slower and shallower. I noticed that he was taking only tiny, weak breaths. I asked the nurses if they thought I should call your grandmother and Simon to tell them to come back. "Yes, probably . . ."

I did.

Then I approached the bed. Papa was no longer moving at all. What should I do?

In theory, I had ideas. I knew more than I had on the day when Thomas died, when I had been guided only by a strange intuition that I should talk to your uncle.

Since then, I'd read the *Bardo Thodol*, the *Tibetan Book of the Dead*, which is a sort of instruction manual for the journey through death.

But the book is very metaphorical, and laden with Buddhist

symbolism, and your grandfather isn't Buddhist. Still, I remember that its essence resonated strongly with what I had experienced in the Amazon. The experience of an altered state of consciousness induced by ayahuasca seems to follow a path of sensory decline identical to that which occurs, irreversibly, at the time of death. The shamanic experience as I have lived it is a *reversible death*, a temporary changing of worlds.

Tibetan master Yongey Mingyur Rinpoche has summarized the essence of this sacred text as follows:

> The organic degeneration of the dying body offers an unparalleled opportunity for recognizing the true mind. As the flesh-and-blood home of the mind falls apart, the fabricated layers of mind also disintegrate. The mind that has been conditioned by misperceptions, and shaped by habitual tendencies, becomes unglued. The confusion that has obscured our original, innate clarity can no more maintain its vitality than the outer skin layers of our bodies. As confusion dissolves, wisdom shines forth, just as it does in the process of meditation.[1]

This bears a strong resemblance to the beginning of many of my nights in the Amazon, even though I never managed to reach the shining wisdom the lama mentions.

As I've experienced, the tricky part of this process is the part in the middle—the collapse and dissolution of the mind, and its separation from the physical body. Everything I've read lines up with both my own experience and what shamans say: the effects of ayahuasca may be reversible, but they're not significantly different from those of physical death. As Ram Dass writes:

> The moment of death is the veil between the dying person and the afterlife. If the experience of death is in any way parallel to

> the mystical experiences I have had, which entailed a temporary dissolution of the Ego structures, it seems reasonable to expect, at the moment of death, a dissolution of the conceptual map by which we have charted reality. This dissolution is likely to begin slowly and then accelerate, culminating in the final discontinuous experience of passing through a barrier into the Soul dimension.[2]

Psychologically speaking, the mystical experience (in my case, a shamanic one) and that of death are the same.

What would I have wanted for someone to whisper in my ear when I was in the Amazon, experiencing extreme destabilization?

I knelt in front of your grandfather's bed so that I could be on the same level as him. My face was only a couple of inches from his emaciated one, which was turned toward me. His half-closed eyes were already absent. They were no longer tracking movements, no longer looking at this world; they were staring into the void. His breathing was imperceptible, micro-breaths.

Then I began to speak, the words flowing.

I told him I loved him, and that everything he was seeing and hearing were creations of his mind; only the light mattered. I urged him not to be afraid.

"You have always been a kind man—a kind father and a kind husband. All is calm, Papa, calm and gentle. You have nothing to fear. I love you, Papa . . . sweet Papa. All is calm, peaceful, still.

"All is equanimous . . ."

Equanimous. A word he used to use all the time. When my brothers and I were horsing around, he'd order us, with an amused smile, to be equanimous. He'd even use it when the dog was barking at the mailman, commanding, "Be equanimous!"

"Do you find it funny that I'm saying equanimous? It's exactly the right word. All is calm, equanimous."

My face close to his, I talked to him in a calm voice without stopping, repeating the same simple words over and over, careful not to say anything that could have a negative or worrying connotation. I didn't say "Don't be afraid"; I said, "All is calm and peaceful. Try to see the light, let yourself slide toward it, dive into it, allow yourself to be surrounded by it. All is still and calm. I love you, you're a wonderful person. Let yourself float in the light . . ."

He was lying on his left side, completely still.

This went on for almost an hour.

From time to time I was overcome by intense emotion.

"I love you. You gave me life . . ."

Tears sprang from my eyes; my body trembled with emotion.

"I'm crying because I'm very moved, but I'm not sad. I'm moved because I owe you my life, and because very soon, we'll no longer see each other in this existence, in these bodies, but I'm not sad."

And it's true, Luna, that it wasn't sadness I was feeling. There was a strange energy in the room; it was filled with a light that I couldn't see, but which I could feel traveling through my body and his, and the space around us, like a whirlwind. I could feel it physically, shaking my whole body. It radiated through me with wave after wave of . . . joy. I know, it's an odd word to use, but that's really what it was. I was profoundly moved, and my immense sadness was juxtaposed with indescribable happiness.

Our souls were speaking to each other.

I really think that's what was happening.

I was so present that I was no longer thinking. During this time-outside-time, as I was bathed with impalpable energy, I could sense that Thomas was not far away, nor was your great-grandmother Lise, my father's mother. I was no longer asking my nonstop journalist questions—how could I be sure? I couldn't care less. I could *feel* that they were there.

I remained in this incredible communion for over an hour. I never stopped talking to him; everything was just right, the words coming easily and obviously, and I was filled with a feeling of great serenity. When your grandmother entered the room, she found me just like this, on my knees, my face against your grandfather's.

She sat right next to me and listened to me talk, guiding the love of her life. He was now completely rigid. His skin no longer twitched, his chest was motionless, his lips parted, his eyes half-closed. Inaudible breathing. Silence. Only the tiniest of muscular movements on his neck accompanied his breaths, which were increasingly far apart.

And then they stopped.

But we weren't completely sure. There was no muscle relaxation, no physical sign of any kind of change.

I put my glasses in front of his mouth. There was no fog. I searched for his pulse. It had stopped. His heart was no longer beating. That was it. He was gone. Papa had died.

An imperceptible death. A discreet one.

It really was a mystery to behold. Why was there life one minute, and not the next?

Simon arrived.

Our father's face was peaceful. We stayed around him, not knowing what to do, sitting in contemplation with our emotions. A few minutes later, his skin had gone slightly rigid and was starting to cool down. There, the mask of death; his life was no longer in his body, his complexion was getting pale, and yet his face was still so familiar. It was so strange to see this unmoving body; it wasn't my Papa anymore, but he looked so much like him. It was surreal.

I wondered what he was now. Where he was now. What he was doing, what he was seeing. If he could hear us.

Night had fallen by the time we returned home. Papa's body had been taken down to the hospital morgue. Everything happens quickly after someone dies. After several minutes of remembrance, we have to leave the room. The body is washed quickly while the skin grows cold and takes on an increasingly yellow hue, there are a few basic preparations for the sake of decency, and then it's down to a dark fridge.

I explained all this to your grandfather before we left him. "Now you are dead. Don't worry about your body. It will be taken care of, and you don't have to remain attached to it. This body is no longer you. Pay attention to the light. Thomas and Lise aren't far away; try to see them and allow yourself to be guided by what they tell you. You aren't alone, Papa, there are a lot of people there to help you. They're in the light. Go join them."

It was nearly midnight. I was alone in his studio.

I already missed him. His intelligence. I could feel the staggering intellectual void he'd left behind. On his desk, I found pages covered in his handwriting, expressing his violent uncertainty about death.

They dated back several weeks, to before his hospitalization. He'd finally accepted that fear in his last moments.

Everything is possible, up until the very last second.

I wanted him to confirm to me someday that he did, in fact, leave in peace. During his last hours, I didn't sense any distress or agitation, but rather a deep calm, a kind of acceptance. But I wanted to be certain.

That was why, on the day of his funeral, without telling anyone, I placed different objects in his coffin, with the idea already in mind—I even wonder if he was the one to give me the idea?—that they would guarantee that I be able to communicate with him when I went to test out some mediums.[3]

19
Mediums

Some people claim that they can see the dead, and sometimes even establish a form of communication with them. Generally, this ability reveals itself in an intrusive way in childhood, which is destabilizing both for the child and those around them.

During these early years of a child's life, their fundamental consciousness is not yet completely inhibited. Their sense of separation from both the visible and invisible outside world is less pronounced, and they still have extrasensory perceptions, to varying degrees. Children are still open to the "other world" from which they've only recently come. They haven't yet learned to distinguish it fully from what they can perceive with their five senses.

But in general, when children talk about what they've seen, we don't listen to them with the right discernment. Admittedly, it's hard to do so. Their stories tend to be very rich, brimming with imagination and fantastical descriptions, so it's hard for parents to know how to identify what's truly imaginary and what might be a matter of perception. We end up lumping them all together. If a child talks about a person whom only they can see, we deem it an "imaginary friend," and that's that.

Yet sometimes there's nothing imaginary about these "imaginary friends." The clinical psychologist Patricia Serin explains,

"Imaginary friends are constructs that help a child to develop. When we say 'imaginary friend,' we're referring to a character that's created by a child, a construction of what the child might experience in relationships with others; through that imaginary friend, the child can practice and grow. It's a kind of mirror that allows them to practice interacting with others. An 'entity,' on the other hand, is something that imposes itself on the child; it's not their own creation. I recognize that it's not easy to make the distinction. As therapists, we have to spend time with the child in order to be able to tell the difference."[1]

As the child gets older, their brain and cognitive development will progressively limit these perceptions, except for in the case of a select few. We don't know why. Perhaps their brains are structured differently.

This cognitive shutdown in adults is an adaptive mechanism. What this means is that those who leave the door open have a harder time adapting to our world. Being sensitive in this way can be extremely difficult to live with on a daily basis, making it difficult to maintain one's psychological integrity.

Heightened sensitivity can be a real burden when it lasts into adolescence; for most of us, our mental boundaries have been constructed by then, except for those for whom they remain inexplicably open. Taming this porosity is no easy task. Many choose to stay silent, quickly realizing that it's better to keep to themselves any experiences of contact they've had with the deceased, most of which they never wanted in the first place.

Others decide to make a profession out of it. It's a strange career, being an intermediary between the living and the dead—a medium.

The first time I consulted a medium, several years after your uncle's death, I was both unnerved by what he revealed to me and frustrated because I'd expected more.[2] Many of the details relayed to me by the medium—who told me that he'd gotten them from Thomas—were so exact that they could not have been either coincidences or flukes.

The medium described the circumstances of the accident and the precise cause of Thomas's death, all from a simple photo. He showed no signs of hesitation, and made no generalizations that could have applied to anyone. Quite the opposite: he systematically gave me a detailed account of my brother's personality, life, and death.

However, alongside this, there were several pieces of information that felt essential—beginning with my brother's name—that the medium apparently did not receive from Thomas, despite the fact that he claimed to be in conversation with him. If he was actually speaking to Thomas, why didn't my brother tell him what his name was? It's a pretty basic fact! I came away from the séance both taken aback and frustrated. This fueled my skepticism for a long time, even though it was impossible for me to explain how the medium could have otherwise given me so much correct detail that day.

After that first experience, I met with other mediums for both séances and interviews, and immersed myself in extensive study of the phenomenon. Several of them allowed me to employ a protocol used by American researchers whose work I had stumbled upon; their studies made it possible to assess the reality of these "communications" in a more objective way.[3]

When a medium is with someone they don't know, someone whom they're meeting for the first time, how are they capable of transmitting any quantity of factual information? Where is this information coming from? Researchers like Julie Beischel of the Windbridge Research Center have focused on this question.

What are the "conventional" explanations?

To start with, we can't rule out fraud: the medium might have gone on the internet, for example, to look for details on their client before the consultation. Social media is a mine of information. In her studies, Julie Beischel provides the medium with the client's name only at the very last minute, and even then, only the client's first name.

You could also legitimately suspect that mediumship is a form of mentalism or behaviorism, and that it's by observing all the physical and verbal reactions of their client that the medium is able to deduce—whether consciously or unconsciously—the information they need. The client's reaction to each bit of information then allows the medium to refine the details. Julie Beischel's solution here is to have the medium questioned by a third party, often even at a distance, by phone, so that the client and the medium have no way of seeing each other.

In the same vein, we shouldn't overlook a bias known as the "Barnum effect." This refers to a person's ability to convince themselves that what they're being told applies to them specifically and accurately, when in reality, it's a vague generality that could apply to anyone. For example, the medium might say that they can see "a person with white hair." The vast majority of elderly people have white hair. The client might then conclude that the medium is talking to their grandfather, the person with whom they're hoping to establish contact, even though there's absolutely no objective evidence to support this.

The medium might also speak in these vague generalities—some of which might even be contradictory—and then adapt to the clues the client provides, giving them the impression that they're speaking to a deceased person when actually they're feeding the medium more and more detailed information without realizing it.

This is known as "cold reading," a technique for obtaining information from someone simply by observing how they react to a series of leading questions.

To mitigate these different interpretative biases in her experiments, Julie Beischel asks mediums to respond to a preestablished list of precise questions about the deceased: physical description, personality, hobbies or activities, and cause of death. The accuracy of the medium's answers is then judged blind: someone who has not taken part in the experiment and who knows neither the medium nor the deceased in question is given descriptions of several different deceased people, and is then asked to choose which one corresponds to the transcript of the medium's reading.

Despite all these precautions and the rigor of Beischel's protocols, the mediums tested were able to obtain indisputable and inexplicable results.

Beischel and other researchers following similar protocols have thus been able to demonstrate that mediums have an ability to obtain information beyond all conventional means even under these controlled circumstances. "The results suggest that certain mediums can anomalously receive accurate information about deceived mediums," Beischel confirmed.[4]

I remember talking about mediums with French mentalist Fabien Olicard during an interview, knowing that he was interested in the subject and that he's an expert on the different ways in which the human brain can be deceived. When I asked him if he thought mentalism could explain mediumship, he told me that he didn't think so. "In my opinion, a medium is not using mentalism." I explained Julie Beischel's methodology to him and asked whether he thought he would be capable of obtaining the same results as the mediums she'd tested. His response was unequivocal: "None of the techniques I can master, whether they're psychological, cold reading, illusionism, etc., would give me the accuracy I'd need to pass that test. For me, it would be impossible."[5]

Julie Beischel replicated her initial studies, once again obtaining the same convincing results. In an article published in the journal *Explore*, she concluded that these new findings

> successfully replicate and extend previous findings demonstrating the phenomenon of anomalous information reception (AIR), the reporting of accurate and specific information without prior knowledge, in the absence of sensory feedback, and without using deceptive means. Because the experimental conditions of this study eliminated normal, sensory sources for the information mediums report, a nonlocal source (however controversial) remains the most likely explanation for the accuracy and specificity of their statements.[6]

A *nonlocal* source.

These results do, however, raise a major question, one that has also been raised by the researchers themselves: is mediumship a form of clairvoyance?

Could the information that the medium believes they're receiving from the deceased person actually be coming from their client's mind, or a nonlocal informational field? In other words: the results of these studies may be attesting to the mediums' ability to perceive information that can be verified, but does that necessarily mean that the mediums are really communicating with the deceased?

I raised the question with several mediums as well as with Julie Beischel.

Could mediums be using—without necessarily being aware of it—a form of clairvoyance, telepathy, or precognition to pick up on the information they provide? Even this hypothesis would be extraordinary in and of itself. Either way, we're talking about extrasensory abilities and the capacity for a consciousness to access a nonlocal space and obtain data from it.

According to Beischel, research has been butting up against the apparent impossibility of responding to this question for a long time.

"There are two different interpretations of the results," she told me. "The first is that it's 'survival psi'"—"psi" being an umbrella term used to encompass extrasensory abilities and other anomalous mental phenomena—"in which the medium is communicating with a discarnate. The second is that the medium is simply reading information from you or an informational field, and there's no discarnate involved. In that case, it's 'somatic psi.' It's impossible to tell which one is the correct interpretation simply by examining the content of a reading."

"Really?"

"Yes. Everything a medium says could be explained by somatic psi. If they give you information that you don't know at the time, but verify later, it could be precognition. If they reveal something to you that you don't know but someone else does, it could be telepathy. If they mention a document hidden in your grandmother's attic, it would be clairvoyance. In each of these cases, you wouldn't need an interaction with the deceased to explain the results, no matter how exact and unsettling they are."

"So how have you approached this question?"

"We conducted a qualitative and quantitative study on the psychological and physiological aspects of mediumship, and the experience of perception as described by mediums.[7] This approach has proven itself to be the best one for distinguishing 'somatic psi' from 'survival psi.' The mediums we interviewed described 'somatic psi' as a very different experience. With 'survival psi,' the experience is more like a form of communication, just like you and I are speaking right now. It's not that they're having a conversation, but the information reaches them. For them, the difference is a bit like 'receiving' versus 'retrieving.' 'Receiving' implies a sender, whereas 'retrieving' does not. All the mediums said that in a reading where they *feel* themselves to be in contact with the deceased, it's a more interactive experience."

Julie's recent research involved more than 120 mediums. The conclusions she has just described aren't surprising to me. All the mediums I've spoken to and tested on my own, most of whom are able to experience both clairvoyance and mediumship, have said exactly the same thing. The two sensations are very different.

In particular, there's a feeling of "intrusion" that's specific to mediumship.

Over the years, I've spent a lot of time asking mediums about their feelings. Their answers align perfectly with Julie's studies, namely that a clairvoyant perception is like a static image; it's never *invasive*. With mediumship, on the other hand, there's a thought, an *intelligence*, that intrudes, and which they identify as that of the deceased.

Several of them have even told me that some deceased people made their presence known before a consultation, for example the night before, as though they wanted to assure the medium that the "channel" would be open when they met with their loved one.

This demonstrates a form of intentionality, of presence—*something* that has come to meet up with the medium and speak to them. That's what happened with your grandfather. When I tested out six mediums, several other deceased members of the family showed up completely unexpectedly. They had some things to say.[8]

20

PRESENCES

Mediums all say that during a reading with the deceased, they can feel the intrusion of an exterior, intangible intelligence who's seeking to communicate. Sometimes the deceased will even interrupt or correct the medium if they feel they haven't been clearly understood. This does not happen in the context of clairvoyance.

Another experiment I carried out recently supports this claim. I tested several mediums with photos of both deceased and living people, and the mediums could tell whether the person in the photo was dead or alive. I wasn't trying to trap them; I simply wanted to observe the phenomenology in both scenarios.

Without consulting each other, several mediums told me separately that they could feel a certain *resistance* from the photos of the living people, which they didn't feel with the deceased.

This remark intrigued me.

Over the course of my discussions with them, they explained this notable difference in feeling by the fact that a living person's consciousness is still in the grip of the psychological dynamics of their personality—their ego—while death loosens this grip substantially. A living person's active brain maintains this kind of watertight mental seal, which isn't the case for a deceased person—or at least, much less so.

Unexpectedly, this experiment was very instructive. If mediumship were simply a form of telepathy or clairvoyance, it wouldn't matter whether they were working with a deceased or a living person; the results would be the same. There wouldn't be a "resistance" attesting to the fact that the medium was in contact with a consciousness still constrained by the brain activity of a living person.

If mediumship were "only" clairvoyance or telepathy—if the medium were drawing on a nonlocal informational field—it wouldn't matter whether the person was alive or dead, because either way, they wouldn't be the source of the medium's information. The accuracy of the information would be the same, as would the medium's sensory experience.

But this isn't what they describe, especially not Christelle Dubois, a medium I've worked with many times who is always up for an experiment.

A year after your grandfather's death, Luna, when I went to test out mediums to try to objectively establish whether they were capable of communicating with him—which led to surprising results that were unquestionably in line with what I'm discussing here, though I won't go on about them now, as I've already written about them extensively in my book *The Test*—Christelle Dubois was one of those six mediums. It was the first time we met.

Christelle has had extrasensory abilities since childhood, but she didn't choose to become a medium right away. She was first a nurse's aide, specializing in end-of-life support, and now she runs a funeral home; it's a different way for her to accompany families, and the deceased person, as they take their first steps *into the beyond.* When I asked her about the nature of what she experiences during a consultation, she was able to describe it very clearly.

"When you talk about mediumship, you describe physical, sensory sensations," I said to her. "How do you know that you're really in contact with a deceased person and not experiencing a form of clairvoyance?"

"Because, right after I pick up on the first physical sensations and emotions, a deceased person appears to me visually, with body language, facial expressions, very precise things. It starts with sensations but becomes a vision. Beyond a vision, even: there's a presence. The deceased person is there."

"What do you mean by that?"

"The deceased person manifests through their presence. I know where they are, I can feel it. I get goosebumps. There are particular sensations that I don't have when they're not present. It happened with your father."

"During a reading, do you see the deceased in the room?"

"Yes, but not the whole time. I know when they're there. Sometimes they're sitting next to me, sometimes they're pacing back and forth in the room. Sometimes they don't move at all and just stay there, frozen. These visual perceptions are what validate the sensations I have."

"Do they speak to you?"

"I hear them . . . but it's hard to describe . . ."

"Do you see them moving their lips and addressing you?"

"No. I don't see them moving their lips and speaking."

"So they're not speaking?"

"No, they are . . . it's just that, when they're speaking to me, it's more mental, as though their voice is coming straight into my head."

"Do you hear their voices?"

"I often hear the intonation they had when they were alive. For example, I'll say to the client, 'Did your mother have a hoarse voice?' and they'll answer, 'Yes, she smoked a lot.' I can perceive the timbre. The voice takes on a form; it's not a disembodied sound in my head, nor is it a thought that came from my own brain. With a deceased person who spoke with a deep voice, I'll hear a deep voice. But it's not at all the same mode of communication that you and I are using right now. It's a more subtle kind of language. Sometimes, with the deceased, I hear more of their voice; other times, it's more emotional, and they'll cause me to experience certain emotions. It's as though the senses on the other side are even more heightened. They don't have hearing or smell, but they do use subtle channels that we living people don't use. That's why we don't necessarily hear their first names, for example, or sentences that might seem obvious to us. Mediumship isn't a phone conversation with the beyond."

A reading is always a strange moment. The boundaries between two distinct realities, between individual beings evolving in space-time (the mediums and us) and others liberated from these constraints (the souls of the deceased), seem to be partially abolished. But that doesn't mean that communication occurs in the way we understand it, between two living people.

A medium is just a channel. The emotions that the deceased person is trying to convey are layered *atop* the medium's own emotions. The words the deceased person murmurs mix with the medium's thoughts. To be a medium, you have to know yourself well so that you don't confuse the messages of your own unconscious with those of the deceased. You have to work constantly for clarity. Good mediums recognize that there's always a bit of doubt, even if years of experience have strengthened their discernment abilities.

As Christelle said, a medium reading isn't a conversation with the beyond. Anyone who wants to believe that is deluding themselves.

Mediumship is a subtle perceptive ability, and an extremely fragile one. In no way is it similar to the kind of dialogue we have with each other here on earth. When the medium "communicates" with the deceased, it's not an intercom. They're picking up on impressions and feelings; sometimes they might hear a word, or a spontaneous sentence. But as soon as you ask the medium a question, for example, thinking that you're talking to the deceased, the medium's brain is also likely to respond, because it never stops functioning and interpreting.

Of course, despite all of this, they might be able to get a response from the deceased, but it's important to stay constantly vigilant. A medium reading in which the client spends the whole time asking questions and receiving responses from the deceased via the medium is extremely rare. For that to happen, the medium would have to be either a charlatan or fooling themselves.

Imagining that a medium is capable of speaking to a deceased person for thirty minutes is just that—pure fiction.

While I'm at it, I'll add another note of caution: a medium will not predict the future. A mediumship consultation isn't a clairvoyant reading; it shouldn't be used to ask a deceased person for life advice. Why not? Because it's always possible that, without realizing it, the medium will be the one to offer their advice unconsciously, and it may not necessarily be wise advice.

Going to see a medium to find out whether the deceased is okay with our selling the house might help us make a business decision; going to see a medium to ask about the future is dangerous, in the sense that it's impossible to guarantee the reliability of the answers.

The second problem, which is not a small one, is that, even

if some of the answers do come from the deceased, why should being dead mean they have all the answers? Why should we assume they're right? I'll come back to this shortly. The answer is not obvious.

I can't stress enough how important it is to ask ourselves why we're going to see a medium, and to question our own motives. If it's for existential answers, it's not the place. If it's in the hopes of making an unbearable pain go away, I think it's more pressing, and most importantly, more effective, to see a therapist.

Grief is a form of heartbreak, a psychological wound. This wound will not be healed by a medium. Despite the profound kindness of many mediums I know, that's not their skill set, and it's not their role.

If a mediumship consultation has a positive impact on the grieving process, it's because of the hope it provides—the possibility of knowing whether the person we've lost is doing well. But they're gone. They won't come back. The medium is not going to fill the void they left behind. Quite the opposite: seeing a medium regularly to "get a new message" runs the risk of trapping the person in what's called pathological grief.

A mediumship consultation is always possible, and it may soothe the pain for a few moments, especially in a situation of great distress, but under no circumstances should it be a substitute for therapeutic support.

Mediumship is extraordinary, not magical.

The research on mediums, after death communications, the nonlocal extrasensory capabilities of consciousness, near-death experiences, phenomena observed at the end of life, etc., all reinforces the hypothesis that a form of existence continues after the death of your body.

I tried to share all of this with your grandfather before his death, Luna. Some of it unsettled him, but I don't think I managed to dispel his fears. At his bedside, I kept looking for the right words, the most objective argument, and yet I still felt powerless in the face of his distress. Why weren't words enough?

I really wish I knew then what I know now. Since your grandfather's death, I've been exploring further, drinking from other fountains of knowledge. I've found other answers, and another way of sharing them.

The fundamental nonlocal consciousness that Pim van Lommel referred to seems to be demonstrated by all the phenomena I've just mentioned. In my quest to gain a better understanding of it, not just intellectually but also through personal experience, my trips to the Amazon have proven crucial. Especially when I took them to the next level.

For my fifth journey, I decided to follow the method that shamans use in their training in order to confront the depths of my unconscious. This deep work involves a formative "diet," or "dieta."

21

Master Spirits

It was an ineffable pleasure to be back in the stifling heat of the *selva*, the Amazon rainforest. By that point, the demands of my career had kept me away for several years.

Since I was last there, your grandfather had passed away, joining Thomas. Now there were two beloved beings, two allies, two soul friends who were waiting for me—*perhaps*—behind the veil. But in order to meet them, I had to face the fears that were blocking me, and most importantly, understand where those fears came from.

The little hut that would be my only view for the next several weeks was located on the side of a mountain. It stood on a platform of about two hundred square feet, which itself was constructed on stilts.

There was a kind of balcony made of planks jutting out from the hut, several yards up from the thick vegetation below. In the back, the forest touched the palm roof. The entrance faced south and looked out onto an astonishing landscape of wild peaks. The panorama was incredible.

A river flowed below.

As the sun began to rise, I was awakened by rustling coming from the foliage a few yards from my bed. It was a group of young monkeys the size of large squirrels with long, thin tails. You'd have loved them, dear Luna. Their fur was either black or dark brown, and they watched me with round, white-rimmed eyes that, from a distance, made them look like tiny ghosts.

They squawked, chirped, and clucked, leaping from branch to branch and quickly forgetting all about me as they foraged for food.

Coffee. I was entirely awake now.

From dawn onward in the Amazon, the air is saturated with humidity, like a warm, suspended drizzle. It gets into your eyes, plasters your hair to your forehead, and makes your skin slick and soft. I was sitting on the doorstep when the sun suddenly pierced through the languishing clouds. The silhouettes of the mountaintops were thrown into relief against a luminous bluish haze.

The Amazon is sublimely beautiful. I hope to be able to show it to you one day, Luna.

I had arrived five days earlier in this isolated spot in the middle of nature, circled by these uninhabited, humid hills, to begin my long *dieta*.

The *dieta* is the foundation of Amazonian shamanism. I'd heard about it on my previous trips here, but I didn't grasp right away just how important it was. It's an ancestral practice that demands a lot of you both mentally and physically, so it doesn't tend to be a priority for short stays.

It was a young French shaman who taught me about its importance. Born to a psychiatrist father and a Colombian doctor mother, Yann discovered shamanism as though he were reconnecting with past knowledge he'd lost temporarily. Trained in the Shipibo tradition in the Amazon, he left France more than eight years ago to live near the village of San Pedro de Cumbaza in the

Tarapoto District of the Peruvian Amazon. Our conversations changed my own shamanistic practice and worldview.

The *dieta* refers to a formative period, or apprenticeship, that can last from several days to several years. It begins with a "dieta opening," the goal of which is to increase the person's sensitivity and energetic and mental porosity. This is performed by a shaman during an ayahuasca ceremony.

Then, during the dieta, you must follow a number of strict dietary restrictions: no alcohol, no red meat, no salt, no sugar. The dieta also requires a certain amount of psychological discipline; you have to completely abstain from sex, for example.

By involving both the body and mind, the dieta is intended to foster a teaching relationship between the person following the regimen and one or multiple "master plants."

The dieter consumes the plant daily—whether in the form of roots, fresh leaves, an infusion, or a tea, depending on the kind of plant—and in doing so establishes an exchange that's both organic and spiritual. Unlike ayahuasca, master plants don't contain any psychoactive ingredients. Their power lies elsewhere. They can also be trees, whose spirits will become the dieter's allies, guides, and teachers.

The plant's teachings manifest subtly, through dreams, intuitions, visions, synchronicities, and other signs. The plant's world is said to be *opening up*, like a kind of intuitive guidance. The plant works upon our energies and unconscious, shining its light from time to time into our darkest corners. It awakens parts of our being that are usually dormant or under control.

It brings disorder.

Dismantles our mental illusions.

The dieta apprenticeship works on our inner self, the different layers of our unconsciousness. At the same time, it brings us into contact with external forces.

It breaks down the person we thought we were.

It brings light to our shadows. In doing so, it profoundly transforms our inner energy, which is usually stuck in the circuits selected by our autonomous mental processes, redirecting it to newer, subtle circuits.

Throughout the Amazon, anyone called upon to become a shaman isolates themself for a year while following this strict dieta. Alone in the heart of the rainforest, the only thing they can rely on is the help of the spirits, particularly those of the master plants.

The dieta apprenticeship is a strange alliance with the plant world. It allows us to progressively acquire a new lucidity, liberating our unconsciousness gradually.

The mind loses its hold; intuition grows stronger; extrasensory perception develops. The boundaries between us and the outside world dissipate. Illusion gives way to greater clarity. The result is a new mastery of our inner strength and greater receptiveness to the hidden dimensions of our world.

When Yann offered me the opportunity to try this prerequisite to shamanic experience, I didn't hesitate for a minute. I had to explore this path, had to follow the method all the way.

Yann was guiding me through this new journey in the middle of a mountainous region in the Andean foothills of the Peruvian Amazon, where he had been based for years.

He suggested I work with a plant locally known as ajo sacha. *Mansoa alliacea*, or garlic vine, is a species of tropical vine in the Bignoniaceae family, and is considered one of the most powerful master plants. During this dieta, it would become my guide and help me to explore my unconscious. Yann opened my dieta with a ceremony during which I drank only a teaspoon of ayahuasca, and he drank a little more.

Half an hour later, Yann was sitting facing me with his legs bent, his head tilted slightly to one side. In the darkness, lit only by the light of the moon, he began to sing the same Shipibo songs I'd heard over and over again in the malocas to set the dieta process in motion for me.

These songs are *icaros*, ceremonial songs that shamans say are the language of plants.

Like all Amazonian shamans, Yann had gone on very long dietas that allowed him to accumulate the energy of the plants he worked with. Their energy mingled with his own. *That* was the energy that was singing right at that moment. The spirit of the plant was expressing itself through him, in melodic form. The songs are a tool that allows us to travel, to "see," to explore our bodies as well as our minds. To act upon subtle energies. And they open up the world of visions.

I was awed by his astonishing concentration and the delicacy of his singing, despite the intoxication caused by the ayahuasca. He explained to me that in this particular state, his perception of people changes; it's as though he can see *through* them.

The shaman doesn't choose the melody, he told me. They are in such a state of trance and fusion with the dieta plants that they have merged. The plants are the ones to heal, act, and express themselves through the human being who's made this pact with them.

When the song was over, my connection with the ajo sacha was open. Yann had *energetically* introduced us to each other. Now it was my turn to receive the spirit's teachings. My turn to learn to grasp the subtilities of this unique relationship.

The next day, I headed off to my hut, where I would be spending more than a month totally alone.

On retreat, I'd gotten into the habit of infusing several leaves of ajo sacha in a simmering pan of water every evening.

This was my daily encounter with my plant. I let it cool down, then drank the infusion slowly while sitting on the stoop, watching the clouds float across the sky and the night fall. The bond that the ajo sacha and I would form over the next few weeks would cement an alliance that will last for the rest of my life.

Before I left for my hut, Yann gave me a little bottle containing about eight ounces of ayahuasca. I didn't know if I would have the courage—or the recklessness—to drink it alone. I'd never done that, not without the strict supervision of shamans. Yann suggested I take it from time to time, starting with a very small dose, as he believed my familiarity with the effects of the drink and my mental stability would allow it. And then I could drink more if I felt like it. I hadn't touched it.

I approached my yearslong commitment to shamanism in the same way as everything else I've undertaken in my life: I wouldn't stop until I got the answers I was looking for.

I viewed my current journey as an evolution of the inner calling that's always been there for me. The desire to explore beyond boundaries.

In the early years of my career, well before you were born, it was geographical boundaries that I crossed in secret. I ventured into dangerous areas, sometimes at great risk to myself, always with the goal of gathering information and photos to bring back, of understanding geopolitical situations and bearing witness to them. During those years, I mostly traveled alone.

Now, my desire for exploration was focused on the remotest areas of consciousness.

My shamanic experiences had already taught me a tremendous amount, and this dieta was the next step. By following its principles and immersing myself in the revitalizing landscape of the Amazon rainforest, as I'd been doing since my arrival here,

I could sense that my consciousness was expanding. I was reconnecting with primitive sensations, communing with the lush nature that surrounded me; my sensitivity was strengthening, my intuition sharpening. I could calmly continue just like that and consider those benefits precious enough. But now that I was there, I was realizing I wanted more.

I'd already learned a lot from the ceremonies. About myself, especially, but also about how these experiences require absolute commitment. I'd begun to perceive the complex reality of these dimensions of consciousness, but had I gotten all the answers I'd been seeking in the Amazon? No. Far from it. Some of them, perhaps, but over the course of my travels, new questions had arisen.

I'm sure you can predict where I'm going with this, Luna. I was thinking about the bottle of ayahuasca that Yann gave me, currently stowed in the bottom of my bag, and about what I might be able to discover if I drank it.

Although I didn't think I would do it at first, the inner peace I'd been feeling since my arrival, combined with the irrepressible desire to push myself beyond my limits, led me to think that I might attempt to drink ayahuasca without someone next to me. Unguided, but with the delicate freedom that solitude offers.

By then I had a good understanding of how the plant affects me. On many occasions I'd had the opportunity to see my fears, and I'd experienced the profound destabilization, both physical and psychological, of that altered state of consciousness. The universe of ayahuasca was no longer foreign to me. I was aware of the stakes of a decision like this.

Curiosity has always motivated my decisions. I've thrown myself into the unknown several times in my life without a safety net.

A new opportunity had arisen, and that's what I was there for: trying it all out. Going as far as I could.

Yes, the time had come to take this strange quest of mine to the next level.

That night, I would drink ayahuasca alone.

22

A Solitary Experience

As twilight fell, I closed the door and settled down in the dark. My plan was to proceed with caution. I knew very well how the Madre could make the world spin.

I picked up the bottle. The contents looked like an opaque, ochre-colored syrup. Opening it, I brought it to my nose. No sooner did the unmistakable aroma enter my nostrils than my body *remembered* and spasmed. It wasn't the pungent smell that provoked this reaction, but something more animal, more organic—a spontaneous reconnection with the power of a memory.

The ayahuasca was *already* in me. It had been for years. Just the scent wafting out from the bottle was enough to awaken the energy coiled in my body.

I could also feel its force spreading instantly through the hut, like a passionate, invisible cloud. This was powerful stuff.

Delicately, I poured the equivalent of a sip of ayahuasca into a small glass that I brought to my lips. In deference, I held it there for several minutes.

I tried to express out loud and as clearly as possible what I wanted from the night. I asked the sacred plant and the ajo sacha for their help. I also whispered to your grandfather that I'd like to see him again. Was he there, somewhere in the silence? Was Thomas with him?

I drank down the thick liquid in one gulp. The bitterness made me retch. I concentrated on my breathing, then, very slowly, I relaxed. No more thinking; time to *feel.*

After several minutes, I seemed to feel the uncertain sensation of a presence in the room. I didn't see anything, but I *felt the presence* of two shadows. Was it my imagination? A projection? *Stop thinking.*

Suddenly there was fear in my stomach, threatening. Maybe I shouldn't be drinking ayahuasca alone. But it was a little late now . . .

Breathe in, breathe out. I kneaded various parts of my body with my firm hands to reaffirm the groundedness that was relentlessly slipping away. My heart calmed down, and the apprehension left my mind and stomach.

Minutes passed, time went by. Nothing seemed to be changing. I decided to drink another mouthful, directly from the bottle, then immediately rinsed my mouth and resumed my position. I waited for it to kick in, maybe another half hour, but again, nothing.

Well, I'd started, and I was not going to give up now. I had to go all the way.

A third mouthful.

I decided I wouldn't have any more, no matter what. I dozed off.

Everything after that was blurrier. Had I fallen asleep? How much time had passed? I didn't know, but I suddenly realized that it had taken effect. I was swept away by a kind of intoxication; it felt like I was mentally and physically floating, but at the same time, my visual acuity seemed to have improved. My movements were awkward and jerky, and I realized that I could perceive the energy moving within me, in circuits made of tiny phosphorescent dots that crisscrossed my skin. The sight was luminous, magnificent. It was like a network of previously invisible energetic vibrations had appeared on top of the reality I knew: my body, the hut in the twilight. The energy circuits trembled with constant movement, and the thought occurred to me that this was my dieta plant, the ajo sacha, *cleansing* me.

I breathed. The sensation wasn't unpleasant, just some tension in my stomach and a bit of nausea; it was manageable. The effects intensified as indescribable images appeared before my closed eyes. I opened them, called for my father, scanned the room. I couldn't see anything with my eyes open, no perceptions at all.

No *signs*.

Was my father there, even if I couldn't see him? I was overwhelmingly cold, and tired, too. I was full of expectation, probably too much, as usual. I didn't know what time it was, or how long it had been since I'd drunk the ayahuasca—maybe two hours? Three hours? A little discouraged, I admitted to myself that the effect was probably already wearing off.

Nevertheless, I was still *mareado*, as the shamans call the particular intoxication caused by ayahuasca. It was hard for me to stand up; I was a clumsy puppet tottering on its legs. I wanted to sleep. I lay down, motionless, curled up and trembling on the foam mat.

But sleep didn't come.

Quite the opposite: *I left.*

At first I heard what sounded like bells chiming, an otherworldly, crystalline melody; this sound I knew. Generally it marked the beginning of the experience. I straightened up, and suddenly everything went wobbly. I turned onto my side, slumped over on an elbow, but then froze suddenly because I realized that if I kept moving, I was going to lose all sense of where I was, any notion of space at all. For a fraction of a second, I told myself, *Okay, let yourself go*, but the sensation of panic was growing, so I tensed up and stopped moving, breathing desperately to fight against the dizziness. I was going to vomit.

I feverishly grabbed for the basin I'd had the good sense to keep beside me, straightened up slowly to sit cross-legged, and slid the basin between my legs, leaning over it. The effects were still intensifying; I was sweating by then from both heat and cold. All the space around me was disappearing. And I was being sucked in, carried off by the crystal bursts of sound that were becoming more and more apparent, strong, *alive*.

I was going to be engulfed by a universe of geometric forms. I could see lines and reflections; matter was simultaneously light . . . My bed was evaporating, I was losing even the physical sensation of being in the bed, of being in my body. At the same time I had the sense that I was being carved up and eaten. I'd experienced this before. But when? In a dream? It felt like a reminder, the revival of something I already knew.

And yet I was still *me*, witnessing this fragmentation from another vantage point. Viewing my body's disintegration from *another dimension*. The most unsettling thing was that I was still lucid. I could observe what was happening, and at the same time, I was powerless.

I was both profoundly conscious and totally confused; I didn't understand anything. I was battling endless dizziness. With all my might I resisted a hurricane of energy, it was spinning, I refused to let myself go, I was too scared, though of what, I didn't know—of vomiting, of losing my footing—I wanted at all costs to avoid being swept away into the unknown, where I could tell I was going to lose consciousness. An absolute refusal to lose control. I was desperately weak, I was freezing, the blood had drained away from my face, I was sweating profusely.

Immobility saved me.

Clenching my muscles as tight as they would go. Concentrating with a strength born of despair. Breathing. What was incomprehensible was that at no point did I feel like I was in danger. It was a total paradox: I didn't perceive any threats, and yet I was paralyzed by an unbearable fear, like always.

Why?

I observed this strange fear with a kind of detachment. I was in a state of dissociation. It seemed further away, less insurmountable and deafening than in previous ceremonies, and yet it had me in just as strong of a grip. Then I managed to block it out. In a last-ditch effort, I breathed and pushed away just a little, millimeters from irremediable chaos. Should I have let myself be carried away? It was impossible—something in me was resisting. I refused. I *couldn't* "leave."

After a period that seemed to go on forever, I managed to move a finger, and then my hand, without the dizziness returning. Extremely slowly, I took hold of my gourd and drank a little water. Very gradually, the indescribable feeling of being swept away began to fade.

I managed to regain my composure. The experience had lasted hours. My mattress was soaked. Despite my exhaustion, it was difficult to fall asleep.

In the middle of the night, I was rudely awakened by an insanely violent storm. I was no longer intoxicated. All the water in the sky was pouring down into the darkness around my hut. An invisible deluge. The ground thirstily lapped up the falling sea. Would my hut make it through the storm? I didn't have the strength to worry about it any more than that, and I fell unconscious once again.

I woke up at dawn by noise coming from the foliage a few yards from the hut.

Monkeys.

I dragged myself out from under my mosquito net. It was beautiful out. I could hear the unusual roar of the river from down in the valley.

Why couldn't I let myself be swept away? Once again, the effect of the ayahuasca had completely thrown me off, and I'd panicked. A survival reflex, probably. I'd exhausted myself trying to block the experience. I didn't see anything with my eyes open, not Papa, nor did I even feel like I was able to communicate with him or Thomas. But I was incapable of letting myself go. It was beyond a question of will. I found myself in an astonishingly clear dissociative state, helplessly observing an unconscious protective mechanism put a stop to my journey. I had no control over it; it was as though my will had been obliterated by this totally panicked part of me. Again!

A light lunch, not much of an appetite. I went outside to get a little air. Walked around for a bit and then lay down in the hammock slung between two beams on the wooden deck, a small paperback in my hand.

I'd brought very little with me on this trip. Just a few books to inspire me, in particular two by the iconoclastic Tibetan Buddhist master Chögyam Trungpa. I turned the pages of *The Myth of Freedom and the Way of Meditation*, letting chance lead me to rediscover passages I'd previously highlighted. In one, Trungpa mentions the "six worlds of the *bardo*," which are not literally stages in the journey after death, but psychological models to which we humans, in our confusion and blindness, cling. These "worlds" are also psychological descriptions of the six major personality patterns we unconsciously identify with.

Buddhism insists that these "worlds," these "personality

types," are mental illusions, reassuring archetypes formed by our desires and aspirations. We think that we're like this or that, but in reality, the person we believe ourselves to be is a form of illusion, a mask we've forged over the course of our existence that hides our true dimension, our true nature.

"A person's psychology is usually firmly rooted in one realm," Trungpa explains. "This realm provides us with a style of confusion, a way of entertaining and occupying ourselves so as not to have to face our fundamental uncertainty, our ultimate fear that we may not exist."[1]

I put down the open book and lifted my head. I'd suddenly had an obvious intuition.

My fear.

Wasn't it the *ultimate fear that I may not exist*? Of course it was! That's exactly what it was last night: I felt like I would "cease to exist" if I gave up control. Now, for the first time, I could see the source of the problem very clearly: I was terrified at the thought of *disappearing*.

Fear of disappearing.

The organic fear of "no longer existing."

I understood that this fear lived not only in me, but in every human being, like a ghost haunting our hearts. A seed left in our psyches at the moment of our birth. Its magnitude varies depending on the person. For some, it's a daily handicap, a source of suffering, depression, even all kinds of unbearable mental illnesses. For most of us, on the other hand, it's generally kept at bay by the powerful mechanisms of our unconscious. But not always. In times of fragility, it reappears, and because we can't understand it, it's unsettling.

The fear of disappearing.

It's not just the abstract fear of dying. It's more physical—the terror of being erased, of being separated from our identity. A visceral fear that lives in the part of us that identifies with our body. The ego. The mental structure attached to our personality.

The ego fears everything it perceives as a threat to its integrity, defining our lives. The fear of changing jobs or partners, the fear of current events, the fear of the state of the world. The fear of the future. The fear of confronting other people, or life itself. The fear of leaving familiar shores behind, even if we don't think they're right for us. The fear of something new, the fear of watching even an unhappy existence unravel, because we've already invested so much time and energy into it, and we don't want to step outside the reassurance of our comfort zone. We're safe there.

As people, we don't like change. We do everything we can to minimize risk of instability, but this approach only imprisons us. Moreover, it doesn't work: isn't the impermanence of our world the very thing that defines it? Nonetheless, we never stop building walls around ourselves, locking up our own souls. An ego-fortress. The shell I mentioned to you earlier. Our bodies change and grow older; our friendships and romantic relationships evolve; the world is unpredictable—and yet our egos continue to cling to the idea that the source of happiness is stability, a life that's unchanging and *under control.*

The fear that caused me to freeze whenever I was in an altered state of consciousness was connected to this apprehension that we feel when we're facing the unknown. It was caused by the fact that during these journeys, my shell began to crack, threatening to shatter completely.

It wasn't me who was scared, it was my ego.

Because it's mortal.

Humanity's two greatest fears—death and madness—take possession of us when our egos, the architects of our identities, begin to fall apart, particularly under the influence of psychedelics. "Madness" in this case corresponds to when we venture outside the confines of our cognitive prison, and "death" is the fear that we won't be able to go back to it.

Trungpa's words were a revelation for me, one that allowed me to see the intensity of the emotions I experienced during the ayahuasca ceremonies in a new light.

However, while his words were inspiring, I found it difficult to grasp what I needed to do to stop being a prisoner to my fear. I kept reading without finding any answers. As usual, my reflex was to turn to a book!

Ayahuasca forced me to leave behind the intellectual, mental, distant relationship I had with death and confront its emotional reality. And emotions were something that my personality structure preferred to keep at a distance. Why?

On a day-to-day level, death remained an abstraction, unreal and far away. When my ego wavered, it foreshadowed the total dissolution of the shell that occurs, with varying degrees of intensity, at the moment of death. I knew this perfectly well—I'd read about it in Greek philosophy, Buddhist and Hindu texts, and accounts of near-death and shamanic experiences—but it's quite a different thing to experience it myself. And I wasn't emotionally ready.

"Understanding" isn't enough.

I thought I'd acquired this information, but I'd only done so in theory. And theoretical knowledge could not "convince" my ego that it could die without putting me in danger, because for the person I am today, on an emotional level, "I" and "my ego" are inseparable.

Fundamentally, though, they shouldn't be.

That night, I found myself on the threshold of a powerful shift in my state of consciousness. My ego was weakening, beginning to die. This brought me closer to a change in "worlds," to refer back to Chögyam Trungpa's psychological concept, and I was overcome with a sense of powerlessness, simply because my altered brain was fighting to regain control.

I could feel that my body refused the experience, refused to *change*, refused to abandon the person I believed myself to be. "Change, from the Ego point of view, is suffering. Change, from the Soul point of view, is just change," Ram Dass wrote.[2]

That was my problem. My ego didn't know what lay beyond that threshold, because it didn't know that on the other side, life goes on. That *my* life would go on.

My fears demonstrated that I was still a prisoner of my ego. And it didn't know that the experience was safe, even though, as Ram Dass reminds us, our egos—the personalities that our brains create and then defend fiercely—are "merely a fragment of who we are."[3]

Neuroscience has provided us with objective confirmation of this point. The ego has no immutable essence. It would be more accurate to say it's a process of control and identification developed by the brain. We are not our egos, just as we cannot be reduced to any of our adaptive functions.

The ego is first and foremost a brain mechanism.

The question is: how can we peacefully liberate our brains from its grip?

23

The Psychedelic Revolution

There's nothing imaginary or symbolic about the traumatizing experience of having the feeling that *you might not exist*. Neuroscientific research on the effects of psychedelics on the brain has drawn attention to a particular cerebral mechanism connected to this intense fear of ego death.

Prestigious universities around the world, but especially in the US—Harvard, Johns Hopkins, Yale, NYU—now have major research programs dedicated to studying psychedelics, and the use of these drugs has been decriminalized in several cities in the US, Canada, Australia, and Switzerland.

Most research focuses on the therapeutic effects of psychedelics to treat a wide range of situations including anxiety, addiction, depression, eating disorders, end-of-life care, and bereavement. The possible applications are endless.[1]

Despite the many promising studies on psychedelics, they were deemed illegal in the early 1960s for purely political reasons.

As psychiatrist Stanislav Grof, a pioneering researcher in the field, said, "The drastic legislation that killed serious legitimate research of psychedelics for four decades was not based on any scientific evidence, but actually ignored the existing clinical data."[2]

Psychedelics had a considerable impact on an entire generation of scientists, doctors, and psychologists. Eminent figures in psychology and psychiatry, including Nobel Prize winners, have revealed that they have had experiences with them that they consider absolutely foundational. The research that's being done now is a sort of return to that era.

Why are researchers so excited about the therapeutic potential of psychedelics? As I've come to realize, they affect the mind, allowing us to gain access to feelings and parts of our unconscious that might otherwise remain hidden.

With conventional therapeutic approaches such as dream analysis or psychotherapy, it can take years to reach those inner corners of our mind, whereas psychedelics can grant us access much more easily—and much faster—for several hours at a time. They change the way information flows through our nervous system, allowing our conscious and unconscious to interact with unprecedented clarity. Psychedelic-assisted therapy helps us reconnect with our bodies and untangle the psychological and emotional knots from our childhood.

MDMA, for example—a substance that increases the production of serotonin, a neurotransmitter that plays a key role in our emotional states, including reducing anxiety levels—acts on the amygdala, a part of the brain closely associated with fear. MDMA "unplugs" this part of the brain, putting us into a state conducive to healing from the harmful effects of trauma.

Psychedelics have a physical effect on our body's levels of serotonin, hormones, dopamine, and oxytocin, helping us be more in touch with our inner emotional world.

For many therapists who use these substances in their work, the spiritual dimension is crucial. The substances allow us to access what certain traditions call "the realm of the dead," enabling a kind of alliance and communication with it. Researchers at Johns Hopkins and NYU studying end-of-life anxiety have reported that their patients' fear of death disappears after using psychedelics.[3]

Stanislav Grov used LSD in end-of-life care with the same results: "The most important effect that LSD had in dying cancer patients was the significant reduction or even disappearance of their fear of death. This happened in spite of the fact that they knew they would die within days or months."[4] He went on to say, "The potential significance of LSD for psychiatry and psychology is comparable to the importance of the microscope for biology and medicine, or the telescope for astronomy. The microscope revealed the existence of the microworld and the telescope revealed the depth of the universe, domains which had been previously unknown. LSD makes it possible to study deep processes in the psyche that are not normally available for observation."[5]

There's more to say on this point, but in a nutshell, this is why large-scale research has now resumed on these subjects: dimethyltryptamine (DMT) in ayahuasca, mescaline extracted from cacti including peyote, psilocybin from various species of mushroom, LSD, and MDMA.

Some of them are revolutionizing neuroscience.

During our conversations about NDEs, Steven Laureys, the Belgian neurologist, told me about some surprising comparative research he'd been collaborating on with the Centre for Psychedelic Research at Imperial College London, founded by the psychopharmacologist Robin Carhart-Harris. The Centre has been conducting brain-imaging research on the effects of psychedelics.

These studies have demonstrated that several types of psychedelic substances, including DMT, psilocybin, ketamine, and LSD, can induce very powerful states of ecstasy that resemble certain aspects of near-death experiences.

They're also comparable to mystical experiences, which can occur spontaneously—during an NDE, for example—as well as for spiritual practitioners. These experiences are characterized by a feeling of inexpressible unity and awakening, often accompanied by a very clear intuitive access to profound knowledge—a connection to a consciousness greater than that which we experience on a daily basis.

We know from previous studies that mystical experiences induced by psychedelic substances are indiscernible from spontaneous ones.[6] This was the finding that led Carhart-Harris to launch his first psilocybin research program with volunteers, in an effort to better understand what happens in the brain during these experiences.

Steven Laureys was once a guinea pig himself, receiving an intravenous psilocybin injection in Carhart-Harris's lab in London while his brain activity was observed via fMRI.[7] He confessed to me that the experience was difficult for him, having never taken any psychedelic substances before. Nonetheless, he added, he was eager to relive what he, too, described as the loss of his ego. "When we study consciousness, we neglect this side of it—experiencing it for ourselves by taking substances or otherwise inducing a trance state," he told me. "This kind of first-person experience is not in our medical and scientific training, but I think we should push ourselves much further in that direction. I can read plenty of publications about the effects of psilocybin, and talk to people about it, but experiencing it for myself is a completely different thing. I'd like to try it again. I need to relive the experience. I feel like a colorblind person trying to understand color vision. Sure, I can know everything there is to know about how color is perceived by the retina, I can identify all the relevant neurotransmitters in the brain, but actually *seeing* it really adds something."[8]

It's a lovely metaphor. It's true: knowing something in theory is different from experiencing it directly. I've been discovering this for myself ever since I began traveling to the Amazon.

The article that Dr. Robin Carhart-Harris and his team published in 2012 in the peer-reviewed journal *Proceedings of the National Academy of Sciences (PNAS)* caused an uproar, to say the least.[9]

As Michael Pollan explained in his book *How to Change Your Mind*, the study involved putting a volunteer who'd been injected with psilocybin into an fMRI machine. "Carhart-Harris's working hypothesis was that their brains would exhibit increases in activity, particularly in the emotion centers. 'I thought it would look like the dreaming brain,' he told me. . . . But when the first set of data came in, Carhart-Harris got a surprise: 'We were seeing *decreases* in blood flow'—blood flow being one of the proxies for brain activity that fMRI measures. 'Had we made a mistake? It was a real head-scratcher.' But the initial data on blood flow was corroborated by a second measurement that looked at changes in oxygen consumption to pinpoint areas of elevated brain activity. Carhart-Harris and his colleagues had discovered that psilocybin reduces brain activity, with the falloff concentrated in one particular brain network that at the time he knew little about: the default mode network."[10]

Not only were these results unexpected, they were also very strange. Ingesting psilocybin leads to reduced activity in several parts of the brain (the thalamus, the anterior and posterior cingulate cortices, and the medial prefrontal cortex), and the extent of that reduction in activity is correlated with the intensity of the subjective effects reported by the subjects. The more the activity decreases, the more intense the effects.

What's more: in addition to this reduction in activity, Carhart-Harris's team found evidence of a reduction in functional connectivity in the "hubs," central regions belonging to the *default mode network*.

What do we know about this neural network?

The default mode network is active in a variety of circumstances: when we're self-reflecting, recalling events we've personally experienced, imagining the future or hypothetical scenarios . . . Basically, it's always working, and it prepares us for changes in our environment on the basis of lived experience.

It's the ego network.

The default mode network inhibits cognition to protect us from an influx of stimuli that could potentially overwhelm us. It's particularly affected in diseases such as Alzheimer's where the person *loses* their history and identity.

In weakening this network, psilocybin also alters what we call "self-awareness," the consciousness that shapes and limits our cognition. It allows these constraints to ease up, leading to a kind of expansion of consciousness.

In short, what we're witnessing is the opening of the "doors of perception" as a result of a reduction in brain activity and functional connectivity in the "hubs" belonging to the default mode network.

These results have been replicated and thus confirmed, first at Imperial College,[11] then, over the course of several years, by other research teams working with other categories of psychedelics.[12]

These results caused a veritable thunderclap in the world of neuroscience. While everyone expected to observe a massive increase in brain activity in correlation with the intensity of the volunteers' subjective experiences, it was exactly the opposite that occurred. When the volunteers were at the height of their ecstatic experience, their brains displayed a significant drop in activity.

This is exactly what happens with NDEs, some of which, as I explained earlier, are linked to an identical cause: a partial or total cessation of brain activity.

This observation runs counter to neurological models. The accepted wisdom is that a more intense conscious experience should be accompanied by more intense neural activity. And yet the facts remain: when we look inside the brain for the source of the ecstasy, we find out that the brain has nothing to do with it.

Psychedelics trigger ecstatic states of consciousness, but what Carhart-Harris's study results show quite clearly is that these experiences are caused not by brain activity but by its cessation.

This research confirms William James's hypothesis that the brain's role is like that of a filter, a *reducing valve* for fundamental consciousness—something that NDEs had already led some to suspect.

When the brain is functioning normally, its strong constraints prevent us from perceiving the nonlocal dimension of reality that's always around us. It blocks us from using our extrasensory abilities. But when the brain's activity diminishes—that of the default mode network that underpins the ego, in this case—the doors of perception will open.

Death corresponds to an irreversible shutdown of the brain. Psychedelics allow us to imitate this experience—in a reversible way!—by artificially putting to sleep the part of the brain that filters material reality: the default mode network. In death, this is almost certainly one of the first parts to shut down.

This was the source of my terror during the shamanic ceremonies.

To borrow a comparison from Natalie Sudman of the U.S. Army Corps of Engineers, who had a near-death experience in Iraq and wrote a profound and deeply moving book on the subject[13]: the ego is like someone watching a film in a movie theater, comfortably installed in their seat and completely absorbed in the story, who identifies so strongly with one of the characters onscreen they begin to believe they are that character themselves, and that there's no world outside the film. The ego can't bear the idea of the film being over; they've forgotten they're just at a movie theater. To them, stopping the film means causing the character they've identified with to disappear forever.

Yet psychedelics stop the film. The character fades away.

This generates a flood of anxiety.

To make it through the fear stage, we have to let this fading-away take place. We have to convince the ego-character that it's safe for the consciousness it's concealing.

The good news is that we can train and alter our brains. They're malleable. The influence of the default mode network, which is also hugely dominant in rumination and depression, can be lessened through just a few weeks of meditation, for example. Studies show that experienced meditators seem to have reduced activity in this neural network.[14]

Michael Pollan draws a parallel between meditation and psychedelics: "Judson Brewer, the psychiatrist and neuroscientist who studies the brains of meditators . . . discovered that the brains of experienced meditators look much like the brains of people on psilocybin: the practice and the medicine both dramatically reduce activity in the default mode network."[15]

But whereas psychedelics take a forceful approach, meditation is gentler, working to *train* the brain to be less beholden to this particular network of survival and anticipation.

Meditation is a sort of permanent brain reeducation.

This is why I'd been dedicating myself to it since my arrival in the Amazon; meditation goes well with the sobriety of the dieta. Would I feel the calming effects during my next ayahuasca sessions? Would a few weeks be enough to calm my automatic psychological reactions to the reduced activity in my default mode network? It would be interesting to see whether the dieta also has a neurologically observable effect.

After reading Trungpa's book, and with my new neuroscientific knowledge, I understood that what I was experiencing wasn't imaginary. It wasn't just a "bad trip." During these ayahuasca sessions, I was actually beginning to experience what death is like, because the network underpinning my ego was shutting down. It wasn't symbolic; it was neurological.

But the fact is that this doesn't lead to unconsciousness, to nothing. Quite the opposite: it opens up an infinite world and a vast array of *real* extrasensory perceptions. I needed to soothe my ego, reassure it, and increase my structural connectivity by meditating in order to free myself from this neural network of fear.

I'm sure you've guessed already, Luna, that it wouldn't be long before I was drinking ayahuasca again.

24
The Wound

Time slowed down. The Amazon rainforest. The sky that had been cobalt blue in the morning turned to a dark gray over the course of just a few minutes, and rain began to fall. Then the sun returned, shimmering on the billions of damp leaves, from the lush grass on the ground to the broad foliage of the canopy. Its scorching rays caused the excess water to evaporate into filaments of steam that danced around in the air, pushed by the breeze.

My mood was as changeable as the weather. At times I was serene, at other times overwhelmed by rumination. I couldn't stop thinking about my first solitary ceremony. I was both eager to try again so that I could put what I'd learned into practice and anxious at the idea of finding myself blocked once more at the same stage.

The isolation had forced me to confront myself in a way that was very unsettling, especially given the sensitive state I was in thanks to the dieta plant. But meeting our solitude head-on is a prerequisite for inner exploration, the first step toward those invisible worlds.

I'd been living in my cabin for two weeks now, surrounded by monkeys, eagles, and geckos. I left it only to go down to the river or explore the forest. The rest of the time, I read and wrote. I'd also been practicing a sort of slow qigong routine in the mornings that helped the energy circulate throughout my body. It did me a lot of good. Too often, I forgot that I had a body, a vessel that carried me through life. I'd come to realize that taking care of it was as essential as paying attention to my mind if I wanted to perceive the reality beyond. I had to take care of my body so that I wasn't its prisoner. I had to take care of my body so that any physical blockages I may have allowed to develop didn't monopolize all my energy. I had to take care of my body so that I could distance myself from it, and in doing so, feel how we're all much more than this reflection of aging organic matter.

I devoted time every day to meditation, simply sitting in stillness, watching my thoughts flow through me as well as I could. It's very simple to meditate, Luna, did you know that? You just have to sit with your back straight, either on the ground with your legs crossed or on a chair. Your eyes can be open or closed, whatever is most comfortable for you. And then you stay like that for, say, fifteen minutes. That's enough. But doing it regularly is essential. Fifteen minutes a day is doable, right?

You don't try to "think about nothing" when you're meditating; that doesn't work. Just leave your mind alone. Thoughts may come, and if they do, don't hold on to them. Just let them go. Imagine that you're a rock in a river, and the thoughts are like leaves swept along by the current. They arrive and then they pass by. That's all. If you devote yourself to this every day, in just a few weeks, you're going to start feeling a change in yourself.

In the rainforest, I could tell how much my regular practice was freeing my mind, even if I wasn't particularly skilled at it. Time passed. A barrier had been broken down.

My research on death constantly brought me back to life. Death is about life, when all is said and done. What we make of it, the individual we think we are. When the unreal event that is death barges into our existence—as it did for me when your uncle Thomas left us, or more recently, when I was with your grandfather until his last breath—it places a mirror in front of us, and the reflection in that mirror can be brutal and uncompromising. Who are we, really, we who are *also* going to die? What are we doing with our lives?

I ate lunch. Finished it off with a sweet pink fruit. Jotted down a few sentences in my journal. Then I went outside, wanting to walk, to get into my body a little.

There I was under the shade of the trees.

The sounds of birds singing, insects humming, and wind stirring the canopy all seemed muffled to my ears by the density of the vegetation as I climbed the narrow pathway. My body warmed up quickly with the effort required to climb those slippery slopes. I took deep breaths and tried to maintain a steady pace. After walking for an hour, I saw through the gaps in the foliage that the sky was growing dark.

I stopped, breathing heavily, face angled toward the sky. From far away, thunder rumbled. I turned around, scanning the edges of the thick vegetation that surrounded me.

A drop of rain hit my face, then another. In an instant I was caught in a downpour.

I began to walk again, aiming for a clearing still invisible from where I stood but which couldn't be more than a hundred yards or so up from where I was. Rain ran into my eyes and made the ground even more slippery.

Then the storm intensified. Soon, torrents of rain were pouring onto the canopy, making it impossible to see more than a few yards in front of me. Low branches brushed against my legs sensually and I was caressed by thousands of lukewarm tears that slipped into my hair and down my cheeks, streaming down my shoulders, my back, my burning skin. I was flesh and bone, free among my brethren made of flesh, feathers, shell, fur, bark, and leaves. The water melded me into the mountain, abolishing all that separated me from my environment. I wanted to dissolve into the life pulsating around me. To slip underneath the bark of that tree, melt into it, roll around in the thick, damp earth until I disappeared.

Under the warm rain, unyielding in its intensity, I could feel the vibrations of powerful, transforming energy circulating through me. I felt liberated, as though I'd been granted a new lucidity. A new strength, too. That of Nature, which was welcoming me. Peacefully.

Suddenly, even the light seemed more intense. The subtle effects of my dieta were becoming more and more perceptible. It's as though the boundaries were disappearing, both those that were within me—as though my various inner ghosts were getting to know each other—and those between me and the worlds around me.

The storm disappeared as abruptly as it came.

In the end I did reach the clearing, and I decided to take advantage of its several large rocks to sit down and let the newly reappeared sun dry me off.

The clarity of mind that I attributed to my dieta allowed me to see the ambivalence I harbored. For close to twenty years, I'd been living with death. I'd been investigating it, following an approach I tried to make as scientific as possible, with interviews and a lot of research. I'd also absorbed a wealth of thoughts and reflections from the reading I'd done on philosophy and various spiritual teachings. My intellectual knowledge about consciousness and its dimensions was by that point quite wide-ranging.

The hypothesis that life is not limited to our existence, but continues in another form after our body dies, is becoming more and more obvious to me.

But then there was the wound.

The emotion and the heartbreak caused by death's sudden entrance into my life.

Picking up my brother's body.

As I sat motionless in the sunshine, staring into space, my thoughts suddenly took me back to Afghanistan, to the day when I had to call my parents to tell them about Thomas's death. So many years ago. Ever since then, we'd been living with his memory instead of his presence. His memory instead of the warmth of his embrace. An imperceptible breath instead of the vibration of his laughter. What strange lives we lead! We're jostled this way and that, desperately trying to find meaning in the saddest parts. For years I'd been consumed with doubt and obsessed with seeking answers.

I was suddenly overwhelmed with emotion.

Sitting on my rock, I literally relived that morning in April 2001. I was in Kabul. Thomas had just died instantly in a car accident, and I had brought his body back to the house we were staying in, in the Kolola Pushta district; I was preparing myself to call your grandparents.

With Thomas's body on his bed, I decided to wait a few hours so that it wasn't the middle of the night in France. Two rings, and Maman picked up. Papa was still sleeping. "Can you go wake him up? I'll call you back in five minutes." I hung up.

Pain. I waited. Those never-ending minutes. Waited for them to both come out from the bedroom, obviously not knowing what could have motivated this morning call; how could they have guessed that a tragedy had occurred that would change their lives forever?

One ring. They picked up. Both of them next to the receiver. What to say? I didn't know, so I got straight to the point: "I have some bad news . . . Thomas is dead." Maman: "What?" I repeat: "Thomas is dead . . . an accident this morning . . ." I no longer remember what happened next, what we said, the details, useless phrases, powerless to erase that unthinkable dawn.

What were they thinking then?

I had to endure, for them.

I had brought my brother's lifeless body back three hours before, I'd carried it, covered in a sheet, and my guts ripped open again when I heard the silence at the other end of the line, the shock, the astonishment. I was the messenger, I was the one to announce the death. To my own parents.

That was the moment, I think, when I stopped wanting to be happy. All the joy in me was extinguished, and sadness took possession of my body; my emotions became the enemy.

Sitting on my rock, I began to cry, carried away by a flood of sadness as I remembered with startling acuity every detail of that incredibly difficult moment. I hiccupped, shocked to be feeling the infinite suffering that enveloped me that morning all over again, the infinite suffering I'd inflicted on my parents. It was as though I'd just hung up the call with them, even though it had been so many years before.

How could I recover?

How could I recover from the burden of making that announcement? From having convinced both my brothers to accompany me in the midst of a civil war to Afghanistan, a place from which one would never return?

"Are you angry with me, Thomas?"

I said this out loud in the small, damp clearing, addressing him directly with a sob. "Are you angry with me?" I couldn't stop crying. “Forgive me . . .” *Forgive.* The word came to me forcefully. “Forgive me, Thomas . . .” For a millisecond he was there, wrapping his warmth around my shoulders, enveloping me with a brother’s love, embracing my guilt. The guilt. And yet I didn’t kill my brother.

Still shaken and trembling with emotion, I made my way back down to the shade of my cabin through the vegetation. In the silence of twilight, I spoke to my dieta plant, and also the spirit of ayahuasca, out loud: “Help me bring joy back to myself. I won’t be able to live anymore if I can’t find that joy again.”

When had I ever taken care of myself? I’d written books, given talks, and appeared on TV shows to share what I’d learned, but when had I taken care of myself? When had I taken care of my wounded heart?

My mind was being blocked by a journalist’s persona, and my emotions were being held at a safe distance by a formidable psychological mechanism. The fortress I needed to take down had some thick walls.

25

An Out-of-Body Journey

Second solitary attempt. I drank a mouthful of ayahuasca even though night had only recently fallen. Outside it was almost stormy. Wind and rain, with thunder and lightning in a nearby valley. After a beautifully sunny day, the elements had been unleashed.

Once I'd taken the ayahuasca I settled in comfortably and asked the ajo sacha and ayahuasca to unfold within me gently. The cabin was becoming increasingly dark.

After half an hour, that subtle feeling of a presence returned. The apprehension was there, but I felt particularly good this time, so it remained at a distance. On the other hand, my nausea was increasing. I resisted it as long as I could so that I could give the DMT molecules enough time to enter my cells, but eventually, I vomited. The plant's effects grew stronger as soon as I did so.

Concentrating on my breathing seemed to help me cling less to my thoughts. They arose, but then they passed by like leaves on a stream, just like when I meditated. To my great surprise, my apprehensions didn't grab hold of me. They approached and receded without further consequence.

My intoxication grew stronger. Visually, I couldn't perceive much; it was in my body that I felt the dizziness. The effect was extraordinarily strong.

But it was no longer accompanied by fear.

From time to time my body spasmed, trembled. I was unable to restrain the uncontrolled movements. And then suddenly I had the irrepressible desire to let sounds come out of me. A kind of primitive chant, a vibration coming up from my rib cage. Overcoming my shyness, I began to let out long, simple, modulated sounds: *eee, ooo, ohh*. It was the first time that I was daring to "sing"; the desire surprised me. It's as though I had been *invited*. I was stunned to realize that this spontaneous chant was intensifying my intoxication. My trance.

The long, monotone sounds that came out of my mouth echoed in my lungs and throat. And I *felt*. I felt that it was there. I hadn't been *carried away*, but very subtly, very indistinctly, my state of consciousness had changed. It was a very slightly different sensory acuteness, a heightened sensitivity—the sensation of *coming together*, of entering into myself and at the same time being in resonance with my environment.

I lost all concept of time. I don't think I dozed off, but I don't know what happened in the next few minutes, which may not have been minutes at all but hours.

And then suddenly, without knowing how it happened, I found myself at home, in southwestern France, where I lived at the time, in the middle of the cluster of hundred-year-old oak trees that was fifty yards or so from my front door. I was facing one oak in particular, the one in front of which I often went to sit. The lighting was surreal. It wasn't exactly nighttime, but it wasn't daytime, either. I felt profoundly happy to be in the trees' presence. I had the sense that they *lured* me here, those trees I loved, by their strength and energy. Lured me home. I floated through the air to the house, in front of which stood the old linden tree with its long branches.

The light was so strange. Like an illuminated night.

Stunned by the force of the experience, and completely aware of what was happening—I knew perfectly well it wasn't a dream, and that I was awake—I decided to enter the house. Instantly I was in our bedroom, a little above Natacha, who was sleeping on her stomach, her body positioned slightly diagonally across the bed, with her head turned toward the side where I usually slept.

The scene was stunningly realistic. It wasn't like a dream at all. Nor was it like a vision. Nor a memory, let alone a hallucination. Was I *actually* at home? The experience was so richly textured.

My perception was sharp and realistic, and yet when I tried to focus on details, it grew vague. How could I know if it was *actually* real? What *proof* could I find to convince me? I could look to see which book was on the chair next to the bed. I didn't know what Natacha was reading at that moment; I'd left France nearly three weeks earlier. I could just read the title and then call her the next day to verify.

My vision honed in on the spot. I could perceive what seemed to be a small pile of books, but it was a little blurry, as though my efforts to control what I was seeing were interfering with my vision. As though my desire to *verify* was reactivating a part of my brain, restarting a mental mechanism that inhibited my extrasensory perceptions.

I thought I could make out the name "Crichton," or something like it, but I wondered if my brain wasn't just inventing it in its feverish desire to verify the experience.

As I focused on this task, I began to unintentionally move backward, getting more and more distant. It seemed to me now as though the bedroom were on the other side of a whirlwind or a vortex of smoke, as though we were inside a cloud, and the opening that had allowed me to go to France was closing.

Clearly, my mind was returning, reestablishing its habits of control; in doing so, it was slowly shutting down this nonlocal experience and bringing me back to its own position in time and space. I wasn't entirely in control of either my movements or my perceptions, but when I released my desire to see the book, I did manage to draw closer to the chair again. I avoided trying to make out the title at all costs. Why was I incapable of bringing written words into focus? But what did it matter, after all; the scene was so real. How strange it felt to be floating above my wife!

I descended gently and moved even closer to her, just a couple of inches away from her skin, and whispered "I love you" into her ear. I could feel the power of the love that bound us unfolding in my body.

Did it ultimately make any difference whether I could read the title of the book? What was happening was so beautiful. So moving. I needed to make the most of the experience! My emotions were so heightened. Something was vibrating intensely inside of me. I kissed her bare shoulder, exposed above the comforter.

I remained still for a moment, stunned by the magic of the moment, and then, slowly, very slowly, I began to drift away from her. There I was outside, above the house. I got higher still, my vision now caressing the group of oak trees. Overflowing with joy and pleasure, I continued rising, there I was a few hundred yards off the ground—and that was the last image of that strange journey, in which I was brought to Natacha by love and oak trees. Soon, only the memory of the vision was left.

And then I was back in the cabin.

The chirping rainforest, the heat.

For several more minutes I stayed in the magic of the memory of what I'd just experienced. I was euphoric. Couldn't wait to be able to call Natacha and tell her about it. For the moment, I was still completely *mareado.*

The experience was far from over. My sensations were indescribable. Fragments of visions that got lost in my memory; powerful synesthesia, when sounds become shapes, surreal colors, abstract and moving visual patterns. But not once had fear come over me.

Light. I opened one eye. It took a few seconds for my brain to readjust. A gentle wind blew through the small valley, bringing with it a slight crispness. I heard whistling; other animals were waking up with the dawn.

Natacha!

I turned on the prepaid phone I'd bought upon arriving in Peru. She was surprised to hear from me. We hadn't been communicating much since my arrival so that I could concentrate as much as possible on my dieta, and she on her writing.

"Hello? It's me. Something crazy happened last night!"

"What was it?"

"Before I tell you, did you notice anything this morning?"

"Like what?" she asked.

"I don't know, did anything unusual happen?"

"No . . . what are you thinking of?"

"A feeling? A dream?"

"I don't think so. If I dreamed, I don't remember it."

"What book are you reading right now?"

"The one about the bees, by Jacqueline Freeman. *Song of Increase*. But are you going to tell me why you're asking me all this?"

I told her about "going" to France, how I saw her sleeping

on her stomach, my attempts to read the title of the book by her bedside, my emotion. Like me, she found the experience incredible.

But I hadn't seen the book she was reading. When I fixed my attention on it, everything became blurry. Curiously, the lack of objective validation didn't diminish my feeling that I had just had an unprecedented extrasensory experience.

I couldn't explain it; it was unusual for me not to be flooded with doubt. It's as though the intensity of the experience had swept away my never-ending objections.

It was such a departure from the visionary effects of ayahuasca I'd come to know well, that abundance of images and sensations gushing forth chaotically. This was something completely different.

My "visit to France" was perfectly linear, with a beginning, a constant presence in the room, and an end. Far from a dream, or a vision, in which scenes bump up against each other and overlap, and in which settings are constantly changing, sometimes in a matter of seconds.

Plus, there was that unusual clarity. And texture. It was all so stable. The trees, the house, and the bedroom weren't fleeting images; it was really as though I'd gone to a real place. My home.

Accounts of "out-of-body experiences" are very similar to what I lived through that night.[1] They're accompanied by perceptions that are both very vivid, marked by a feeling of heightened reality, and also somewhat confused when it comes to elements that require analytical processing from the brain.

The explanation is simple: interference occurs automatically when the brain's analytical circuits are called upon to process extrasensory perceptions experienced by our nonlocal consciousness.

It's no longer our usual senses that are perceiving—in which case the brain would know how to process the input—but our nonlocal consciousness. As we've seen, the brain isn't the source of this dimension of consciousness, which manifests only when the brain's filtering activity decreases or stops. It isn't involved at all in this kind of perception, even if it's still obviously there afterward, when it tries to memorize and interpret the experience.

I have no objective proof that I actually left my body that night, but the next day, as I walked back down to the river, I recalled the joy and profound happiness that I'd felt throughout. It truly had the intensity and texture of a real extrasensory experience. I'd had such a strong feeling when I suddenly found myself in front of the oak trees in my yard, then in my house, above my sleeping wife.

It was so real. As though I'd finally managed to find my soul's nonlocal capabilities, without constantly letting myself be brought back into my body or overwhelmed by confusion.

My mind was still present, but it took up less space, and was less domineering.

A strange intuition whispered to me that my feelings for Natacha may have acted as an *attractor*. As though love had magnetized me. The idea stuck with me for the rest of the afternoon. Love opens the door to a greater reality.

Love is energy.

I saw the experience not as a waking dream but as confirmation that I had made great progress in liberating my nonlocal consciousness from my brain's grip.

It's been demonstrated that extrasensory perceptions are real; we've seen it with verified near-death experiences, for example.

But these abilities manifest in different ways. What they reveal is enormous: the human mind has no limits. Researchers have tried to categorize these extrasensory perceptions according to their phenomenology, a project that's still in its infancy, given the perplexing nature of its subject. Their classification is undoubtedly imperfect, but all the same, it's helpful for organizing our thoughts.

Out-of-body experiences share some similarities with the type of extrasensory perception we call "clairvoyance." They differ in a few important respects, but both are predicated on the assumption that it's possible for the nonlocal consciousness to perceive information beyond our normal senses, whether that's by *leaving the physical body* or *seeing from a distance*, as though the limitations of space no longer exist.

What we call "remote viewing" is a way of enabling our consciousness to receive information without being constrained by the physical limits of our bodies and sensory organs. We've seen that out-of-body experiences can occur during exceptional circumstances like near-death experiences, such as Dr. Greyson's patient who literally "oversaw" his own heart surgery when under anesthesia. This often happens accidentally. However, it seems that we can induce and even develop some extrasensory perceptions, such as clairvoyance. By using our brain's analytical capacities, we can actually free ourselves from its grip rather than needing a substance to shut it down.

In 2009, in Paris, the artificial intelligence researcher Alexis Champion, who'd been fascinated by the subject since he was a teenager, founded the only school in the world for remote viewing: iRiS Intuition.[2] Their curriculum is designed to help us analyze and optimize our intuitive perceptions so that we can exploit them for a specific purpose. Anyone who wants to practice remote viewing can learn.[3]

You know me, Luna. As soon as I learned about the program, I enrolled in it. The prospect of learning this incredible method, which on the face of it is so different from what I'd experienced in the Amazon, was perfectly in line with what I've been trying to do this whole time: understand how to overcome my mind's limiting inhibitory activity so I could personally experience the nonlocal dimensions of consciousness. Shamanism confirmed for me that theoretical knowledge wouldn't be enough. Past a certain point, personal experience is the only way to keep exploring this spiritual reality.

In 2019, I took a training course at iRiS Intuition.

It was a shock!

In the first week of the program, the goal was to try to describe the place pictured on a photo that was hidden in an envelope. The envelope was selected at random among dozens of others. I knew in theory that the technique worked, because I'd talked about it with several people who had mastered it, but I was blown away when I realized that I, too, had become capable of "seeing" the hidden target and describing it with precise, sensory detail.

I did several sessions, and each time, the results were so conclusive that it was impossible to dismiss them as coincidences or the result of unconscious analytical reasoning. I was able to "receive" so much information specifically linked to the targets—I even drew sketches, just from my intuition—that turned out to match what was inside the envelope so precisely it was as though I'd had the image in front of me the whole time.

Experiencing this myself made it absolutely clear to me, Luna, that I was intuitively accessing information that couldn't be accessed from my five senses. And in such a short period of time, too. Does that seem crazy to you?

Yet this incredibly impressive ability and its potential strategic applications caught the attention of one institution that could hardly be suspected of fantasy. To design his training courses, Alex Champion drew on the tools of remote viewing as they were defined within the framework of a program developed by . . . the CIA. For national security purposes, at the height of the Cold War.

It sounds like something out of an unrealistic Netflix series, but it's absolutely true—I swear. And I'm going to take a quick break from narrating my shamanic retreat to tell you about it.

26

"PSYCHICS" AT THE WHITE HOUSE

On September 20, 1995, former president Jimmy Carter gave a talk to students at Emory University in Atlanta. As he was speaking about his time at the White House, sharing stories and confessions and answering questions, he revealed publicly for the first time the event that had been most intriguing to him during his presidency.

In doing so, he drew back the curtain on one of the army's most secret programs, one of the famous "black projects" shrouded in mystery and fantasy: Stargate.

It was March 1979. At the height of the Cold War, a Tupolev TU-22 military aircraft, the first supersonic bomber to be produced in the Soviet Union, crashed in Zaire, now the Democratic Republic of the Congo. The Americans desperately wanted to recover the plane so that they could examine the Russian technology, but the wreckage was undetectable by all ordinary means; the surrounding vegetation was so dense it was impossible to spot it from the sky.

Jimmy Carter explained that the intelligence services called in a psychic, and that as strange as it seemed, this enabled the Americans to track down and get their hands on the aircraft wreckage.[1]

In reality, it wasn't one but three "psychics" who carried out this feat. And it wasn't an isolated initiative. It was actually just one of *hundreds* of missions carried out by "remote viewers" in the Stargate Project. These viewers were "psychic spies," also known as "intuitives," who worked in this very official department in the US intelligence arsenal.

For this particular mission, three viewers, all of whom worked separately and without any coordination among themselves, used their clairvoyance—the ability to perceive things or events from a distance—to locate the wreckage. Despite the colossal size of the Zairean forest, the locations designated by each of the viewers were all within a zone about eight miles in circumference. American military personnel were sent to the area, and they found the plane. One of the viewers later reported, "Search teams on the ground said as soon as they entered the circled area on the map they began encountering natives on the trail carrying pieces of the wreck to use in the construction or reinforcement of their village huts."[2]

Bear in mind that the country spans over 1.4 million square miles! Yet all three locations given by the viewers were within five miles of the site of the accident. You can hardly call that a coincidence.

How did they do it?

One of the two civilian scientists who recruited viewers for Stargate, Russell Targ, described how a viewer named Joe went about the task:

> Joe was given a large map of Africa on which he could try to match and record his mental pictures as they emerged. The first thing he saw on his mental screen was a river flowing to the north. Working with his eyes alternately open and closed, he followed the river until it flowed between some rolling hills.

> After a half-hour's work, he drew a circle on the map and said the plane was between the river and a little village shown by a dot. Within two days, the TU-22 was found by our ground forces within the circle that Joe had drawn.[3]

The Joe to whom Russell was referring was Joe McMoneagle, the most tested and certified viewer in history. He enlisted in the army in 1964, joined the intelligence service, and then became one of the first extrasensory spies to be recruited for Stargate under the code name Remote Viewer #001. Now retired, he lives in Virginia.

I've known him for more than ten years.

From all the examples I've mentioned, Luna, you may have noticed that a considerable number of people experience instances when the barriers of space and time seem to break down: NDEs, terminal lucidity, perceptions during a coma, etc. Other types of unusual phenomena are even more frequent: seemingly prophetic dreams, intuitive phenomena, a physical sensation of impending danger to oneself or one's loved ones, remote perception of something involving a family or friend, the sense of "picking up on" the thoughts of people around us, or even just thinking of someone minutes before they call us. There are countless stories just like this, and they all have to do with extrasensory perception.

Extrasensory perceptions have been categorized—albeit arbitrarily, a qualification we'll come back to—according to their effects: telepathy when information is exchanged over a distance; clairvoyance when information is perceived without time or space being an obstacle; precognition when information about an event is perceived before it occurs; and psychokinesis when the mind acts on matter. Researchers use the term "psi," after the twenty-third letter of the Greek alphabet, to refer to these abilities.

All of these experiences bring us to the farthest reaches of the human mind, where it's easy to lose our bearings. This tends to elicit one of two opposite reactions: rejection or fascination.

But what do they say about our abilities? What is *actually* experienced?

Extrasensory perceptions suggest that we have the ability to obtain information without being limited by ordinary constraints of space and time, and without using our regular five senses. It was this realization that led the American intelligence services to take a closer look at them. In a very pragmatic sense, if extrasensory perceptions were real, they would be hugely advantageous in spying on the enemy from afar, without needing to send an agent.

The willingness to incorporate this strange human capacity into the arsenal of conventional intelligence tools goes back to the early 1970s. It had nothing to do with a sudden CIA or military interest in philosophical or spiritual matters. Stargate was launched because it was proven, under operational conditions, that it was possible to perceive events even at a spatial or temporal distance.

It's astounding that clairvoyance has been used by US intelligence, but it also reveals that some of the senior officers were highly pragmatic. If it works, why not use it?

But how did clairvoyance—intuition, in the etymological sense of the word—become a functional intelligence tool? How could something so intangible, subjective, and spontaneous be used repeatedly and on command during those hundreds of Stargate missions? How could this ability be mastered to the point that it could even be taught?

27

The Stargate Project

It began in the same way as any counterintelligence story begins. In the early 1970s, US intelligence services heard a strange rumor: the Russians were using "psychics," although it was unclear for what purpose. Was it a practical joke? If not, was it actually effective? And could it be a potential threat?

The CIA set out to learn more about it. At the same time, two researchers, laser physicist Russell Targ and engineer Harold Puthoff, launched a program at the Stanford Research Institute to study and evaluate extrasensory perception.

Their work was intriguing.

Under controlled conditions, subjects were able to describe places and situations from afar, as though they had been there, even though they hadn't left the lab and had absolutely no information about the target. It seemed that it was possible to acquire information *psychically*.

US intelligence services found these two scientists' research so convincing that they decided to support their work at the SRI and evaluate their results regularly.

In the winer of 1977, a scientist affiliated with the CIA's Office of Research and Development named Kenneth Kress published an article in the CIA's internal magazine, summarizing the remote viewing experiments that had been carried out at the SRI since 1972. He also wrote about a few of them in more detail.

One was a remote viewing session in which the target was a vacation home in the eastern United States. Two viewers (one of whom was a particularly gifted retired police officer named Pat Price) were given the property's geographical coordinates and instructed to spontaneously report what they *intuitively perceived* about the target location. Without consulting each other, both described a kind of military facility.

It didn't fit at all. But because the two descriptions were identical, the CIA officer was intrigued enough to go look at the location for himself.

To his surprise, he discovered that there was a sensitive government installation just a few miles from the vacation home. This strange coincidence led him to request a second session at the SRI, inviting the viewers to provide information about the inner workings of this particular location. That information was then reviewed by the CIA and the relevant government agency.

Pat Price, who had no military training or prior intelligence, was able to provide a list of projects that were associated with current or past activities at the site, one of which was extremely sensitive. He also provided the code name for the site and some other descriptive information. Everything was correct.[1]

These were the kinds of inexplicable results that motivated the continued collaboration between the CIA and the SRI.

Targ and Puthoff were convinced that extrasensory perception was a skill that anyone could acquire with the right training. As I myself experienced, the future would prove them right.

Kenneth Kress's report, which included details of other missions with equally incredible results, concluded that the results of SRI's remote viewing experiments defied explanation. It was highly unlikely that they were coincidental—if it were one time, that would be one thing, but this was hundreds!—and no fraud had been uncovered.

In the same report, Kress explained that the CIA wasn't the only intelligence agency interested. The Defense Intelligence Agency was also intrigued by these phenomena, which they described as "paranormal" and which they had observed during the Vietnam War.

Kress wrote:

> Certain individuals called point men, who led patrols into hostile territory, had far fewer casualties from booby traps and ambushes than the average. These point men, needless to say, had a loyal following of men and, in general, greatly helped the morale of their troops under a brutal, stressful situation. The army gave extensive physical and psychological tests to a group of unusually successful point men and came to no conclusion other than perhaps that paranormal capabilities may be the explanation. The Army was most interested in CIA results and wanted to stay closely informed.[2]

Within the DIA, First Lieutenant Frederick "Skip" Atwater, who was then a counterintelligence officer with the 902nd Military Intelligence Group at Fort Meade in Maryland, was deeply impressed by Kress's report on remote viewing. Skip was probably one of the only ones to understand its real importance.[3] Thanks to him, with the collaboration of the SRI, the DIA began to recruit internally, with the goal of launching their own ESP research program.

The first step was to find people in the military who already had "Secret" security clearance—agents or other members of the intelligence services—who had demonstrated above-average intuitive abilities, the "point men" mentioned in Kress's report.

That's how Joe McMoneagle's military file came into the hands of the recruiters.

During his deployments to Vietnam as part of the intelligence services, Joe told me, he'd experienced five major offensives, including the 1968 Tet Offensive—and on multiple occasions he would have died had it not been for his sixth sense. When we last met, at his home in Virginia, he told me about it.

"In Vietnam, I got into the habit of always listening to the voice inside my head. I knew when I should or shouldn't do something—I just *knew* it. For example, one time, I was sitting on an old lawn chair outside a bunker, reading. I liked to sit behind the wall of shelter. I was enjoying the sun, totally calm, and then all of a sudden, I had this feeling that I had to move. Right away! I got up, taking my chair with me, and went into the bunker. Two minutes later, we were targeted in a mortar attack. The two shells landed right where I'd been sitting just minutes earlier."

"Couldn't that be considered a coincidence?"

"If it happened once, yes. But my life has been saved many times simply because I did what my inner voice was telling me to, even if it seemed stupid or even embarrassing at the time. It happened so often that the soldiers who were with me began to notice, and started doing whatever I did. I seemed to make the right decisions intuitively. Going left instead of right, going into that bunker. Things like that."

One day in the fall of 1978, when he was back on American soil after having been stationed in Germany, Joe received an order to go meet up with two military intelligence officers at the military base in Arlington. The two officers were Skip and Scotty Watt.

"I remember in the first meeting they invited me to, there were thirty people whose files had all been pulled and analyzed. One of the criteria was that we had an above-average ability to survive the dangerous situations we'd been in. They must have felt that this was the case for me during my deployments in Vietnam."

"What happened in the meeting?"

"They asked all thirty of us to raise our hands if we thought we were 'clairvoyants.' I looked around and not one person raised their hand. None of us were nuts enough to admit something like that and risk losing our Secret clearance. We were all dismissed, and then they called us back for individual interviews. At the end of that, twelve of us were selected to go on to the next stage of being interviewed by the researchers at the Stanford Research Institute studying remote viewing, Harold Puthoff and Russell Targ."

"At that point, did you know what the interviews were for?"

"Not really, no."

"What did Targ and Puthoff say when you met them?"

"They took some documents out of a briefcase and asked me to take a look at them. The documents included both classified and unclassified documents. Some were about psychic research programs in other countries, others were newspaper articles about the same thing. I sat down and took a few hours to read it all through."

Afterward, the researchers asked Joe what he thought about what he'd just read. Cautious and unsure of which tack to take, he answered carefully that he wasn't sure what they meant by their question.

"'Do you believe in it or not?' they finally asked me. I said that I wasn't sure whether it was real, but if it were, it posed a threat for the country, and we should study it to see how good or bad it was. That was the stance I took. What they didn't know was that I'd had these clairvoyant abilities since the age of four!"

Several weeks later, McMoneagle received a call from Scotty

Watt, who told him straight away that he'd passed every part of the interview.

At the time, Joe was beginning his second year on the staff of INSCOM (Army Intelligence and Security Command), and his career was looking promising. But he had a swift intuition that his life was about to take another direction. Selected along with five others who met the criteria, he was sent to the SRI to be trained by Harold Puthoff and Russell Targ, who shared what they had been studying since 1972. Joe had never heard of remote viewing before.

In October of 1978, the US military intelligence's extrasensory spying program was officially created. It was called a number of names—Gondola Wish, then Grill Flame—before it became known as Stargate.

It was top secret, with access restricted on a need-to-know basis. During the first year, the viewers' abilities were tested on targets based in the US and therefore easy to verify. The reports were then sent to an independent agency for evaluation and found to be astonishing. As Joe recalls, "the accuracy of our viewing against ground truth targets was beginning to be noticed in the Office of the Assistant Chief of Staff for Intelligence. Some details we were able to provide about ongoing US intelligence operations were, to be frank, scary."[4]

"Why 'scary'?"

"Remote viewing works so well that it scared some people in intelligence agencies. You can't prevent a remote viewer from picking up information. It doesn't matter how far away they are, in space or time—none of that makes any difference. A remote viewer can target pretty much anything and give you information about it."

If the Russians really were using remote viewers, the Americans had to assume that no secret of theirs was safe. Their primary motivation in developing their own remote viewing program was to study how it worked so that they could try to identify ways of protecting themselves by doing exactly what they suspected their enemies of doing: psychic spying.

Quickly, requests began to flow in from all the other organizations in the intelligence community: the CIA, the DIA, the Secret Service, the Air Force Intelligence Agency, the Naval Intelligence Command, the FBI, the DEA, the NSA. One after another, the missions put the remote viewers through their paces.

This went on for sixteen years. To this day, no one has access to the entire archive. There are more than a hundred sealed boxes at the CIA headquarters in Langley, Virginia, containing hundreds of reports still classified as top secret. Over the years, however, viewers and employees have revealed some of the missions to the public, such as the one Jimmy Carter mentioned to the Emory students. Joe McMoneagle described several of them to me in detail; they correspond to tragedies that occurred over those years.

What did they consist of? Essentially, the goal was to obtain "psychic information" in situations where classic spy tactics weren't possible. Joe and the other Stargate viewers were called upon, for example, during the Iran hostage crisis in 1979, when more than fifty American diplomats and citizens were held in the US Embassy in Tehran. They were able to provide information that was impossible to obtain otherwise about the identities of those present at the embassy the day the hostages were taken, how the hostages were separated into different diplomatic buildings and under what conditions, and the locations of personnel who were able to escape. They even "saw" that three CIA agents, whose presence in Tehran at that time was a secret, were among the hostages.[5]

They also carried out missions in other tension zones: in the Middle East, Central America, the Eastern Bloc, etc. They spied on Soviet sites and located drug labs; few places escaped the viewers' "mind's eye." They could "see" secret sites, "receive" information, foresee *future* events, and even help liberate people who had been kidnapped.

Sometimes, remote viewing is even more astonishing, to the point where the viewer feels as though they are actually *at* the target location—exactly like I felt during my "visit to France."

28

Remote Viewing Discoveries

One of Joe's first missions was in September 1979. It was commissioned by a naval officer assigned to the National Security Council (NSC), whom Joe had previously met on an operational security operation, and who was very interested in testing remote viewing as part of an intelligence-gathering mission.[1]

The officer provided them with a photo of a large industrial building near a body of water. Nothing about the building's exterior gave anything away, except that it was massive and located somewhere in the Soviet Union.

Joe would learn later that it was located at the port of Severodvinsk, on the White Sea, at the edge of the Arctic Circle. The officer told them that the NSC wanted to know what was going on inside.

When Joe began his remote viewing session, he hadn't seen the photo, and had only the target's geographical coordinates. All he could deduce was that the target was "in the north," probably in Finland or the Eastern Bloc.

His first impression was of a cold wasteland with a large industrial building that had huge smokestacks. It was by a sea encrusted with a thin layer of ice. As this description suggested that

Joe had clearly hit the target, Skip Atwater, the analyst working on the mission, decided to show him the photo. It comforted Joe to see his initial perceptions confirmed.

Joe then resumed the session, closing his eyes and relaxing. He imagined that he was on site at the target location, drifting down through the roof of the building and entering its interior *in spirit*.

Inside, he could see very clearly what was going on, and what he found was astonishing. The building was the size of two or three giant malls. In giant bays were what looked like cigars, varying in size but all massive. One of them was bigger than Joe could have ever imagined. It was covered with scaffolding, and at the heart of the maze were two immense side-by-side cylinders being welded together. Joe had the unmistakable sensation that it was an enormous submarine with two identical hulls. There was a lot of noise and movement, and flashes of blue light. He could see so much it was hard to keep track of it all. When he ended the session, he sketched what he'd seen, writing in the margins that he personally thought it was a submarine under construction.

Two or three days later, Skip asked him to visit the same target again. What Joe didn't know was that in the interim, the report from his first session had created quite a stir within the NSC. At the time, several American intelligence agencies were of the firm belief that the building was being used to construct a new type of assault ship that would carry troops. The submarine hypothesis was deemed highly unlikely.

In his second session, Joe returned to the enormous building, where he was again overwhelmed by the size and height of what seemed to him to indisputably be a giant submarine inside. Looking at it more closely, he estimated that it was about the length of two football fields, around seventy feet wide, and six or seven stories high. It was being built from two elongated and parallel tubes. Positioning himself above the submarine's platform, he could see that there were eighteen or twenty missile tubes placed side by side.

At the end of this second session, Joe took his time making another, more detailed sketch of the submarine, noting its dimensions and pointing out the missile tubes. The sketch and the report from the session were again sent to the NSC.

This second report wasn't deemed any more relevant than the first. The NSC officers saw it as proof that the viewer's "findings" were nothing more than fantastical stories. One of their objections was that the building was half a mile from the sea, and they couldn't see how a giant submarine could be transported that far. Nonetheless, the officer who made the initial request asked if Joe could do one more session to provide further details, like how far along the project was.

During the third session, Joe could *feel* that the submarine would be operational four months later, sometime during the month of January 1980—in the midst of the Arctic winter, a time that seemed particularly unlikely for launching a submarine; the sea would be frozen, and the building wasn't even connected to the sea. But Joe "saw" it and reported that bulldozers would be digging a canal to launch the ship.

This third report wasn't taken any more seriously than the first two, as no other conventional source was able to confirm or refute Joe's claims.

But four months later, in mid-January 1980, satellite photos of the site revealed the existence of a canal that hadn't been there previously that ran alongside the building and out to sea. At the dockside was an enormous submarine that no one had seen before. Tied up alongside it was an Oscar-class attack submarine. The size difference between the two was striking. The new submarine was enormous. The photo also clearly showed that it had twenty missile tubes.

The satellite photo was the Americans' first glimpse of a new class of Soviet submarines, the Typhoons. These submarines were so unusual that the NSC officers had considered them impossible when Joe reported having *seen* one four months earlier.

They were the biggest submarines ever built, and still are to this day. We know now that the first one (there would be six in total) was indeed created in the Severodvinsk installation and was moved out to sea for its first trials in early 1980, thanks to a canal built at the last minute. The hangar was located far from the sea on purpose, to throw off American satellites.

Joe had seen it all four months before!

The first Typhoon was officially put into service in 1981. It was a multihulled vessel consisting of five segments within a superstructure composed of two long parallel segments. The Typhoon was 564 feet long and 75 feet wide. It would enter popular culture ten years later in *The Hunt for Red October*, in which Sean Connery plays a Soviet Typhoon captain who wants to defect to the West.

Some within the NSC—including Robert Gates, who would become CIA director several years later—continued to dismiss Joe's sessions as a "stroke of luck."

This attitude is a testament to the unease that the Stargate Project provoked in some intelligence officials, who believed—just on principle, and without having done any real in-depth analysis—that the "paranormal" had no place in a serious institution.

Given its still-unexplained nature, it's no surprise that the subject of ESP provoked the same reactions within the intelligence community as within society at large. There are those who will reject it and refuse to hear anything more about it, and then there are those who take the time to really study the data and are stunned to find that something so unusual could be real, and more importantly, useful.

Joe told me that in general, field officers were appreciative of the new and valuable information provided by the Stargate viewers, because it was so useful and sometimes even helped them make decisions. They asked for more. However, at higher levels, where politics were often more important than operational logic, the existence of the program tended to evoke sarcasm, if not outright hostility.

This ambivalence toward the Stargate Project, like that of part of the scientific community with regard to clairvoyance, comes in part from the implications of human extrasensory abilities. However, even if they've been proven to be real, that doesn't mean that they're some kind of superpower granting a form of infallible omniscience. They're not a magic wand.

Clairvoyance is a perceptive sense, meaning that our mind's cognitive biases influence its manifestation. No matter how skilled or "gifted" the viewer, the information gleaned through clairvoyance is not always reliable, which can lead some to deny that extrasensory perceptions are ever real. But that's throwing the baby out with the bathwater.

The goal of the remote viewing technique is to optimize this subtle ability. But while it can lead to amazing things, it can't do everything. This is an essential point. The ignorance and fantasy that still surround the use of extrasensory abilities have contributed, then and now, both to its discrediting and to the overestimation of its possibilities.

It took Joe McMoneagle a long time to grasp the operational potential of remote viewing.

"It takes a lot of practice. It's essentially a method of analysis that enables you to better understand how your unconscious interacts with your conscious. Intuitive perceptions enter the unconscious as sensory information in just milliseconds—it's very fast. But the problem is that your unconscious instantly turns these perceptions into things it understands, things you've already seen or experienced. It interprets them on the basis of whatever in your memory is closest. And these interpretations aren't necessarily accurate."

"So if I'm understanding correctly, even for someone like you, who's had these abilities since childhood, your mind can still interfere?"

"Yes. That's the case for all of us. Even the most gifted psychics. And it's extremely difficult to tell the difference."

"The difference between what?"

"Between intuitive perception and mental interpretation."

"But you said that you have 'images,' 'flashes,' 'visions.' With the Russian Typhoon submarine, for example, you said you were actually there, weren't you?"

"Yes, that can happen, but not every time. And to be useful, you need to able to access information each time with a workable reliability rate. Remote viewing is a reasoning-based technique that relies on awareness of our unconscious mechanisms of interpretation to help us differentiate conjecture from perception. That's why it takes a long, long time to learn. The more you practice, the better you'll be able to understand how your unconscious interacts with your conscious. Remote viewing is a martial art. You're picking up on little bits of information that you know come from your intuition."

"That makes more sense. You have to be capable of providing, on demand, small pieces of information that you can vouch for?"

"Exactly. That's how intelligence works. The convergence of little bits of information from different sources makes it possible to see the bigger picture and make operational decisions accordingly."

The Stargate Project was officially terminated in 1995. This was a political choice that had nothing to do with the project's results; the field of ESP was still controversial.

That same year, 1995, the US Congress asked the CIA for an evaluation of the program's activity. The report, titled "An Assessment of Evidence for Psychic Functioning," wasn't made public until five years later, in 2000.[2] The audit was performed by Professor Jessica Utts, head of the statistics department at the University of California, Irvine. In the introduction to her report, the scientist warned that "it is too often the case that people on both sides of the question debate the existence of psychic functioning on the basis of their personal belief systems rather than an examination of the scientific data."[3]

The report submitted to Congress explained very clearly that the data from the statistical study of remote viewing proved that it was real:

> Using the standards applied to any other area of science, it is concluded that psychic functioning has been well established. The statistical results of the studies examined are far beyond what is expected by chance. Arguments that these results could be due to methodological flaws in the experiments are soundly refuted. Effects of similar magnitude to those found in government-sponsored research . . . have been replicated at a number of laboratories across the world. Such consistency cannot be readily explained by claims of flaws or fraud.[4]

The conclusions of Jessica Utts's report for the CIA are unequivocal: "It is clear to this author that anomalous cognition is possible and has been demonstrated. This conclusion is not based on belief, but rather on commonly accepted scientific criteria. The phenomenon has been replicated in a number of forms across laboratories and cultures."[5]

If we're capable of perceiving information at a distance, despite gaps in space or time, this is further confirmation that our consciousness has access to a nonlocal dimension, and is therefore itself nonlocal.

Do you know what Descartes called these nonlocal abilities of our consciousness?

Intuition.

29

Intuition: The Soul's Language

Extrasensory perceptions are the "anomalies" of our era. They can't be reduced to mere coincidences, illusions, magical thinking, or anything else of the sort. Clearly that's not what they are.

We often refer to them with the catch-all term "sixth sense," but there's already a word that perfectly describes the faculty underpinning nonlocal perceptions: intuition.

René Descartes defined intuition as a form of immediate knowledge that doesn't involve reasoning.[1] According to philosopher Henri Bergson, intuition even grants us access to the spiritual dimension of reality.[2]

See, Luna, it's all there in plain sight.

Descartes's historical definition helps us understand where the materialist approach to these inexplicable manifestations of consciousness—dismissing them out of hand, without further study—goes wrong. According to psychology and neuroscience, intuition is linked to our cognitive processes, and therefore to the development of our brains; it's the natural and instantaneous ability of our neural networks to sort through the colossal mass of knowledge we've acquired over our lifetimes in order to extract—without our realizing it—whatever will be useful in any given situation. This mechanism does exist, of course, but it's not the "form of immediate knowledge that doesn't require reasoning" described by Descartes.

If we return to this original meaning, intuition is a property of consciousness—the ability to access nonreasoned and nonlocal knowledge. It has nothing to do with intelligence, analysis, or mental processes linked to a field of expertise or prior knowledge.

The time I spent at iRiS practicing remote viewing successfully convinced me that intuition is a real extrasensory ability.

It took only several days of intense training to awaken my own nonlocal abilities, and for me to discover that it was possible to communicate with the fundamental dimension of my consciousness.

How did I do it? It wasn't by meditating for hours on a cushion. I sat at a table, pencil in hand, in front of a pad of paper, and I patiently learned to use a number of reasoning tools to identify how my mind worked. From then on, if a mental construct or analytical interpretation came into my head, I could identify it as such and push it away, with increasing ease. Thanks to this slow, methodical exercise, I gained the ability to discern unconscious interpretative mechanisms from raw sensations—my intuitive perceptions.

These intuitive perceptions are always there, behind the intensely heavy filter of our minds. Like a violinist's delicate melody within an orchestra. The violin is the fragile whisper of our intuition, and the rest of the orchestra is the analytical mental noise of our brains.

My remote viewing training helped me better understand what intuition is. The *inspired* ideas that suddenly spring into our minds aren't necessarily intuition, even if sometimes they resemble it.

The deputy director of iRiS Intuition, Marie-Estelle Couval, a lawyer by training, gave me an illuminating example of how to distinguish between unconscious analytical reasoning and non-local perception:

> Imagine a customer walking into a clothing store. A saleswoman greets her and they exchange a few words. During this period of time, which might be very brief, the saleswoman is analyzing how the customer is dressed and how she speaks and acts, without even realizing she's doing so. She might then think to herself: "I'm sure that she's going to buy that red cardigan I've just put out on display" and call that intuition, without realizing that she's unconsciously picked up on, analyzed, and processed a large number of cognitive signals in order to reach that *pseudo-intuition*. If the customer then buys the red cardigan, the saleswoman will be amazed: "Wow, I sensed that! I always thought I was intuitive." But that's not intuition, it's just unconscious reasoning. True intuition would be if the saleswoman was alone in the store, arranging her wares on a shelf, and then all of a sudden has a flash and thinks, "Hey, I can sense that in five minutes, the next customer will enter the store and will buy the red cardigan I've just put out." And five minutes later, that's exactly what happens. That would be intuition, because the saleswoman had no prior information.[3]

In day-to-day life, we often mix up unconscious reasoning and intuition. This is for two reasons. The first is that we've been trained since childhood to value reflection and analysis over listening to our strange little inner voice. It's pretty funny for a Cartesian society not to believe in intuition as defined by Descartes, Luna, wouldn't you agree?

The second reason is that our brains aren't hardwired for it. They're actually hardwired to play the opposite role. As we've seen, their function is to help us adapt to the functional and social reality of the world we were born into. When we're born, our brain has already been formatted by our genes, which carry the heritage and knowledge already acquired by our species, but its fundamental development will be shaped by the billions of stimuli it receives from our environment. Every cognitive request, every perception, helps to create new neural links. Incredibly complex networks develop so that we can improve how we process, analyze, and understand the information that comes to us through our senses. If a child's brain has developed correctly, they will have built up a solid mental map of their usual external and internal reality well before the age of ten, and that map will continue to serve as a reference for all their cognitive functions.

It's their default model for relating to the world.

Our brains rely on these models to become more efficient, focusing on an essential adaptive function: anticipation. When we anticipate, we can react faster, protect ourselves, and prepare ourselves to face the unknown. But our ability to anticipate is based on the data we've already acquired and our capacity to process and analyze new data.

What this means is that as our brains become more efficient, they begin to need less and less data to understand our environment and suggest solutions accordingly. When our brains are fully developed, they don't use many of the sensory signals they receive; they rely on previously learned patterns to take cognitive shortcuts, which are more economical and faster.

These cognitive shortcuts are a form of unconscious reasoning.

Our brains never stop reasoning and interpreting. Ever. Adult humans largely operate in a closed circuit. Cognitive stimuli from the outside world become almost secondary on a day-to-day basis. This is yet another indication that we're locked up by our own brains.

Our brains aren't looking at the world anymore, nor are they listening to it. They're taking in only a tiny part of the mass of outside data, and the first data to be ignored are the subtlest: intuitive data.

Intuition—the perception of nonlocal signals that we incidentally never learned to detect—shows up through sensory perceptions that are instantly overwritten by our minds. These fleeting, subtle perceptions tend to dissolve as our brains carry out their unconscious mechanisms of filtering, analysis, and reasoning.

To open ourselves up to intuition, we must first understand that we're interpreting the world rather than seeing it as it really is. Without that understanding, we'll continue to confuse our intuitions with our interpretations, which are the result of our unconscious mental patterns shaped by our beliefs, fears, fantasies, and desires.

Intuition is the "language" of our souls, a preverbal form of expression for the nonlocal dimension of our consciousness that's usually muffled by our brain activity. Rediscovering intuition means reconnecting to our sensory perceptions; we have to listen to their signals before they're interpreted and deformed by our subjectivity, deductions, abstractions, and emotions.

To do this we have to either silence our minds or, in the case of remote viewing, learn to use our minds to identify those signals right away.

Intuition is a little bit like stars. Stars are always there, but in broad daylight we can't see them, because the sunlight masks their radiance. The subtle light of our intuition is masked by the blinding brightness of our minds at work. If we can either put those minds to sleep or teach them, the starry skies of the world of intuition—the nonlocal dimension of reality—will appear.

Joe McMoneagle's hundreds of missions, and the rest of the missions in the Stargate Project, reveal that all information—whether it's past, present, or future—is perceptible on a nonlocal level. Our consciousness has access to all of it. As Albert Einstein said, "Our separation from each other is an optical illusion of consciousness."[4] This raises staggering philosophical questions.

30

Science vs. Anomalies

How can we "capture" these extrasensory perceptions? Is it possible to bring them into a laboratory setting so that we investigate their causes? Can we study these extraordinary experiences—which are, by nature, spontaneous and nonreproducible—the same way we would study a more conventional phenomenon? And if we can, what are they likely to teach us?

Do you remember that day? The high-speed train had been speeding along for some time. I remember that we were sitting across from each other, both of us bored out of our minds. I can still see us looking up from our respective books and peering out the window at the Burgundy landscape flashing by. Then I had an idea.

"Do you want to experiment with telepathy?" I asked you.

You looked at me, surprised. "Is that possible?"

"We can try."

"How do we do it?"

"I'm going to think of something, and you're going to guess it."

"Really?"

With what I'd learned from my remote viewing training still fresh in my mind, I explained:

"Don't try to think in words. Instead, pay attention to what you feel—colors, images, anything sensory. We're going to use a simple method. I'm going to think of a fruit, any fruit, and instead of saying its name in my head, I'm going to imagine its taste in my mouth, visualize its color and texture, and concentrate on those sensations to *send* them to you."

You looked even more taken aback than before. "And what do I do?"

"Nothing. Most importantly, don't think. Close your eyes, breathe, and try to connect with what you're feeling, the sensations you're experiencing."

"Okay, go ahead!"

"You ready? Okay, I'm thinking of a fruit . . ."

I closed my eyes and let myself be swept up in the sensory details of the fruit I'd just chosen. A banana. Yellow. I was thinking "yellow," visualizing the crescent-shaped fruit, trying to mentally feel the thick peel, the flesh, the sweet and mild flavor in my mouth, when suddenly you exclaimed:

"A banana!"

"Sheesh! You're good."

"Was that it?"

"Yes!"

You couldn't believe it. "Let's do it again!"

"Okay. I've chosen a new fruit . . ."

This time, I thought of a pineapple. I visualized its rind, the juice flowing from it, the taste that was both slightly bitter and very sweet, the consistency of its flesh . . .

"A pineapple?"

This time, I was the one who was blown away.

We repeated the experience with a total of ten fruits and you answered correctly nearly every time. Neither of us could believe it. After a while, we both retreated into our own thoughts. You went back to looking out the window, and I could see in your eyes something that wasn't there before. A gleam of amazement.

Both of us were perturbed by how well you did on that train, but a scientific mind might object that it could have all been coincidence. Objectively, the very small number of attempts we made could have been explained by chance.

The classic scientific approach is to try to transform these extraordinary stories from everyday life into usable, objectifiable data to better understand them. This is the aim of parapsychology, a scientific discipline dating back to the end of the nineteenth century that focuses on the psychic phenomena that are linked to the interactions between our consciousness and the environment, improperly classified as "paranormal."

So how could we turn our train game into science? First question: were your correct guesses simply a stroke of luck? There's a mathematical tool we can use to try to answer this question: probabilities.

To simplify things, let's say we do an experiment in which you have to guess between four fruits. You would have four possible choices—three wrong, one right. One chance in four to guess correctly. The statistical probability is that you would guess the right one 25 percent of the time.

With ten tries, as we did, the probability calculation isn't significant; it leaves too much to chance. We would have to try a ton of times in order to obtain a significant statistical probability. A million, let's say—but don't worry, this is purely hypothetical!

Statistics are at the heart of the scientific method. They're used in medicine, psychology, climatology, physics, neuroscience, and many other areas of study in which everything is a matter of probability.

Important point: no matter the domain, statistics don't offer proof that the results aren't due to chance. They offer only a "degree of certainty."

Let's assume that after our million tries, you guessed the correct fruit 32 percent of the time. This result would be seven percentage points higher than what you would have guessed by sheer chance. Given the enormous number of tries, the probability that this incredible success rate was due to chance becomes very low, statistically speaking. In fact, we could say with a high degree of certainty that it *wasn't* due to chance. So *something* occurred during the experiment. Something we can't explain but which impacted the result. What conclusions can we draw from this?

What is that "something"?

This is where the speculation begins. That result would indicate the presence of an anomaly. Could it be telepathy, as one might suspect, because my intention had been to mentally send you the name of the fruit? It could also be precognition, in which you had guessed in advance the fruit I was going to pick. Or perhaps it could be something else altogether. As you can see, the explanation for this "statistical anomaly" doesn't magically arise from the results. Many different hypotheses are possible. But no matter what the explanation is, it must take into account the fact that something unusual has unquestionably occurred.

Let's stick with the telepathy hypothesis, because that's the one we had fun testing on the train. Telepathy, if it indeed exists, is a state of resonance between people. It's somewhat akin to empathy—a visceral form of communication in which you perceive another's world as if you were in their shoes, feeling in your own mind whatever is present for them, irrational as that feeling may be. Clearly, it's a nonlocal perception.

Surveys of the general population show that a majority of people believe that they've experienced telepathy. It happens every day. Many therapists report having inexplicably experienced telepathy with their patients, for example. Twins also mention the phenomenon frequently,[1] as do mothers with their children, couples, siblings, and other people with a particularly close relationship.

These experiences occur in regular life, both in innocuous moments—like when someone thinks of a friend seconds before they receive a phone call from them[2]—and also, more frequently, in situations of imminent danger.[3] Psychiatrist Diane Hennacy Powell notes:

> Telepathy has been reported to be more common in people who have a close social bond and high level of intimacy. This implies that the barriers people erect to intimacy may also be barriers to telepathy. One intimate relationship where the barriers are down is that between mothers and their newborns. In fact, mothers often report a sense of telepathic connection with their young children, especially infants who are too young to have formed their own sense of identity or personal boundaries.[4]

There have been a considerable number of parapsychological experiments on telepathy over the past century. The resulting statistical data confirm the presence of an anomaly that could be explained by some form of entanglement between human consciousnesses, as the subjects' reports suggest.[5]

Many other statistical studies on various types of extrasensory abilities underline the fact that there is empirical data to support the validity of psi phenomena, and that this data is further backed up by countless accounts.[6]

Why, then, is the validity of psi phenomena so contested? Diane Hennacy Powell points out that if the statistical results applied to a less unsettling subject, they would be accepted without question. So why aren't they?

There are a number of reasons, but the most important one is this: science doesn't know what consciousness is. We don't know its source, and we don't have any theories capable of explaining its nonlocal capacities, which means they remain incomprehensible to us. As a result, the statistical results, however significant they are, remain open to interpretation.

Scientific research on these unusual subjects is a real challenge, and obviously, it leaves us with more questions than answers. As I reminded you in the introduction to this book, we too often forget that science grants us access to only a relative reality. "Relative" is not an empty term here. It's essential for us to bear this in mind. We live in a society that gives us the illusion that we can master everything, first and foremost understanding the world we live in.

This is very far from the truth.

We seem to think that scientists can simply wave a magic wand and come up with an answer to every problem, phenomenon, and question that presents itself. I often hear this word being used: "scientists," as though they're an omniscient and unified group.

They're not.

Science isn't a religion, it's a formidable method of questioning what is real. It's constantly evolving, but nonetheless it's constrained by the tools it has available. And since its previous findings are constantly being called into question, it tends to bring researchers face-to-face with doubts and hesitations more often than certainties.

Having spent more than fifteen years in the world of scientific research, I'm well aware of the subjectiveness of its progress. Science is carried out by humans, so it's partly ideological. I know I'm repeating myself here, but the results of even the most methodical experiments will be interpreted subjectively, according to a theoretical model. And the major problem when it comes to the nature of consciousness is that we don't have one. A theory, that is.

Moreover, the term "proof," which we tend to think of as indicating certainty, doesn't exist outside of mathematics. In other disciplines we use the term "evidence." Evidence is not proof. It's just one piece out of many, and it's only when the many reach a certain threshold—when all the evidence points in one direction—that we can begin to formulate a hypothesis, or even a theory. Then we can say that that hypothesis, or that theory, has been demonstrated *beyond reasonable doubt*.

It often happens, especially when it comes to controversial subjects, that some scientists will consider that they've proven their hypothesis beyond reasonable doubt, while others will disagree. These are problems found in many scientific disciplines. But with parapsychology, the debate tends to get stuck there. Its opponents resort to the appeal to authority fallacy, citing arguments that aren't relevant to the subject at hand simply to defend their own beliefs. It's a shame.

Professor Etzel Cardeña, director of the Centre for Research on Consciousness and Anomalous Psychology at the University of Lund, Sweden, called for an open, informed study of all aspects of consciousness in 2014 in the journal *Frontiers of Human Neuroscience*.[7] The vast amount of empirical data supporting psi phenomena, she wrote, should make psychologists want to consult the primary sources—the data, the criticism of the data, and the responses to the criticism—instead of rejecting it arbitrarily.

Unfortunately, it's not just opponents of parapsychology who resort to the appeal to authority fallacy. Its defenders do, too, when confronted with legitimate objections from competent and open-minded scientists. I've observed it myself. Bad faith is not limited to the skeptics. I've witnessed heated arguments from experts on both sides in which their beliefs took precedence over a real exchange. This only makes Dr. Cardeña's appeal all the more important: listen to both the criticism and the response to the criticism. *Both sides*.

In this polemical context, I can't ignore that there is a more irrational element at work. Sometimes, criticism of parapsychology is not based on any examination of the research, but on preconceived beliefs and ideas. Many scientists regard the results of psi experiments as *necessarily false* without even looking at them.

When it comes to extrasensory perceptions, for example—a phenomenon that radically changes how we see the world we live in—we can see that there are cultural, psychological, and cognitive mechanisms at work that lead to willful blindness and rejection.

One of those mechanisms is cognitive dissonance, the internal psychological tension that occurs when new information—parapsychological data, for example, or Stargate remote viewers' reports, or near-death experiences—conflicts with previously held beliefs, emotions, and knowledge. When we experience cognitive dissonance, we tend to reject the new information out of hand, a rejection that doesn't come from either rational reasoning or a lack of intelligence.

It feeds our unconscious denial of anything that's too unusual, anything that threatens the interpretative frameworks through which we make sense of our world.

I've observed it in myself over the course of my investigations. On several occasions, when new data has forced me to question what I thought I knew, I've felt a kind of internal tension. Reconsidering my previous convictions has never come easily. Even if I knew that the new data was corroborated, at the same time, *something* in me resisted.

Cognitive dissonance isn't bad in and of itself, provided that we're aware that it's an emotional, *unreasoned* response, and that we try to work through it. For me, it's been a driving force rather than a handicap, motivating me to go further and further into my investigations, with more and more scientific rigor.

The best way to reduce cognitive dissonance is to study the new information carefully, without letting preconceived ideas get in the way. This way we can gradually reduce the tension caused by the gap between what we know and what we've just learned.

31

Firsthand Accounts

Let's get back to what is perhaps most important: the phenomena. It is an undeniable psychological and sociological reality that people do experience these anomalies, and laboratory experiments and statistics aren't the only scientific methods at our disposal through which to explore them.

These unexplained phenomena may not be as indisputably objectified as we might wish, with their sources identified and their mechanisms understood, but that doesn't mean they don't exist. Millions of stories validate that these spontaneous, extraordinary experiences are more widespread than we might think: dreams, premonitory feelings, telepathic experiences, times when we can *viscerally* feel that we must or must not do a particular thing, strong intuitions . . . the list goes on.

This was what led me in 2007 to found INREES,[1] a research institute for extraordinary experiences, on the advice of a psychiatrist friend of mine named David Servan-Schreiber.

The initial goal of INREES was to bring together a large number of healthcare professionals who were familiar with these extraordinary experiences and who were eager to share their observations and clinical knowledge. They formed a welcoming, open-minded network that became a resource for people who had undergone such experiences, many of whom were isolated and distressed, or seeking explanations. This network is still around today.

In the years that followed INREES's creation, I received literally thousands of firsthand accounts. Some even came from people close to me, who had never spoken publicly about the strange thing that had occurred to them; the rigorous and yet caring framework of the institution made them feel comfortable enough to open up.

I'm thinking, for example, of your grandfather's best friend, Claude Collin Delavaud, also a geographer, member of the Société de Géographie and president of the Society of French Explorers. Claude and my father met in college and went on several trips together, including as far as Afghanistan, in the mid-1950s. One day he confided in me about an experience he'd had one afternoon in April 1968, which he'd never been able to explain but which had a marked impact on him:

> I went out in a boat with my two children off the coast of the Lérins Islands, in Cannes. Without warning, our sailboat flipped over. At the same time, my mother, who was still back at the house, suddenly got up and went to the window. Seized with uncontrollable anxiety, she called out to my stepfather, "Claude and the kids are in the water. Something happened to them." We were two miles from the shore, totally invisible from the window. "But you can't even see anything from here!" my stepfather answered, trying to reassure her. And it was true that even with a pair of binoculars, my mother wouldn't have been able to spot a sailboat on its side and three heads from so far away. She begged her husband to rush her to the port, but despite her insistence, he refused to listen. Stubbornly, she went anyway and found a little boat she could take out to help

> us. As unbelievable as it may seem, she was able to guide her boat to where we were without even seeing us. After having spent over an hour in the cold water, we were relieved to see her. How could she have possibly known we were in danger? I don't know, but I'll never forget that moment.

There are an infinite number of these stories from everyday life, each one a powerful testament to the fact that neither space nor time is an obstacle to our consciousness.

I've been blown away by accounts with even more dramatic outcomes than Claude's, as though some inevitable piece of information has been "captured" from the future. A woman named Laure wrote to me the following:

> One morning, I got a phone call from my sister-in-law, who was in a panic. She asked if I had heard any news about my son, who was in the military. When I asked her why, she said, "I dreamed that army officials had come to your house to tell you that your son was dead. Everyone was crying except you." Filled with dread, I called my son. Everything was fine. I told him about the dream and we laughed about it. But two weeks later, he died, and police officers came to my house to tell me. He was twenty-five years old.[2]

Another story, this one from a woman named Catherine:

> Several months ago, when I was in the car, I had a vision of an accident. My son was in it, and his car had been overturned in a ditch. It was nighttime, and he was crying . . . I saw myself get into the car and sit down next to him. I held his face in my hands, telling him he had to hold on, he had to fight, he couldn't let go, but it was of no use. He wasn't listening

to me. Afterwards, I tried to put this macabre vision out of my mind. It was inconceivable to see the death of my own child. Maybe a month later, my son drove over to his studio. It was around 6 p.m., and it was dark and rainy outside. His father and I were worried, but he told us, "Don't worry, I can handle it." Those were his last words. The accident happened on the same road where I'd had the vision—not exactly the same spot, but the same road. I wasn't the one caressing his face and telling him to hold on, it was a woman who had been driving behind him and who stayed with him until the ambulance arrived. Whenever I talk about this vision now, I get the sense that people think it's the pain of grief talking. But what would be the point? I blame myself for having seen my child's death and not having been able to prevent it. He was nineteen years old.[3]

This one is from a grandmother named Louise. "On October 15, my grandson died suddenly. At the moment of his death, his mother—my daughter—was sitting on the bed with me. She suddenly fell backwards, saying to me, 'Mom, my chest hurts. I don't feel good.' Her son had been hit by a car at that exact moment, which obviously we didn't know at the time."[4]

Sometimes, people have a perception that allows them—as with Joe McMoneagle in Vietnam—to avoid an accident. Amandine, for example, explained to me:

One winter night a few years ago, I was sitting in front of my fireplace. The fire was blazing, and I was watching the flames without thinking about anything in particular. Suddenly, a thought popped into my head, as though a voice were saying to me, "Get up and move away from the fireplace, the glass is going to explode . . ." Why did I comply? I have no idea . . . I

> went to join my husband in the next room over and told him about it. Of course he started to laugh! Then a few seconds later, the glass from the fireplace insert shattered into pieces! The fire wasn't out of control, and the glass was in perfect condition. Is that what they call intuition?[5]
>
> Yes, Amandine, that's precisely what it is!

Very often, people report a kind of extreme sensitivity that can be difficult to live with on a day-to-day basis. Florence is one such person. "I'm thirty-eight now, and since childhood, I've had what we call 'flashes' that often foretell accidents, illnesses, deaths, etc. What's disturbing is that I can't control them. And the older I get, the more of these perceptions I have."[6]

And then there's Élodie, who was forced to shut down her business because these perceptions were too intrusive. "I used to own a restaurant. I was constantly in contact with customers, and therefore constantly besieged by 'visions' of their lives. It was like I was a receiver. I couldn't ever stem the flow of information, so it stopped only when I was alone. I finally had to give up the business. Now, I think of it as a help more than a handicap."[7]

These types of perceptions don't always occur in such a dramatic context. In some stories, they're simply evidence of a kind of psychic porosity, such as with Nathalie:

> My niece and her husband were coming over to eat raclette. In the days leading up to it, a phrase kept coming into my head: "Buy champagne!" It was like it was stuck there, and it irritated me to no end. The day of the dinner, I went to the store, and the "buy champagne" got even stronger and more

> annoying! I kept thinking to myself that it would be silly to have champagne with a simple raclette, so I didn't buy any. That evening, when my niece arrived, I immediately thought, "She's pregnant!" It was as though someone had implanted the words in my head. It was only after an hour or so that they proudly announced that they were going to be parents in eight months! Then, I understood why I was supposed to buy champagne![8]

One last short account, from Agnès, about a phenomenon that's more widespread than one might think:

> I had a friend named Guillaume, who I used to see regularly just a couple of years ago, but then circumstances drove us apart. One day, as I was driving to an appointment, I kept thinking of him, wondering how he was doing; it was like his face wouldn't get out of my head. I even kept looking to see if maybe he was on the street. When I arrived at my appointment and got out of my car, I suddenly heard someone shout my name. I turned around and it was Guillaume. I wasn't surprised to see him, but I didn't tell him why, because he wouldn't have believed me.[9]

All these experiences are unsettling. Some were particularly memorable for those who experienced them. *They're real.* Are there other scientific tools available for studying these phenomena and trying to understand them better? Yes. I'm thinking of the so-called qualitative approaches, those that focus on listening to and analyzing these stories, or even direct experimentation, like what I've been doing for years in the Amazon.

Many different fields of science are interested in the subject. For example, psychology: psychologists, psychoanalysts, psychiatrists, psychotherapists . . . Who could be better when it comes to exploring what many consider to be "ridiculous stories," or delusional beliefs and interpretations?

There does seem to be an apparent closeness between how these extraordinary experiences might manifest (hearing voices in one's head, seeing a dead person, sensing events before they happen, out-of-body experiences) and mental disorders as described in the *Diagnostic and Statistical Manual of Mental Disorders (DSM)*,[10] the "bible" of psychiatry. This might lead some to suspect that experiencers are lacking discernment in some way, or even that they're mentally ill. But this suspicion rarely holds up to a serious psychological examination. This is even noted in the latest edition of the *DSM-5*.

The *systematic* link that too many people still make between "extraordinary" and "delirious" or "magical thinking" is illusory. It can be a diagnostic error, particularly when a hypothetical pathology is evaluated too superficially and too quickly.[11] The content of the experience isn't in and of itself synonymous with a disorder or an error in judgment.

This clinical observation approach means that we can approach these witness accounts in a radically new way, allowing us to gradually see a coherence emerge: the experiences share unsettling similarities, and often, there is no conventional explanation for their occurrence.

I've met many psychologists eager to explore these extraordinary experiences without preconception, and with only their own clinical tools at their disposal.[12] I've also met anthropologists who are doing the same through shamanism.[13] Their groundbreaking work is invaluable, and it contributes to the advancement of our public knowledge. And it's science.

Our default stance should involve open-minded and benevolent listening. That goes not just for scientists but for all of us. It frees us to move away from binary ideological positions and see just how important these inexplicable phenomena are; they're an integral part of our reality even if we can't yet measure them. They're the subtle signs of our fundamental consciousness.

Even before Galileo discovered them in 1610, Jupiter's four largest moons had been orbiting for millions of years. That's almost so obvious it goes without saying—and yet. We seem so confident in the idea that if our own tools haven't proved something yet, it doesn't exist, even when so many signals remind us otherwise.

Consciousness and its nonlocal capacities present a formidable challenge for science. When we stubbornly try to understand these phenomena with scientific methodologies that exist today, we only become stuck in our debates and our thinking, completely missing the point of what these phenomena have to teach us. We should consider that any potential rushed attempt at explanation is heavily influenced by our unconscious beliefs, our culture, and our expectations—so many interpretative biases that we have to set aside. The nature of consciousness is such a vast subject that it requires a multidisciplinary approach if we want to understand it better.

Neuroscientists are interested in the correlations between conscious experience and neural activity, but it's clear that their scope of approach is quite narrow. Knowledge of the mechanism (neurology) does not lead by analogy to knowledge of consciousness (subjective experience). And these limitations apply to all disciplines, not just neuroscience. It would therefore be best if scientists working in different fields were to collaborate and explore complementary approaches. Philosophy, psychology, and social sciences in general are some of the fields that could work well together, given that they all explore our subjective experiences.

And I would be remiss not to mention spiritual teachings, the fruit of diverse practices from contemplation to shamanism, from meditative introspection to mystical revelation. They open up new perspectives that are just as enlightening, especially when they allow us to induce nonlocal experiences—as shamanism does. And to experience them ourselves.

On that note, perhaps it's now time for us to head back into the forest.

32

On the Threshold of the Spiritual World

The Amazon rainforest. I was still on my journey, though I wasn't moving; the days were hot and unchanging, and yet each morning I thought I had reached a new degree of inner clarity. For example, the boundary between my nighttime dreams and my waking state was becoming increasingly blurred, as though the unconscious messages I received during my dream-waking were becoming more and more comprehensible. I was more conscious when I dreamed, a semi-lucid observer.

The confusion was dissipating like fog evaporating with the rising sun. Every day I appreciated the effects of my dieta more and more.

Ajo sacha had become a kind of friend, an accomplice. I took pleasure in our daily meetings, when I slowly sipped the tea made from its leaves.

I'd begun to pay attention to details I hadn't noticed before. A rustling in the leaves that synchronized with a particular thought. A ray of sunlight that sliced through the clouds and caressed me as I read a sentence that moved me. A passing butterfly. A lizard that stood still. A bird that appeared and indicated the way toward a path through the vegetation I'd been looking for to no avail. A deer that raised its head when I was out on a walk and stared at me insistently.

Birds of prey crossed the sky constantly. On several occasions I watched them emerge from the forest and soar over the cabin. They slipped soundlessly between the trees, sometimes circling the nests of other birds; then there were sudden movements in the uppermost branches, frantically thwacking wings, and loud screeching and squawking.

One morning I discovered that a young snake had shed its skin on the threshold of my cabin overnight. He'd left it for me, entirely intact and still in one piece. Right in front of the door. I received it as a message. I, too, would leave a former skin there.

I loved those poetic, intimate little signs of synchronicity. I saw them as gifts, encouragement from the living intelligence around me, and was moved by them. What were they saying? Perhaps quite simply that life was as it should be, and that the path taken was the right one. I was undergoing a transformation of my own, shedding my mind's old skin. How many of these signs do we ignore, distracted by the control we exert over our own lives?

In the peaceful days that followed, a profound confidence radiated through my body. I could feel that I was ready. For what? It wasn't very clearly defined, but I had an intuition that something important was about to happen. I'd never lost sight of my goal: to go to the world of the dead. Was this finally the time?

The morning of my twenty-eighth day on the dieta arrived. The heavy downpours seemed to be over, and the bright sun was dazzling as I stepped outside the cabin. Underneath the surface of my reason, my soul peeked through, an intelligence revealed through the increasingly frequent silences in my mind. My body, thin from a month of discipline, was filled with gentle energy.

I decided to try ayahuasca alone again that night.

In the middle of the afternoon, I ate a bowl of fresh fruit. A little before sunset, I drank my ajo sacha tea as I sat on the stoop, watching the valley disappear into darkness. Nocturnal animals emerged one by one. I felt good, lightly euphoric, ready to receive ayahuasca's medicine, more confident than I'd ever been before.

The darkness of night blanketed the valleys and ridges, and the celestial vault was studded with stars. I felt a tremendous inner peace. My mind was calm, my body awakened from fasting, meditation, and the dieta.

I rested comfortably on the mattress, legs stretched out, bottle of ayahuasca in hand. My movements were slow and assured. The sacred moment. I unscrewed the cap, placed the neck of the bottle on my lower lip, closed my eyes, and began a modulated whistle, barely audible at first. My prayer.

With my breath, I nonverbally infused the concoction with my intentions. My mind usually cut me off from the infinite field of reality, and that night, I wanted ayahuasca to grant me access to other dimensions. I wanted it to allow me to perceive beyond time and space, for it to open my eyes to the other worlds I barely knew anything about.

My eyelids were closed, and the whistle came out of my mouth and entered the bottle. After a long pause, I raised it delicately, closed my lips around it, feeling the liquid come into contact with my tongue. I let it fill my mouth, running down my throat, then swallowed a second thick mouthful. It slipped down easily.

I put down the bottle and waited. I'd already had more than in previous ceremonies, but this time there were no spasms or retching, no pungent unpleasant taste. Harmony right from the start.

As usual, I began to feel the first effects after about thirty minutes. Light, barely perceptible vibrations started to take over my body. The less I moved, the more intense they became, as though *something* was opening up and unfolding. *Don't move. Let it grow.* A ripple of organic fear began somewhere in my chest, threatening to grow bigger. I breathed, and the fear diminished, then subsided. I wasn't afraid of anything. Nothing was going to happen to my body. It wasn't going to stop working, I wasn't going to suffocate. I could breathe, and my organs weren't actually going to shut down. *Relax.*

My physical sensations became distorted. I had the sense that my body was stretching out, becoming thinner and thinner, my arms and legs growing very long and extremely skinny. I kept my eyes closed so as not to clutter my brain up with visual perceptions. To be able to see what is invisible, what is visible must also disappear. Motionless, with my eyes closed, I reduced the demands on some of my usual senses.

Again my heart rate accelerated, the beating of my heart resonating throughout my body. That was usually the point when I began to lose control of my reason and became overwhelmed by fear and panic.

But not this time.

My heart was hammering in my chest, every beat an explosion, but all I had to do was remain still and breathe for the fear to immediately vanish. I held myself in alignment, symmetrical: my legs straight out in front of me, my torso upright against the mattress against the wall, my arms by my sides, my hands clasped together on my thighs. Nothing could happen to me. Even if I were to lose consciousness, I would continue to breathe, and my heart would continue to beat. I was reassuring my body, because *it* was the one that was scared; I was no longer scared at all.

Vibrations passed through me with even greater intensity, and I remained calm and serene. I was beginning to understand that the vibrations weren't coming from the outside; they were born inside me, in each one of my cells, the depths of my very being. The movement came from every molecule, each of the billions of atoms that make up my body. My entire body was changing frequency, in perfect, coordinated harmony.

Each one of those billions of cells began to vibrate progressively. It was completely incomprehensible for my mind, and I realized that that's where the fear had come from. But tonight, the medicine was so powerful, and my state of mind so calm, that my protective ego had been lulled to sleep in loving arms.

The intensity grew even stronger. My whole body was vibrating in unison, and then it left, it *moved*. As each atom changed frequency in perfect coordination with all the others, my entire body began to slide into a parallel dimension.

A part of my face and shoulder had swung into a non-earthly world. My upper body was covered in indescribable geometric lines, like circuits of light and energy. It's not that my mind was leaving and dissociating from my body; it was both of them together, mind and body melded into one, entering another universe.

I was in two worlds at the same time. Mine and *theirs*.

I could hardly make out anything, no color. My face was a lifeless gray, and the energy circuits glowed bright white. I found myself in an environment without space, color, or dimension.

A tremendous vibration had taken hold of my mind-body and literally carried me into another world. A nonhuman world, foreign to this earth.

I was conscious.

But I was far away from "myself."

I'd lost my bearings completely. It was so intense that it became more and more difficult for me to factor in the magnitude of what I was perceiving. Too many things were happening, too much information at the same time, as though the floodgates of a gigantic reservoir of knowledge had been opened. I was drowning in it. As soon as I tried to focus on one thing, just one of the countless pieces of information, I became overwhelmed, incapable of committing anything to memory. It's like having a magnificent dream and then trying helplessly when you wake up to remember it, to put it into words, when it's simply impossible to describe. What I was perceiving was so unfamiliar that much of it didn't fit into any of my cognitive patterns and remained inaccessible.

It was all too strange, too new. I'd entered a different dimension of reality, but it appeared to me an incomprehensible maelstrom; my brain didn't know the code. And yet it didn't stop—to the contrary, in fact. I had an extremely hard time staying focused and present.

Love . . .

I could feel that energy again. Overwhelming harmony. Throughout my whole body, I sensed an avalanche of knowledge that was too massive. My consciousness couldn't decipher it. I was a spiritual being made of matter . . . no, that wasn't it . . . matter was a vibratory state . . . it was impossible for me to remember everything that was happening . . . as soon as I tried to put it into words, it was as though I *fell back into my mind*; everything shrank and curled up. If I wanted to continue perceiving, I knew I must not try to "understand."

The knowledge that was revealed to me was beyond words, beyond my limited capacity. But nonetheless it was there, in me, around me. Knowledge emerged from the depths of my system, from my mind-body, from each one of my cells, from the furthest reaches of my soul. I was on the threshold of other worlds; they were there, they existed, within sight.

Breathe.

My body was growing tired. Too much energy. Moments of pure perception alternated with slightly calmer intervals. During those tiny periods of respite, I tried in a hesitant voice to describe into the tape recorder in my trembling hand what I was feeling, what I was seeing, what I thought I was understanding. But the very act of speaking out loud made me come back, cut me off from an immense part of that other reality. I could capture only fragments.

With whom was I in contact?

Who were these energies around me?

Other beings?

Be quiet. Stop trying to understand everything. I could feel the oneness of life. Everything was made up of living light. The whole universe was alive; it was life. It manifested in an infinite number of forms, one of which was me. I was so far away from "myself." I could sense how everything that was alive was part of one indissociable whole. "I" was dissolved into it, into this whole, and yet the "individual" that was me continued to exist.

I could perceive that Papa and Thomas were still individuals, but much less so than I was. The "dead" just have one less layer of individuality than we living do. I couldn't see my father, but I knew he was there.

I knew he was there. It was obvious and right. A fact that was more sensory than anything I'd ever experienced.

His world was in my own. He was not in a far-off *beyond*; he was there, existing on a plane that was superimposed over the one in which I existed. So close.

The words I was speaking into the recorder brought me so

far away from the knowledge to which I had access, that radical otherness. It was heartbreaking that all I was able to say were a few dull, faintly ridiculous phrases.

I understood that the universe is made of energy.

The stronger our biological and psychological casing, the less possible it is for us to connect to it. Our shells cut us off from the universe, from what is external. By protecting me, it was preventing me from accessing the world's energy.

I was deliriously intoxicated. The ayahuasca was open. Running my hand through my hair, I felt the vibrations, the surface of my skin trembling. I was vibrating from the inside.

I was in another dimension, another time.

This lasted for hours—well into the night.

33

Understanding the Inexpressible

Oh, Luna, I wish I had the words to describe that night for you! It was nearly 4 a.m. I was gradually coming back, still gently rocked by a wave of exhilaration. I managed to stand up and take a few hesitant steps. I opened the door onto the night. Lightning flashed silently and intermittently across the sky, far to the south. Dark clouds advanced overhead, obscuring parts of the celestial vault. My senses were dramatically heightened. I could see the animals crisscrossing the darkness, and hear them breathing, rustling, shrieking.

I was so calm, so at peace, luxuriating in a feeling of such happiness and fulfillment. I savored every second of it. I slid down the doorframe and sat down on the stoop, fascinated by the magic of the moment.

The effect had barely started to wear off, and already, I had a hard time believing what just happened. And yet it was so intense. Still, I "brought back" so little. I had found myself in contact with a knowledge that was impossible to "keep." It felt like I had reached a threshold from which I was able to contemplate an inexpressible landscape, but now that I was back, I wasn't able to remember it.

When I was in that space it was indisputably real; I didn't have even the slightest bit of doubt. I knew that I was experiencing something more real than my everyday life. But now that I was partially out of it, when I tried to remember the myriad details, feelings, perceptions, and information that emanated from that other plane of consciousness, the little pieces that my brain could reconstruct felt very far away.

I realized that when I was in direct contact with that knowledge, *I knew*. But as soon as the contact was broken, I could remember only tiny details. The knowledge didn't come back with me.

But the feeling was there nonetheless. The feeling of having *lived* something profoundly real.

The nonhuman dimension part of me had had entered the space where Papa and Thomas were—those worlds were real. I didn't have the slightest doubt about their existence when I was experiencing them. They are here. Not "beyond," in some far-off space, but here, in our own reality, simply vibrating on a different frequency that our brains ordinarily can't pick up. They're so close. The physical and psychological shell created by the pronounced feeling of our individuality is the only barrier that separates us from them.

In our usual state of consciousness, we're cognitively limited, hypnotized by our belief in ourselves. Our psychological personality imprisons us and blinds us. As soon as we can step outside the boundaries of our individuality, we can see, touch, and make contact with these worlds. And we *know*.

I slept for part of that morning. At noon, I picked at my food. There was bright sunshine flooding the valley. Two birds of prey called out to me; I stepped outside and they tore across the sky like two arrows, only a few yards above me. Hunters, with light beige plumage.

The days that followed were peaceful. I spent a lot of time writing down the details of that incredible night.

Soon, my solitary journey came to an end. I prepared myself to leave the tranquility of that isolated cabin. I was a little nervous that when I returned to my usual life in France, the inner clarity I'd acquired would fade away. I was cheered by the thought of seeing you again, Luna. But I didn't want to leave behind this open connection with my dieta. I kept thinking about the idea of pursuing it. Not right away, but perhaps in the near future.

I had a feeling that the spiritual world, the world in which "the dead" live, was as volatile as the dream world—a fluid space in which it's difficult to grab hold of something solid. An identity, a place, a situation. It all seems to be continuously dissolving, the thoughts from one moment evaporating in the next without a trace, just like in a dream. I wanted to go back to that world and learn how to remain stable in it. To stay there, and understand it.

During my last experience, I got the sense that the crystalized shell of my personhood had dissolved completely, leaving me open to a vaster reality.

As though "I" were a gallon of water inside a balloon floating in the ocean, and the balloon had popped, allowing the water to empty into the ocean, to become the ocean, all while retaining a kind of identity—which is what happens at the moment of death.

With some confusion, I'd perceived that the wholeness I was entering—the balance of the universe—was connected to love. In this case, "love" referred to a form of harmony fundamental to reality. I'd realized that the more we identified with our individual self—with the balloon—the denser we became, a vicious circle, and the more difficult it was to connect with the universe as a whole and with this love. With the ocean.

Over the past few weeks, I'd sometimes felt this immortal

part of me. It was unclear and murky, and I still wasn't sure I'd fully understood what happened; my doubts and uncertainty remained. And yet these subtle experiences were so intense that they'd begun to forge a new path for me.

I'd managed to distance myself a little from my expectations and my desire for objectification without feeling like I was giving in to preconceived ideas. I now *knew* that these other worlds existed, because I'd experienced them.

I'd sensed an intelligence in me that went far beyond the one formed by my brain activity. An intelligence that couldn't be reduced to my biological existence alone. An intelligence that didn't seem to be constrained by space or time. An intelligence that we call a "soul"—that term is so apt.

I'd felt my soul. But also the souls of others.

I'd become my soul again. For a few moments.

The existence of this spiritual part in us isn't just a matter of belief. It can be experienced directly. I'm now convinced of that.

For centuries, we've been assuming that the question of the soul is exclusively a religious one, as though it were limited to that human realm full of dogma, contradictions, paradoxes, and divergences.

A very large proportion of the human population adheres to one form of religious belief or another. According to science, religion is a philosophical construct devoid of objective reality, and its various theological systems are complex and abstract theoretical models. But this overlooks the fact that the religions that bring together billions of people around the world are all rooted in direct human experience—by believers, shamans, mystics, prophets, meditators, awakened beings, and so on—of the spiritual, transcendent dimensions that are so impossible for our rational minds to accept.

In our Western society we have a tendency to look at religion through the narrow lens of materialism, which prevents us from understanding the true nature of the source of spiritual teachings. We pay attention only to the differences between religions, their contradictions, and the wars waged in their name, seeing in these an argument in favor of the naive and illusory nature of faith.

Yes, religion is the source of many conflicts. Yes, there are major differences of opinion on many points between religions; yes, they are contradictory, and sometimes excessively dogmatic. But we cannot forget that their creeds are human creations, influenced by the social, political, and cultural context in which they were developed, and that sometimes these creeds have strayed quite far from the source. Dogmas are attempts to interpret and organize a transcendent reality. Religions are rough drafts, tentative translations—reductive by nature—of what is inexpressible.

This transcendence can also be found through direct experience. That's the essence of shamanism, humanity's first spiritual experiment. I'd just experienced it.

The sensory memory of the vibration that progressively spread throughout each one of my cells is still in my mind, as though now that I've acquired this piece of knowledge I'll never be able to forget it. My body became secondary on that incredible night. I left and went elsewhere, to a place that was real but indescribable. And the experience was intensely physical.

How far can you go like that? Is there a boundary you cannot cross? And if so, where does it come from?

It makes me think of those stories they tell in the Himalayas about Tibetan masters who can sense their own deaths approaching and ask to be left alone so that they can enter into a state of deep meditation. When their disciples open the doors to the cell several days later, the master's body is gone. They dematerialized, the Tibetans explain. All that's left is a garnet robe on the floor. It's as though their physical body had been no more than a reflection, and that once the lama's consciousness stopped projecting into this world, their physical body disappeared. I had always thought that these were just legends, like the great Tibetan flood, until I heard the Dalai Lama himself recount having witnessed such a phenomenon.

Could it really be true that at a certain plane of consciousness, attained by the Tibetan masters through meditation or by shamans through master plants, it's possible to free oneself from the weight of matter so completely?

I really feel that that's what I was being shown that night so fleetingly. I was experiencing the malleability of my body. My body: merely consciousness taking shape. Death, then, would be just the opposite: consciousness changing shape, no longer projecting itself onto a material form fixed in time. Abandoning the body with which it's so often confused in order to become itself again.

Leaving an empty shell on earth: a dead reflection.

The difference between the Tibetan master and us is that he *knows* that his body is a projection. Thanks to his awakening, he harbors no attachment to it and doesn't believe that it's real, so at the moment of death, he can stop the projection without the slightest constraint. For us, on the other hand, our bodies are the repositories of so many of our illusions, first and foremost our identities. Our attachments are embodied in these reflections, and so when we die, they remain on earth, abandoned, like froth after a receding wave. We believe in these dense, organic forms so much that they remain frozen in matter. A three-dimensional memory that will turn back into stardust.

That night, I experienced the illusion of my organism, and the reality of my spiritual consciousness. I caught a glimpse of what it is to exist without a body or a face, outside of time and space, beyond the deceptive appearances of matter. And I wasn't in a void; I was a part of life. Life after "death." Life after life.

Yann gently placed his hand on my plexus, closing my dieta and concluding my alliance with ajo sacha after thirty-four days of isolation. In the exhilaration of the night, we were lulled by the energy of the sacred plant. He was facing me, lit up by moonlight and swaying his torso forward as if trying to observe the effects of the chant he had just finished on my body. His palm was hot and moist. The short ceremony had just come to an end. It was gentle and calm.

"How are you?" he asked me.

"Good . . . Very good."

"How about some cake?" he suggested, and burst out laughing.

"Oh yes, great idea."

After more than a month of restriction, I could now eat sugar again, along with anything else I wanted. I had to ease back in gradually, making sure not to overdo it.

A large fire had been lit outside. We sat in front of the flames after stopping by the kitchen, each of us with a slice of cake in hand. I liked Yann and appreciated his freedom and curiosity, which had pushed him to consider both the strict conceptual and cultural framework of Amazonian shamanism, and to look elsewhere—Western psychology, for example—for insight into what he experiences on ayahuasca. It's invaluable to be able to think about these ineffable experiences, even if it's hard to find the right vantage.

The fire, the glittering dome of the sky, the sensation of being completely in the present. The last suspended moments in the arms of the *Madre*.

I now knew where the door was; it was inside me. I'd partially opened it. I knew the way. I owed this knowledge to the isolation and the dieta, the conditions that were just right for me to profoundly connect with my spiritual side. After more than a month alone in the rainforest, I was on the same wavelength as what is essential. I had rediscovered a form of serenity, and an inner confidence.

"Thank you," I told Yann. "Thank you for the framework you offered me. These weeks of the dieta and solitude have been a truly extraordinary learning experience."

"The energy of your dieta is in you now. It will continue to open up."

"I became aware of my soul's voice. I heard it, felt it in my body."

"It's that immortal breath beyond the masks."

"And it's so hard to describe."

"Words trap us. The sensory experience is so much bigger. When we try to talk about it, we cut ourselves off from what we feel. We just circle around it . . ."

Yes, it was probably best to keep quiet right then. The fire's embers were rising toward the stars, and the night enveloped us. It was my last one in the Amazon.

The next day at dawn, in the midst of a terrifying rainstorm, I left the rainforest in Yann's old pickup truck. The dirt road had turned into mud, and an uprooted tree lay across the road, blocking our way out. Did the rainforest want me to stay? Having forgotten the machete, we had no choice but to try to push the trunk aside. It was a tricky operation, both because of the size of the tree and because of a colony of giant ants hiding under the leaves whose bites were extremely painful.

Soaked to the bone, we were finally able to clear the road.

I managed to get to the airport on time and caught my plane to the Peruvian capital.

Lima. Already the rainforest was far away. I looked out at the ocean from the window of my hotel in the Miraflores neighborhood. How wonderful it was! No more mosquitoes or spiders as big as my hand, a hot shower, a big clean bed that didn't smell damp and musty, a Caesar salad ordered via room service.

Out the window, I could see that one had only to cross a street, a shopping mall, and a strip of beach before reaching the Pacific Ocean. It was no more than three hundred yards away as the crow flew. The view was incredible and the sky was clear. Ocean as far as the eye could see, with the sun setting over it. *I'm going home tonight.*

A taxi in the evening. Lights, traffic jams, Latin music. The Air France long-haul plane took off from the runway at Jorge Chávez International Airport. After several hours in the air, I was back on French soil.

With just one desire: to keep going.

34

A New Opportunity

Despite how serene I felt for the first few days, the return to France was difficult. I felt like I was being plunged back into a society that pushed those invisible worlds away through its infatuation with so-called rationalism. In only a few weeks, the connection I'd forged with my soul, and with the knowledge and serenity I thought I'd found, seemed to slacken.

It's as though I had been torn from a dream that I firmly believed was bringing me closer to the essence of reality. As though I had been interrupted, and was now being pulled between two worlds. There was such a gap between my shamanic experiences and my everyday life . . . it felt like living a double life. Stuck in the inertia of reality. Like a sleepwalker.

There was something missing. I felt like I'd been cut off from what is truly important. Why do our rational minds prevent us so fiercely from being lucid? It's like we're condemned to a lifetime of struggling with the small torments of the roles we play without realizing it. We're obsessed by our reflections and our petty indignities—the no-stakes battles we wage, driven by anger, that take up all our attention and keep us subjugated.

This is the paradox of life: we're imprisoned in our personalities. They're all that we see, convinced as we are that we're nothing more than these mortal masks. The inertia of the real world in which we are immersed stretches thin our link to our most profound self—our soul—and blinds us to the true nature of the ties that bind us to those we love. When death takes us by surprise, we weep for the ephemeral connections forged by our personalities, unable to feel that our souls are still speaking to each other. We go through life isolated in our bodies. Cut off from ourselves, and cut off from others. And we are scared.

However, scientific research on near-death and other experiences at the boundaries of life, as well as extrasensory perceptions and capabilities, has suggested that the fundamental nature of consciousness is spiritual. Subjective experiences in states of altered consciousness have reinforced this model. We are spiritual beings living a material experience.

How can we integrate this into our daily lives? How can we reconcile these two realities—a spiritual path and a life in a physical body, with all its inherent compromises—and lead a meaningful life?

One book indirectly played an important role in my investigation from this point onward: Michael Pollan's *How to Change Your Mind,* in which he explores the large-scale revival of psychedelic research and psychedelic-assisted therapy. Pollan recounts several of his own experiences with various psychoactive substances, which he carried out under the guidance of therapists—a session of low-dose LSD, a session of psilocybin, and a session of 5-MeO-DMT (a psychedelic in the tryptamine family that can also be produced synthetically).[1]

I was surprised by how sweeping his conclusions were, given that his own experiences were relatively limited and modest, as initial ones tend to be. After five trips to the Amazon and more than thirty ayahuasca ceremonies, I still feel like a beginner. And what I thought I understood at first has evolved over the years; if I've learned one thing, it's not to jump to conclusions based on only a few experiences.

For example, based only on his own experiences, Pollan discounts the spiritual side of a psychedelic experience, considering it almost a secondary epiphenomenon. Under the guise of professional skepticism, he opts instead for a staunchly materialist interpretation. It's a little like someone who attends a weekend-long meditation retreat for the first time and decides afterward that the thousands of years of teachings that have informed the practice aren't very important after all.

Nonetheless, his book was how I learned that there's a community of therapists in the West who use these substances in their practice. Connecting with them seemed like a potential new avenue for me to continue my own exploration.

What I experienced during my weeks of isolation in the Amazon wasn't a dream. I had discovered another level of reality. However, despite how intense my nights there were, I'd glanced only very briefly at that reality.

To use a geographical metaphor, after that final trip to the Amazon, I felt as if I'd arrived at the border post of an unknown land, from which I'd observed an almost fantastical landscape. Why not go explore it? I was the son of a geographer, after all, and by then I'd learned to handle the destabilizing experience of ego dissolution a little better.

Psychedelic substances are still classified as narcotics in France. In the United Nations Convention on Psychotropic Substances from 1971, they're part of Schedule I, a list of substances that have "a high risk of abuse, posing a particularly serious threat to public health, which are of very little to no therapeutic value." The fact that this assertion is unproven, and what's more, that it contradicts all the medical and scientific research on the subject, doesn't change anything from a legal point of view. Not yet, at least. In light of the new research from all over the world that reveals the therapeutic potential of psychedelics, the legislation will probably change, as it already has in many other countries.

As psychologist and psychedelics advocate Timothy Leary once said: "Psychedelic drugs cause panic and temporary insanity in people who have not taken them."[2]

However, my intention in writing about how psychedelic drugs became the next phase of my own journey is not necessarily to encourage people to use them. My approach is part of a long tradition of first-person exploration that's also prevalent in scientific research today—from Johns Hopkins to Yale to the Brain and Spine Institute in France to the Faculty of Medicine at Imperial College London.

The German writer Ernst Jünger coined a neologism to refer to those who engage in this particular type of consciousness exploration: *psychonauts*, or "soul explorers," who intentionally enter altered states of consciousness in order to go beyond the limitations of science. The term was then taken up by Stanislav Grof, a true pioneer in this field.[3]

Assisted therapy is merely the tip of the psychedelic iceberg, but it gave me a new, solid, and relevant framework to follow—and as an added bonus, I wouldn't have to disappear into the rainforest for long periods of time.

I began to work with Lennie, an experienced practitioner. During our first session, I told her about my history of ayahuasca and was open about the fact that my goal was to repeat, under her supervision, the experience of ego dissolution and foray into nonlocal reality. She agreed to guide me. Over the course of several sessions, I tried MDMA and then MDMA combined with psilocybin mushrooms.

This particular form of therapeutic support is very different from what is offered by shamans. The emphasis is on accepting and integrating whatever bubbles up from our unconscious, which turns out to be inseparable from the spiritual experience.

As I've said before, experimenting with an altered state of consciousness may open a door to the world of the soul, but it also acts powerfully on our unconscious.

Just when I thought I'd solved the problem, I was confronted again with dark fears. During moments of intense anxiety, Lennie invited me to sit with those emotions and let the most unconscious parts of my personality express themselves. Her quiet, reassuring presence in the room with me was crucial.

With her, the therapeutic aspect became more important. Unexpectedly, it revealed a major childhood trauma of mine.

It hadn't been my first goal for the therapy, but nonetheless my inner invisible world became visible. I was able to pinpoint one of the things that had most profoundly affected my psyche, something that explained the solidity of my mental fortress—the one that, for years now, had been hindering me from being able to listen to my emotions and inner world, blocking me from accessing the dimensions of my soul. I'd managed to extricate myself from its grip during my long dieta, but obviously the reprieve was only temporary. I still needed to definitively free myself from the ultimate source of that mental resistance.

My work with Lennie brought to light the traumatic event that had been its initial cause: the sexual abuse I experienced as a child.[4]

The revelation was absolutely devastating, and at the same time, it was the start of true healing. As a child, I'd had to build a shell that was thicker than most; it was the only method my unconscious could find to keep me from being destroyed by the abuse. My work with psychedelics lifted the dissociative amnesia that had cloistered me for decades.

During those months of work with Lennie, I realized how much I'd been cut off from the world, and from myself, for the majority of my life. Inside me was a devasted child trapped in the physical citadel of my body, and this unconscious suffering had made me a stranger to myself. Once the dissociative amnesia was gone, I was able to begin rebuilding and healing, a process that's still ongoing today.

This therapeutic work radically changed my approach to altered states of consciousness. It made it possible for me to activate a self-healing force—a revitalizing force, an inner intelligence. My experiences with psychotropic substances were never the same again.

I have to insist on this point, even if it means repeating myself: before we can see what is invisible externally, we have to confront what is invisible internally. Before we can see spirits, we have to confront our inner ghosts.

Shamans understand this, and they encourage us to face our hidden fears before we embark on a journey to other worlds. Different traditions around the world, including shamanism in all its forms, have developed practices that enable us to step outside the walls of the cognitive fortresses that our brains have been building since the beginning in order to experience our own nonlocal *inner* dimensions: our souls.

Let's take a little detour to two thousand years ago, Luna. As surprising at it may seem, it's highly likely that ancient philosophers like Socrates, Plato, Aristotle, and Epicurus found their own way into those inner dimensions through a rather strange experience.

35

The Shamans of Ancient Greece

You and I have both always heard that ancient Greek philosophers were the illustrious forefathers of rational thought. This is indeed true. However, for them, the love of wisdom went far beyond ideas.

For Socrates, Plato, and Aristotle, reasoning and thought may not have been the *source* of their wisdom, but rather a tool—a method of ordering, structuring, and thinking about perceptions they'd experienced, especially during a particular spiritual initiation that was an integral part of the Hellenistic world. For those who attended, it was the experience of a lifetime.[1]

A literally shamanic initiation.

In ancient Greece, being initiated into one of several cults known as the *Mysteries* was considered one of the most important things one could do during their life. The most famous was located in the temple of Demeter in Eleusis, one of the five sacred city-states along with Athens, Delphi, Olympia, and Delos. Located twelve miles west of Athens, the Eleusinian Mysteries were dedicated to Demeter and her daughter Persephone, who was abducted and brought into the underworld of the dead.

The German scholar Walter Burkert, who taught classical philosophy at the University of Zurich and became one of the world's leading specialists in ancient Greek myths and religion, defined the Mysteries as "initiation rituals of a voluntary, personal, and secret character that aimed at a change of mind through experience of the sacred."[2]

There weren't any lessons taught in the temple of Eleusis. Initiation wasn't about the priests revealing knowledge. It was where you went to experience a powerful psychospiritual transformation.

In this case, the word "Mystery" doesn't refer to something that can be taught; it refers to a form of knowledge that could be accessed only through the spiritual experience of initiation, transcendent and ineffable.

What's more, it was forbidden to speak publicly about the experience. Athenian laws were very strict in this respect. All the same, there are some ancient writings that can shed some light on it, even if none of them reveal what took place within the temple.

"I came out of the mystery hall feeling like a stranger to myself," the rhetorician Sopater wrote after visiting the Eleusis sanctuary.[3]

Dio of Prusa, born in 40 AD, explained that the initiate would see all kinds of secret visions and hear mysterious voices; darkness and light would alternate before his eyes, not to mention countless other sights. "Something is bound to happen in the soul," he concluded.[4]

Second-century sophist Aelius Aristides, meanwhile, declared that Eleusis is both "the most frightening and the most resplendent of all that is divine for men."[5]

The philosopher Apuleius, in the last book of *The Golden Ass*, gives an account that's even more striking, explaining that he glimpsed the secrets of the lower world through visions. Apuleius was a writer and philosopher from a family of Roman citizens in what is now Algeria. During a trip to Greece, he was initiated into the Mysteries. "I came to the boundary of death. . . . and I returned having traversed all the elements; at midnight I saw the sun shining with brilliant light; I approached the gods below and the gods above face to face and worshipped them in their actual presence."[6]

What was going on in the temple of Eleusis?

What did the initiates see?

What could this absolutely indescribable experience that's had such a considerable influence on the whole of philosophy have been?

In *Phaedo*, Socrates—the father of Western philosophy, and a figure so beloved by your grandfather—evokes the Mysteries with his disciples. "I conceive that the founders of the Mysteries had a real meaning and were not mere triflers when they intimated in a figure long ago that he who passes unsanctified and uninitiated into the world below will live in a slough, but that he who arrives there after initiation and purification will dwell with the gods."[7]

The "world below," Luna, is Hades—the realm of the dead.

An initiation that sheds light on the afterlife and frees the initiate from their slough?

Aristotle confirms that the initiation into the Eleusinian Mysteries has nothing to do with any kind of instruction: "The initiates were to suffer, to feel, to experience certain impressions and moods. They were not to learn anything."[8]

Walter Burkert explains that the goal was for the initiates to experience what was beyond. To *show* them, over the course of those sacred nights, "that death is not only an evil, but good" and "how to live in joy, and how to die with better hopes."[9] He quotes ancient Greek lyric poet Pindar, who says in one of his *Dirges*, "Happy they all on account of the *teletai* [initiation rites] that free from suffering."[10]

Epicurus was initiated into the Mysteries, probably those of Eleusis.[11]

Plutarch, another initiate, also compares the rite to the process of death: "When a man dies he is like those who are initiated into the mysteries. Our whole life is a journey by tortuous ways without outlet. At the moment of quitting it come terrors, shuddering fear, amazement. Then a light that moves to meet you, pure meadows that receive you, songs and dances and holy apparitions."[12]

It wasn't just philosophers: most of the Roman emperors took part in the Mysteries, as Paul Foucart, a leading voice in Eleusinian studies in the early twentieth century, wrote. "The ancient reputation of these Mysteries, and the hopes they provided for the afterlife, were attractive to Romans, who had nothing of the kind in their own religion. Sylla, Antony, Cicero, and his friend Atticus were initiated. Augustus followed suit in the year 21. Emperor Claudius tried to bring the Mysteries to Rome, but failed; Nero didn't dare enter the Sanctuary of Demeter, which was forbidden to murderers."[13]

It was the right call: anyone who spoke Greek, no matter their rank, qualified for initiation, except for those who had killed someone.

Hadrian, the philosopher-emperor Marcus Aurelius, and his son Commodus[14] were also among those who participated in this singular experience.

Word spread far beyond the Hellenistic sphere—Cicero spoke of "Eleusis, that august and holy city, where the world's farthest nations are initiated"[15]—and the initiation brought its participants certainty of a calm entrance into the other world, the world of the dead. But what did it actually consist of?

"The mysteries were 'unspeakable,'" wrote Burkert, "not just in the sense of artificial secrecy utilized to arouse curiosity, but in the sense that what was central and decisive was not accessible to verbalization."[16]

An experience impossible to recount?

Philosophers, historians, and classicists all acknowledge that they don't know exactly what occurred in the secrecy of the temple of Eleusis to provoke such strong reactions. Initiates became completely disoriented, and their mental states ranged from profound perplexity to intense exaltation.

How did they reach the threshold of death?

Excavations in the Telesterion, the great hall of the sanctuary of Eleusis where these rites took place, have revealed that it was bare: there were no underground passageways and no staging rooms. The hypothesis that what the initiates saw and were so impressed by was some kind of theatrical performance by the temple priests is thus ruled out by the archaeological findings.

The majority of works on the spirituality of the ancient world don't shed any light on this question because they skip over an essential point. They all take for granted the idea that these cults are a kind of metaphor, mythology, or symbolic teaching. But this secular assumption doesn't explain how some of the greatest thinkers of antiquity—praised for their intelligence and discernment—could have been so astounded by the Mysteries.

Our Western society interprets thousands of years of history through a strictly unspiritual lens. The mystical past must *necessarily* be metaphorical; religions are *obviously* institutionalized and naive beliefs; and spirituality is, *according to logic*, an illusion born from human's fear of nature's unknown forces.

Guided as we are by materialism, we find it impossible to appraise other realities, and to consider the true scope of the mystical experiences and connection to the spiritual realm that many different civilizations have had at many different points in history. The blindness shown by the majority of anthropologists when it comes to shamanic practices is just one example.

What if the Mysteries really did immerse the initiate in a spiritual reality?

We know now that as Greeks traded and colonized across the Black Sea in the seventh century BC, they were introduced to a culture based on shamanism,[17] traces of which were found across Eurasia.[18]

The Irish classical scholar Eric Robertson Dodds, a specialist in ancient Greece, explained, "In Scythia, and probably also in Thrace, the Greeks had come into contact with peoples who . . . were influenced by this shamanistic culture."[19]

Scythia was a vast territory stretching from Central Asia to what is now the eastern border of Europe. Thrace was situated between the Balkan peninsula and part of Bulgaria. Shamanic culture still exists today in various forms in Central Asia.

But it significantly predates the seventh century BC, and may have inspired Mediterranean civilizations much earlier. Shamanism is humanity's oldest spiritual practice. It's not an institutionalized religion, but rather a set of rituals—song, dance, sensory deprivation, fasting, ingestion of psychoactive substances, for example—that can bring about a sensory, cognitive, and spiritual reawakening for the practitioner. As I've begun to experience, these trance-inducing techniques liberate the fundamental consciousness and connect the shaman to the "spirit world."

It's unclear when the Eleusinian Mysteries were first practiced. The remains of a small temple dating back to the Mycenaean civilization, which flourished from 1650 to 1100 BC, were discovered on the site, but although this archaeological evidence suggests ritual functions, it's not clear that this was the same as the Mysteries.

The beginning of these cults is often said to be the seventh century BC, because this was when the "myth" of the foundation of the Eleusinian cult first appeared in an anonymous poem, "The Homeric Hymn to Demeter." This earliest written account of Eleusis recounts how the goddess Demeter went in search of her daughter Persephone after Persephone was abducted by Hades.

Carl A. P. Ruck, a professor in the Classical Studies department at Harvard and a specialist in mythology and religion, reads the myth of Persephone as an archetypal experience of death, writing, "The Homeric hymn, after its account of Persephone's fatal nuptial encounter, goes on to tell how Demeter came to establish the Greater Mystery. In grief for her lost daughter, she went to Eleusis. Her journey there is a sympathetic imitation of Persephone's entrance into the citadel of Hades, for Eleusis was a simulacrum of the other world."[20]

We know that the Eleusinian cult existed at least as far back as the seventh century BC, and that it lasted until 392 AD, when an imperial decree banned all pagan cults in the Roman Empire and destroyed their sanctuaries. So the Mysteries were celebrated for, at the very least, nearly a thousand years.

There are striking similarities between the descriptions we have of the effect the Mysteries had on the initiates and what we know about shamanic practices. Reading these ancient accounts, I was amazed to discover how much overlap there was with what I'd experienced in the Amazon. Many historians believe that a shamanic influence on the Greeks is highly likely. It's also uncanny that the "founding myth" of Eleusis speaks of a journey into the world of the dead—the very essence of shamanism.

The link between the Mystery cults and shamanism becomes even more apparent to those researchers who have themselves had powerful psychospiritual experiences during shamanic rites.

What Apuleius, Socrates, Plato, Epicurus, Plutarch, and so many others describe—going into the world beyond, the inexpressibility of the experience, the light, the physical and psychological reactions, the fear, the ecstasy, the reversal of beliefs, etc.—is exactly what happens during a shamanic ceremony.[21]

Furthermore, participating in the Mysteries was a once-or-twice-in-a-lifetime experience. Being initiated didn't mean adopting a religion, or joining a brotherhood, or devoting oneself to a particular belief; it was a personal psychospiritual experience.

Exactly like shamanism.

There's another thing that's particularly intriguing: "The Homeric Hymn to Demeter" offers us some detail as to how exactly Demeter went to search for her daughter Persephone in the underworld. According to the poem, she asked the people of Eleusis to make her a drink, *kykeon*, from barley, water, and mint. She drank it and found herself among the dead.

The poem then explains that anyone who wanted to follow her example simply needed to drink this beverage after fasting for nine days, at which point they would be initiated into the Mysteries.

Over the centuries, those who celebrated the Mysteries followed this ritual scrupulously. Several thousand *mystae* (future initiates) participated. Only those who had observed a nine-day fast and purified themselves physically were able to enter the Telesterion, the central temple, more than fifty yards long on each side, where the heart of the initiation rite took place. On the evening of the ninth day, the participants were invited by the hierophant, the priest who presided over the Mysteries, to drink the sacred *kykeon* beverage.

Anyone who wanted to be initiated had to drink. *Kykeon* is at the heart of every account of the rite. It was clearly crucial. After the participants drank, they are said to have been *carried away by divinity*. Ancient accounts suggest that what they experienced were visions. As Carl A. P. Ruck writes:

Then there came the vision, a sight amidst an aura of brilliant light that suddenly flickered through the darkened chamber. Eyes had never before seen the like, and apart from the formal prohibition against telling of what had happened, the experience itself was incommunicable, for there are no words adequate to the task. . . . The division between earth and sky melted into a pillar of light. These are the symptomatic reactions not to a drama or ceremony, but to a mystical vision; and since the sight could be offered to thousands of initiates each year dependably upon schedule, it seems obvious that a hallucinogen must have induced it.[22]

There it is: the word "hallucinogen."

36

The Initiates

This hypothesis has been studied by three renowned scholars. The first, Robert Gordon Wasson, specialized in ethnobotany, ethnomycology, and anthropology. In the mid-1950s, he took part in shamanic ceremonies in Mexico involving sacred mushrooms, and he continued to study these practices for the rest of his life.

The second, Albert Hofmann, was the Swiss chemist who accidentally discovered LSD in 1938.

The third was Professor Carl A. P. Ruck, the Harvard classics professor I mentioned before.

Through comparative research[1] combining the anthropological study of shamanism, chemistry, and ancient Greek history, these three scholars gathered data suggesting that ingesting a psychoactive substance was a crucial component of the initiation ritual in the Eleusinian sanctuary, writing in their co-authored book, *The Road to Eleusis*:

> The ancient testimony about Eleusis is unanimous and unambiguous. Eleusis was the supreme experience in an initiate's life. It was both physical and mystical: trembling, vertigo, cold sweat, and then a sight that made all previous seeing seem

> like blindness, a sense of awe and wonder at a brilliance that caused a profound silence since what had just been seen and felt could never be communicated: words are unequal to the task. Those symptoms are unmistakably the experience induced by a hallucinogen.[2]

Doesn't that sound exactly like what I experienced in the Amazon?

The similarities between accounts of the Mysteries and accounts of experiences with sacred mushrooms in Mexico, ayahuasca in the Amazon, or LSD really are startling.

But should that be so surprising? The practice of using psychoactive substances to powerfully alter our states of consciousness is as old as time. Did the Greeks have access to them?

It's possible that they took hallucinogenic mushrooms, but based on ancient texts, Wasson, Hofmann, and Ruck thought that barley was more likely, given that it was sanctified at Eleusis and was also an ingredient in *kykeon*.

Albert Hofmann's earlier work also encouraged this line of thought: it was rye, a grain similar to barley, that led to his great discovery. Several kinds of grains including rye, barley, wheat, and other grasses can be parasitized by ergot fungus, a kind of fungus belonging to the genius *Claviceps,* which contains psychoactive alkaloids.[3] In 1938, Hofmann was experimenting with rye ergot fungus (*Claviceps purpurea*) to try to isolate active ingredients used in obstetrics for their antihemorrhagic properties when he synthesized lysergic acid diethylamide—LSD-25.

At the time, the substance was deemed uninteresting from a pharmacological point of view. But Hofmann had a premonition, and five years later, he decided to synthesize it again to try to identify other possible properties. In the spring of 1943, he devoted himself to the task.

On Friday, April 16, 1943, as he was crystallizing the LSD, he found himself overcome with unusual sensations. He wrote:

> I was forced to interrupt my work in the laboratory in the middle of the afternoon and proceed home, being affected by a remarkable restlessness, combined with a slight dizziness. At home I lay down and sank into a not unpleasant intoxicated-like condition, characterized by an extremely stimulated imagination. In a dreamlike state, with eyes closed (I found the daylight to be unpleasantly glaring), I perceived an uninterrupted stream of fantastic pictures, extraordinary shapes with intense, kaleidoscopic play of colors. After some two hours this condition faded away.[4]

Hofmann assumed that his condition must have been linked to his experiment that day, and yet as usual, he had been extremely strict with his hygiene, given the known toxicity of ergot substances. "Possibly a bit of the LSD solution had contacted my fingertips during crystallization, and a trace of the substance was absorbed through the skin. If LSD-25 had indeed been the cause of this bizarre experience . . . then it must be a substance of extraordinary potency," he wrote.[5]

To find out for sure, he decided to perform an experiment on himself the following Monday, April 19. Out of caution, he began with the smallest quantity that could have a measurable effect, given his knowledge of the efficacy of rye ergot: .25 milligrams. The first serious effects began to wash over him after about thirty minutes, and he had to ask his laboratory assistant to escort him home.

The experience became more and more intense over the course of the bike ride back to his house. Once he'd arrived, things worsened dramatically. He could barely manage to ask his assistant to call a doctor, and was soon completely disoriented:

> Every exertion of my will, every attempt to put an end to the disintegration of the outer world and the dissolution of my ego, seemed to be wasted effort. . . . I was seized by the dreadful fear of going insane. I was taken to another world, another place, another time. My body seemed to be without sensation, lifeless, strange. Was I dying? Was this the transition?[6]

Was this the transition?

It's unsettling to find that Apuleius put it almost exactly the same way nearly two thousand years ago to describe his initiation into the Mysteries: "I came to the boundary of death."[7]

Hofmann's experiment lasted several hours. By the time the doctor arrived, the effects had already begun to dissipate, and slowly the chemist came back to reality. The terror he had experienced faded away, and in its place he began to feel a sense of happiness and gratitude. When he woke up the next morning, he felt as though a new world had been opened up to him. "There was to my knowledge no other known substance that evoked such profound psychic effects in such extremely low doses, that caused such dramatic changes in human consciousness and our experience of the inner and outer world," he wrote.[8]

The ancient Greeks did not cultivate rye. But Hofmann's laboratory analyses of wheat ergot and barley ergot led him to discover that they both contained essentially the same alkaloids as rye ergot—namely, water-soluble psychoactive alkaloids.

Hofmann concludes from his research that, from a technical point of view, the ancient Greeks "could have arrived at a hallucinogen from ergot . . . growing on wheat or barley."[9]

In and of itself, this proves nothing, but when you look at it in connection with those uncanny ancient accounts, compare the Eleusinian initiation rite to induced shamanic trances, and widen the scope of reflection to include everything we know about Antiquity and the Mystery cults, it becomes fairly obvious that the ancient Greeks must have practiced a now-forgotten form of shamanism, which may have inspired the founders of philosophy.

While I was writing this chapter, I wanted to know what my philosopher friend Fabrice Midal would think of the idea that Socrates, Plato, and Epicurus may have been "Greek shamans."

Socrates didn't leave us any written works. All we know of his school of thought comes from the writings of his disciples, foremost among whom is Plato.

"That's actually exactly what the philosopher François Roustang called Socrates—a shaman!" Fabrice told me enthusiastically in response to my question. "He writes about it in his book *Le Secret de Socrate pour changer la vie* [Socrates's Secret: How to Change Your Life]."

Fabrice grabbed the book off his yellow bookshelf and flipped through it until he found the passage where a reference is made to a text by Plato in which Protagoras, a sophist, is in dialogue with Socrates. In the passage, Roustang explains how Socrates's way of thinking is different from that of Protagoras.

"I'll read it to you," Fabrice told me, and began: "'Readers will understand how the sophist is operating: he reasons, he argues, he proves. He's the philosopher who values thinking and who expresses himself methodically. Socrates, on the other hand, has a different approach: he wants to relate an experience. A human experience can't be deduced; it has to be seen, so you must let all its various aspects appear.'"[10]

"So for Socrates, experience comes before thought?"

"Yes. Socrates was a strange person who believed 'the greatest blessings come to us through madness.'[11] But he was talking about an inspired madness, one that disrupts speech, which is a characteristic of shamans, as Roustang explains. All Plato's writings speak of *experience* beyond thought."

The Mysteries provided access to the Knowledge, allowing initiates to *see* that at the moment of death, the soul separates from the body. That the body's passions, pleasures, and fears are obstacles to truth, and create confusion that only purification can dispel. How could this ancestral knowledge be passed on to non-initiates?

Through philosophy, Socrates and Plato, and a number of the others who followed them, transcribed it into the language of reason. In doing so, they allowed it to reach us.

Their genius lies in the way that they were able to rework the initiation experience of the Mysteries. If they hadn't, that knowledge would have remained limited to the initiates. And perhaps by structuring their school of thought around the sensory and spiritual experience of their initiation, they were also able to skillfully dodge any accusation of having revealed the secret of Eleusis. The Socratic dialogues do not openly break Athenian laws.

For me, perhaps the most convincing piece of evidence that all these texts were inspired by a real, transcendent experience of the afterlife during initiation is how serene Socrates was in the hours leading up to his death. That was what struck your grandfather, too.

Socrates was so calm. Even his friends were moved by his peacefulness.

Plato's *Phaedo* gives us a detailed account of the philosopher's last moments and the dialogue he had with his disciples. In the text, Phaedo is captivated by the tranquility of Socrates's soul under such circumstances:

> I remember the strange feeling which came over me at being with him. For I could hardly believe that I was present at the

> death of a friend, and therefore I did not pity him. . . . His mien and his language were so noble and fearless in the hour of death that to me he appeared blessed. I thought that in going to the other world he could not be without a divine call, and that he would be happy, if any man ever was, when he arrived there, and therefore I did not pity him as might seem natural at such a time.[12]

Doesn't that seem like the description of someone who knows where he's going, not because he's spent his life *thinking* about it, but because he's already experienced it, in the temple of Eleusis?

I'm thinking back now to your grandfather in his hospital bed, immersed in his copy of Plato's works—the same one I'm now holding in my hands.

He'd read it so many times in search of something that would convince him once and for all that his son Thomas was still alive *somewhere*. But no matter what, it seemed like the answer kept evading him. He was looking for a definitive, *intellectual* argument, and was astonished to find none convincing enough to put his mind at ease.

My father was reading the book as he'd learned to read it, educated as he was in our so-called rational society that saw the Mysteries as a form of mythology, barely more sophisticated than a bedtime story for children.

However, in this case, rationality is on the side of the founding fathers of philosophy. Rather than denigrating the higher wisdom they experienced through the spiritual path of initiation, as we do today out of ignorance, they reworked and restructured it in an attempt to make it accessible to all through language.

But Socrates probably intuited that the written word can be a trap, a prison for intelligence, leading us to abandon sensory experience in favor of rhetoric alone. Could this be why he himself didn't write anything?

The fact is that today, we worship words, and in doing so we completely blot out what inspired them. The philosophers' texts are merely reflections of their experience, hollow shells—veiled accounts of their own example.

What's the point of devoting your life to philosophy if, on the threshold of death, you're just as trembling and fearful as someone who hasn't pondered life's great questions?

Your grandfather pored over the pages tirelessly, looking for something that would shed some light on Socrates's peacefulness. He desperately needed to comfort himself. As I mentioned earlier, he even told me that he didn't think Plato had recorded everything. And indeed that was true. But the explanation for Socrates's inexplicable peacefulness lies not in his reasoning during those moments, but in the strange experience that inspired his state of being. The shamanic voyage, the Eleusinian secret. The initiation.

That's the key that opens up the words, giving them their fundamental meaning.

The Sanctuary of Eleusis was destroyed by Alaric and the Visigoths in 396 AD, and today not even its memory remains on the shores of the Mediterranean. But elsewhere, shamanic traditions continue, unchanged since the dawn of time. The thread has never been broken.

To follow in Socrates's footsteps and explore the teachings of the Mysteries, let's put words aside and instead look to the effects of psychedelics similar to those that were likely used by the Greeks. This parallel came to mind when I was reading a particularly enlightening book.

37

Surrendering Ourselves in Order to Learn

Christopher Bache is professor emeritus in the Department of Philosophy and Religious Studies at Youngstown State University in Ohio, where he taught for thirty-three years. He's also adjunct faculty at the California Institute of Integral Studies (CIIS) and an emeritus fellow at the Institute of Noetic Sciences. His interest in psychedelics began in 1978 when, at the age of twenty-nine, he read *Realms of the Human Unconscious* by the psychiatrist Stanislav Grof.[1] Grof's work on altered states of consciousness and the therapeutic usage of LSD before it became illegal in 1963 changed Bache's life, convincing him that lysergic acid diethylamide could be used to explore the depths of the psyche.

Starting in 1979, Chris Bache decided to begin psychedelic experiments on himself using Grof's protocols, without suspecting that the venture would last for twenty years.

Between 1979 and 1999, he underwent seventy-three carefully planned and structured therapeutic sessions with high-dose LSD (500–600 micrograms).[2] His goal was entirely philosophical. He wanted to experience, explore, and attempt to describe the realms of the transpersonal unconscious, and the dimensions even beyond—nonlocal reality.

After his last session in 1999, it took him several years to be able to fully assimilate his journey.

Bache describes LSD as a "high-altitude" psychedelic. He began his sessions early in the morning and they lasted all day. Generally he worked alone, accompanied only by his wife, who was also a therapist.

In his book *LSD and the Mind of the Universe*, he explains:

> High-dose *psychedelic therapy* is a very different form of psychedelic engagement. In this therapeutic modality, consciousness is much more powerfully amplified, and the strategy is to push through the psychodynamic level of consciousness and trigger an experience of ego-death and transcendence. Rather than working through one's personal issues layer by layer, psychedelic therapy seeks to induce an ecstatic state in which the boundaries between the self and the universe are dissolved, allowing one to reconnect with spiritual reality and gain a new perspective on one's life. Verbal interaction during a session is kept to a minimum. This therapeutic protocol is sometimes described as the "single overwhelming dose" approach. At Spring Grove Hospital in Baltimore, where Grof and his colleagues worked with terminally ill patients, high-dose psychedelic therapy was limited to three sessions.[3]

As I've mentioned in previous chapters, these end-of-life sessions with terminally ill patients can be incredibly impactful. They enable patients to overcome their fear and apprehension in the face of death by allowing them to experience the continuity of their consciousness—like a rehearsal before the great leap into the beyond.

Experiencing such a revelation for yourself is undeniably therapeutic, light-years ahead of conventional psychotherapy in terms of efficacy.

It's a little bit like actually vacationing in Hawaii versus staying home and reading the Lonely Planet guide. Mystical experiences are transformative, and for patients with terminal illnesses they are especially invaluable. The intensity and longevity of the beneficial effects they have on people at the end of their lives surpasses anything imaginable. For the patients as well as their doctors, these benefits are a testament to the fact that during the sessions, the space that their consciousness is entering is very real.

They are *actually* experiencing what death is like, living it from the inside. And death turns out to be a passage, a moment of transformation, rather than the disappearance they'd feared.

As Chris Bache says:

> Death is simply the price one is asked to pay to gain access to the myriad worlds that lie beyond the body-mind ego, death not as a metaphor or symbolic enactment but the agonizing loss of everything we know to be real and true, the spasm of our last breath, the terrifying surrender.[4]

Even top scientists, at Johns Hopkins for example, recognize the reality of a cosmic dimension that informs us, and with which we can make contact.

We might use different words to describe it, depending on our beliefs, but the experience is indeed an encounter with what is divine and what is sacred, both within us and beyond.

All the research that's been done for decades about psychedelics being used for scientific or therapeutic purposes has highlighted one essential element: the absolute importance of the framework for how the psychedelic experience will unfold. Anyone who ventures into psychedelic territory should be accompanied, just as the Greeks were initiated into the Mysteries at the consecrated site of the Temple of Eleusis.

The substance itself isn't the only factor. The same psychedelic in the same dosage taken by two people with the same psychological profile but in two different settings—for example, one in a therapy session, and the other at a rave—will have radically different effects. Whereas the former can have profoundly beneficial effects, the second can easily turn into a nightmare. A "bad trip."

That's what psychologists refer to as a "dysphoric response"—when "someone's innate resistance to losing control triggers an intense struggle and possibly paranoid or schizoid reactions."[5] The shock and overwhelm drown out any positive perceptions or ideas they might otherwise experience.

It's not dissimilar to what I experienced those first few times in the Amazon.

To counter the possibility of a dysphoric response, the "set and setting" of assisted therapy are crucial. This term refers to the two essential factors for any psychedelic experience to run smoothly.

The "set" is short for "mindset," and refers to the subject's mental, physical, and emotional state of mind, as well as their psychic makeup, expectations, mood, etc.

The "setting" is the environment in which the session is conducted. It should be welcoming—for example, with soft lighting, an eye mask, and soothing music in the background.[6]

After I'd discovered the richness of psychedelic-assisted therapy and read Chris Bache's inspiring book, it was clear to me that I had to follow his example. It was good timing; I was ready for another exploration. I'd been freed from my personal mental blocks and there was nothing keeping me from taking my quest to the next level. It was time to retrace the steps of Socrates the initiate, to experience what he had experienced in the Temple of Eleusis. And to learn the secrets that my father would have loved to know when he was on the threshold of death.

I began to experiment with LSD before I started meeting with Lennie. Ten or so attempts in all, beginning with very small doses and then building up gradually to familiarize myself with the medicine.

By the end, I was taking very high doses—more than 500 micrograms.

As Bache reports, the first two hours of the experience provoke a powerful dissociative response. In the 1960s, a dose of 500 micrograms was considered a "true initiation." Psychonaut Terence McKenna encouraged those who "really wanted to get the message" to take this kind of "heroic dose."

And that's what I did.

Nine times. Over the course of a year and a half.

Starting from my very first accompanied session at this dose, I witnessed the total dismantling of my psychological limits. I was catapulted far beyond anywhere I could have imagined.

38

LSD

It happened one winter morning.

I was about to swallow six drops of a clear liquid. The quantity seemed miniscule, and I was wondering how such a small dose could possibly have an effect on me. But in that little spoon was more than 500 micrograms of LSD. With a dose like that, the kind of dose that Chris Bache used during his twenty years of self-experimentation, there should be no more resistance. A decrease in activity in the default mode network had been observed in volunteers who'd been administered 75 micrograms, nearly seven times less!

I lay down on the couch, my noise-reducing headphones over my ears and a blackout mask over my eyes.

After about twenty minutes, a feeling of suffocation came over me. The fear of not being able to breathe. A part of me said, "Well, then, don't breathe!" I knew I was safe. I was much more at ease now, even as my mind tipped back and forth between fear and control and between trust and letting go. This lasted for several minutes, and my deep breaths soon restored my sense of inner calm.

On the screen of my closed eyelids I could suddenly see myself on a familiar tropical beach. The water went up to my knees.

Then, slowly, I began to float up and away. My body disappeared, but my *being* grew bigger, expanding more and more rapidly. I became huge, and soon the beach was miniscule; I got farther and farther away, and then it was the entire ocean before my eyes, the horizon becoming spherical; and then it was the whole Earth that I could see from space. In a flash, that, too, became tiny, and I was in the infinite cosmos. After that my memories faded away. I disappeared from my own view. My nonlocal consciousness had awakened.

I was no longer "Stéphane," and that didn't matter. I was alive in a way I'd never been before. I'd made it to the other side. I wouldn't return for a good two earthly hours.

How can I describe what is indescribable?

I left our reality behind. I became exterior to our material world, observing it first from a distance, as though I were in a theater, before it disappeared completely and I went even further beyond. At that point I entered into an ineffable love. It was as though this love was the ultimate nature of reality. There's no comparison between it and the love we feel for our friends and family; it's a million times more intense than that which unites us on earth. Absolute harmony, unblemished clarity, beyond causality, beyond doubt, beyond shadow, time, and space. There was no confusion whatsoever in that love. It was difficult to bring any information back from it, even though I managed a little with practice. But entire parts of my experience were so different, so *other*, that it was impossible to remember them, even three hours afterward.

The dissolution of "me" pulled me out of the cocoon of my identity. I was no longer "Stéphane," no longer "someone" at all, no longer my body, my history, my memories. I even lost the sensation of the material world, melting into immateriality. Yet astonishingly, I was still a "being" observing what was around me—the reality of the fundamental consciousness I'd once again become.

No more dimensions, no up or down, no familiar landmarks; just an infinity that existed outside of space and time. A feeling of well-being as I'd never experienced it before. Absolute harmony. And the energy of that love. It really was as though it were the raw material of the fundamental consciousness's universe—before the forces of causality, isolation, and individuality began to take over.

My dear Luna, the reality of that world is so beautiful . . .

And there's that *energy*.

Chris Bache explains, "*Deeper* states of consciousness are *higher* states of energy. . . . To have a *stable experience* of a given level of reality, one must acclimate to its energy. . . . In mountain climbing, we are adjusting to less oxygen; in psychedelic work, we are adjusting to more energy, and this activates intense purification processes."[1]

I was absolutely captivated by the massive flow of energy that absorbed me every time. Again, words fail to describe it. A harmonious, living energy. On that level alone, each of my sessions was extremely invigorating. I could never sleep the night after a session, for example, because the energy of the consciousness I'd been immersed in for hours was still flowing through me.

In those higher energy levels, there's no form, space, or reality as we know it. Just total consciousness, and sometimes a sensation of waves, of vibrations, of *fission*, which made it so that I could also perceive the presence of other beings, other fundamental consciousnesses, other *observers*, within that fundamental oneness.

What was most striking was that despite the total dissolution of all matter, I continued to *be*, to observe, without either a body or even a precise location. I was both everywhere and nowhere at the same time. Not in a void, but in exactly the opposite: in an indescribable infinity.

In a state of absolute awakening.

Several times, in this spaceless space, in the midst of bliss, I caught glimpses of what looked like small spheres, like tennis balls that I could hold in the palm of my hand.

I could sense that they were *existences*.

In their densest and most limited form, like constellations of the totality of a person's life experiences. Each one was an entire existence. That of someone on earth. As my vision expanded, I realized that I was looking at an infinite field of these spheres. There was mine, your grandfather's, your uncle's, and others still, some of which were known to me and many of which were not. They weren't souls, just the ultimate materialization of our earthly lives, as though the four dimensions (spatial and temporal) that characterized them had huddled into a sort of compact little ball.

As I contemplated the field of those earthly existences—all those "me's," all those temporal stories—I could feel how they had an anesthetizing power on our consciousness, as soon as they huddled in and we became absorbed in them during our time on earth. Was this a real image, or was it a laborious reconstruction of an inexpressible vision? It didn't matter. In this reality, appearances are secondary.

As Chris Bache says:

> Everything we see and learn in these visionary states is shaped in subtle ways by what we are at the moment of contact. This does not mean that the visions we experience are merely projections of our personal psyche, as though

> we were not experiencing something that truly exists in the cosmos. Rather, it means that *all visionary encounter is participatory.*[2]

So what I saw in those spheres was an illustration of the limitation of our life experiences when we are contained in a personality, like wetsuits that cover up our fundamental consciousness on earth and that contain all our experiences, emotions, and memories; the past, present, and future of our bodily existence.

Among all the bubbles of existence I could see were those of the "living" as well as those of the "dead."

As for the fundamental consciousnesses, I couldn't see them because they had no form, but they were there.

They were there, Luna.

Permeating this spaceless space were the consciousnesses of the being whom I had known as my father, as well as that of the being who had been my brother.

In the place where I'd found them, beyond life and death, my fundamental consciousness and their fundamental consciousnesses were no longer imprisoned in one of those dense, limited lives; instead they inhabited infinite space. We were all part of this boundless ocean—Thomas, me, Papa, and billions of other fundamental consciousnesses, all liberated from our attachments and personalities. *My* soul, *my* fundamental consciousness intertwined with all the others, seeing these little spheres—these identities—for what they are: illusory reflections. Experiencing this was a moment of grace. I'd found myself in the ultimate reality of being. With those I love. We were countless, and we were One.

During each of the nine sessions I did with a similar modality and dosage, I systematically and instantly experienced the total dissolution of my ego in a tangible and clear way. Repeating the experience allowed me to begin to truly familiarize myself with the nonlocal dimension of my consciousness. Every experience was further confirmation of the transcendent reality that I had first glimpsed on that intense night with ayahuasca during my dieta.

When we die, we don't die.

This isn't a belief.

I'm not drawing this conclusion solely from my subjective experiences of an altered state of consciousness. Everything I've experienced for years now only confirms what science has already shown.

As I've been saying, Luna, the conclusion that fundamental consciousness is nonlocal is based on facts, studies, and the analysis of countless real experiences. The body of evidence attests to it beyond reasonable doubt. Living this reality for oneself only further reinforces the model's coherence, especially as neuroscience confirms the parallel between a psychedelic experience and the experience of death.

The fact remains—and this is an understatement—that the dissolving of the ego is not an easy thing to go through, nor to observe as though watching a show from afar.

Bache explains:

> In deep psychedelic work, *one learns by becoming*. This is especially true when working with high doses of a powerful psychedelic like LSD. We cannot transport the egoic self into these depths where it can then "have an experience" of how the world works there. In order to know the universe at these levels, we must become *a citizen* of these levels. We must *become* the levels themselves. To do this, our smaller sense of self must cease to be the container of our experience. It must die. Giving up everything is simply the price of inheriting everything else.[3]

Our "observer self" is no longer able to watch from a distance; it must agree to *temporarily* die in order to make way for a more profound dimension of being. The observer has no choice other than to move aside so the fundamental consciousness can be experienced.

During my experiences with high doses of LSD, I was able to enter death, to go beyond the moment of dissolution and just *be* in the place beyond space-time, piercing the membrane of my physical consciousness, becoming a citizen of those levels. In other words, I had to completely un-identify with everything I thought I was: an individual, an "I," a being separate from the world's infinite globality. These experiences were beyond anything I could have imagined.

Several times, during different sessions, I was able to enter one of these concentrates of earthly life, as though I were immersing myself in a four-dimensional film.

Without any will on my part, I became absorbed into a sphere, and could taste the existence it contained. It was as though I were *living* it, experiencing the entirety of its life gathered therein—the emotions, the images, each moment.

In this way I was able to "visit" your grandfather, or your uncle, and live some of their experiences from the inside, as though I were becoming the person they had been during their time on earth.

And on one occasion, without my wanting to or deciding to, I slipped into the sphere of my brother's life as though I'd been transported there, and saw the moment of his death as he had lived it.

39

Fragments of Life

I found myself in a state of absolute ecstasy, and then suddenly I was slipping into his life, and I was in the car. Time slowed down dramatically, coming almost to a stop for those few seconds. The vision was incredibly clear.

Thomas was there, and I could also see Vadim, the other person who died in the accident. I *was* Thomas. I was looking at the scene from the outside and, at the same time, I was present everywhere inside the car, in a scene that had been solidified in time. I could see the entirety of the passenger compartment from different angles, as though I were everywhere at once.

I was following the scene as a whole and also seeing its most infinitesimal details. It was like I was glued to Thomas's body. His right eye socket, which took the first shock, and then his face.

I saw it, I lived it, I experienced it down to the cellular level, in his blood. The slow-motion violence of it, almost surrealist.

The seconds passed in the direction of time, but then went back again, as though the scene were being rewound. The shock in one direction, the injury, and then all of it over again in reverse.

The moment of his death: a few fractions of a second beforehand, then during, then a few fractions of a second afterward, then again during, then before, and so on. This replayed several times over. I could observe every detail, both from *within* Thomas and from the outside.

Why had he shown me this? I wasn't the one who'd chosen it. I could sense, as I was brought into the experience, that there was a benevolent healing process at work. At the same time as I was seeing and living the event, I was also experiencing the consequences it had on me—the sadness that had changed me afterward. The sadness of the beliefs my personality adopted: "Stéphane's" sadness; the sadness of having perhaps betrayed my parents' trust by having been the one to take my brother to this country; the sadness of having caused his death. The sadness at the violence, the blood, the shock.

I was seeing its emotional impact with new eyes; it was both extremely painful and a kind of readjustment. On the level of my fundamental consciousness, it wasn't so much that I suddenly understood the "meaning of the tragedy," but rather that I was seeing it for the first time from a distance, as though I'd been freed from the blind suffering of the moment.

I had reached the mystery, and was reliving, from the harmony of the soul, the moment that had torn apart our family. A healing energy was beginning to unfold, one that would fill my incarnate life with a new kind of peace.

In a different session, I relived a family death that had taken place much earlier. Once again, it was without having thought about it beforehand, without having expected it or sought it out. The condensed, living memory of the life of one of our ancestors suddenly appeared to me and drew me into its fold.

The first things I saw were farms amid the rolling hills of the countryside, tall grass, a woman, and several children. There was the face of a little girl whom I *knew* was my grandmother Lise, and an older boy, her brother Paul.

The vision was evanescent, and as soon as I realized what I was seeing, everything froze and then slowly faded away.

Next I found myself above a battlefield. It was sunny, not too cold, and the air was dry. I was in a body, Paul's body, and it was years later, in 1915, on a front line. Suddenly, I was propelled into the air; I was a broken body spinning in every direction, with no sense of which way was up. There had been an explosion and the air had been ripped apart. A blast of inconceivable intensity, splinters of wood, white earth, stone. I felt like I was in a whirlwind. My skin had been ripped to shreds, but it didn't hurt at all. It was *far away*.

My body was far away. Pulverized. I could see each of its molecules explode, an infernal force causing the whole body to vaporize into red dust. But it was silent, and it wasn't painful.

It was the moment of Paul's death, but there was nothing but life. How can I explain it? The body shattered into pieces, and life was flung into eternity.

The body had vanished into thin air, and it wasn't a big deal. It didn't *interrupt* anything. And especially not life. That body was just matter. And Paul—*I*—was no longer matter. I had just stepped out of time, and I was watching. The mutilated, dissembled body was already invisible, already gone.

All of that unfolded in extremely slow motion, just like I'd experienced Thomas's death. Each second was an eternity.

This is what happens when a fragile, flesh-and-blood human explodes on an artillery shell. There's no more body, no nothing, no distinct organs. Just a red mist in a whirlwind of splinters of wood and white earth.

My body had been torn apart, but it didn't hurt at all. It didn't matter. The scene played over and over again. Explosion, then the blast of air that carried away the pelvis, then the torso. I was experiencing the death of my great-uncle, Paul Lafitte.

The day after that session, as I reread my notes, I wondered why I'd witnessed that scene in such detail. He was my grandmother's older brother, but I barely knew anything about him, other than that he was a painter who went missing in action in February 1915. His self-portrait had hung on my bedroom wall for a long time when I was a teenager.

Shortly afterward, as I searched through my own genealogical files, I discovered that he was presumed dead on February 18, 1915, after being reported missing in the hamlet of Beauséjour on the Marne. He was thirty-one years old.

Launching into further research, I found out that he was a second lieutenant in the 84th infantry regiment. He had led his section into battle before his disappearance, and posthumously received a citation for gallantry. On a different site, I found a list of the battles in which his regiment had fought.

The attack began on the morning of February 16. During the bombardment that preceded the assault, the French soldiers noticed that many of the projectiles didn't explode. Upon leaving the trenches, the soldiers were decimated before they'd even made it a hundred feet. All day and into the next day, one attempt followed the next. It was carnage. Nonetheless, they managed to push back three German counterattacks. The report, which I read with some emotion, mentioned the 84th infantry regiment by name, saying that it had captured an important enemy holding near the Beauséjour fort.

I was struck then by a quote from a soldier who had taken part in the battle: "There's no longer any trace of the January fort—barely even its foundation remains. At ground level, you can almost make out the indistinct parapets, lost in the chaos of the white earth." I read on without paying much attention: "The umpteeth German counterattack weakened our position, forcing a retreat, while the 84th was pushed out of the stronghold they'd captured just hours before. Apart from the fact that the French lost 400 men, the front line moved very little . . ."

The chaos of the white earth.

In these detailed accounts of the heavy losses suffered by my great-uncle's regiment, the 84th infantry regiment, is this seemingly insignificant mention of the fact that the soil at Beauséjour was white. It was probably chalky. And that's exactly what I'd seen: the blast of an explosion, and his dismembered body mixed with splinters of wood and *white earth*, like chalk dust.

My great-uncle Paul was no longer missing; he had just shown me his last moments. *He was no longer missing.*

Over the course of my nine sessions, I visited other earthly lives, including my own, from this same exterior vantage point of fundamental consciousness. Time after time, I realized how much more we are than these individual "spheres" of life—these personalities. The faces we see in the mirror every morning are merely masks.

After several hours, the effect of the LSD would begin to die down, while my brain's filtering processes would start up again. I could literally feel my default mode network reactivating, my mind coming back, my identity reforming.

It gave me the sense that I was sliding into a tunnel, passing from an immaterial space to a reality of phenomenal material density. I could see space and time reestablishing themselves, rebuilding my physical body, the existence of which I had completely forgotten, block by block. It was a dizzying, swirling slide. A contraction into the three-dimensional space of my current life from the free, dimensionless space where everything is fluctuating and vast, ecstatic, harmonious, bathed in an inhuman love.

I could sense that this crossing, this progressive reinstallation of material reality, passed through several layers of worlds. Returning to linear time is intense. It's like returning to *what is hard*. To the body and identity that's so dominant. An individual, a "me."

It may feel like our world is profoundly real and dense, Luna, but I can assure you that where I've been is even more real, even if there's no matter.

These experiences have made me even more certain: I was entering a *true reality* each time, as I freed myself from my brain activity. A reality that's even more real than what we live in here.

When our brains stop, we wake up.

Our earthly world is an illusion of matter. Science is beginning to realize this, and I've experienced it for myself. It's become obvious.

What I have learned from these experiences is something that will stay with me for every second of my life, even if fully integrating it will likely take me many more years. The total erasure of our ego and our identity does not cause our consciousness to disappear. Quite the opposite: once again, we become the whole universe.

Death does not exist.

All the phenomena I've presented in this book about consciousness's nonlocal capacities and the neuroscientific research on the effect of entheogens (substances that promote a spiritual or ecstatic experience) on the brain support the idea that what I have experienced in these experiments, from my first journey to the Amazon in 2006 to my most recent encounters with LSD, corresponds to what the soul experiences after death. It's at once an awakening and a complete destabilization.

There is no longer any notion of reality or unreality. No more time; space, too, is dissolved. There's no more individual identity. We're no longer limited to a "me"; instead, we become an infinitely expanded consciousness, interwoven with other consciousnesses without any illusion of separation.

Everything is fluctuating, changing, unstable. We're carried away by forces—by thoughts that are not mental reasoning, but more like exterior, autonomous energies. There is no longer an inside and an outside. There is no longer matter. Everything is extremely volatile.

On the Earth, we are mere breaths of life, fragments of a larger being whose harmony we are striving to attain. The entire world is contained within our soul.

Dying is absolutely safe.

40

The Soul's Journey

My dozens of experiments with an altered state of consciousness have lifted the veils of my unconscious, enabling me to reestablish contact with my soul and to discover the infinite worlds in which it exists. This acquired understanding is not just limited to my mind; it's not the product of years of *thinking*. My personal subjective experiences have been decisive. I've lived through death. I've crossed over the rampart of fog. I've felt the reality of my nonlocal consciousness.

The adventure I've been on for the last fifteen years borrows from both science and, even more so, my own experience. I'm sharing it with you not as a universal truth but as something that has been imparted to me. What follows is my interpretation. They're only words. Pale reflections of an experience that is ultimately up to us to have for ourselves.

Death concerns only our physical aspect—our body. But that's not all we are. So many things would be inexplicable if this were the case: NDEs, terminal lucidity, mediumship, extrasensory perception, all these proven manifestations of our nonlocal consciousness. For the fundamental dimension of our being, death doesn't exist.

This being the case, then, what is it like now for my brother Thomas, your grandfather, and all the others we've loved, now that they've been returned to the nonlocal dimension of consciousness?

Words, like conceptual thought, limit our ability to conceive of what is, by definition, beyond our understanding. After the physical death of the body, the consciousness leaves time and space. We become infinite once again. The space where the consciousness goes doesn't have the inertia of the material world. Everything there is more volatile, limitless. Death, like altered states of consciousness, reveals that the personality with which we identify throughout our corporeal existence does not define who we are. Our personality is not our consciousness. The big question, then, is: who is it who dies?

As Ram Dass says, our bodies "capture our consciousness."[1] We've seen how much this observation resonates with what we know today through neuroscience and psychology about how human beings develop.

Right from the beginning of our existence, our brains are working to make us functional beings in a material environment. They reinforce the limitations they've imposed on our consciousness, the most significant of which is the inhibition of its nonlocal dimension. Most notably, this leads to the development and maintenance of a feeling of identity, singleness, and spatial localization. Gradually, these personalities reduce what we think we are to the narrow confines of our ego.

Being an individual is an adaptive mechanism that quickly becomes a stubborn illusion. The soul slips into a role in order to live an earthly existence, and that role begins to believe in its own existence. Its own psychological dynamics, thought patterns, and convictions spill onto the soul and soak into it, like a pure mountain stream growing muddied. We're blinded by the mud of our individuality. We are afraid and we suffer because we are fish swimming in murky water.

Our earthly life is a chasm of amnesia. But it's also the stage for our soul's experiences. Everything we go through has meaning for our soul, even if that meaning sometimes escapes our understanding. It's all teaching, all part of a path toward harmony.

Our soul had a plan when it arrived.

Whether death comes at the end of a long existence or suddenly, following an accident or illness in the prime of one's life, may not be the personality's choice—but it's always that of the soul. Ram Dass explains:

> The soul itself has an agenda in taking birth as a human being. It has certain work to do and complete while on the earth plane, and it uses the body and personality to carry out this work. When the work is finished, it leaves this plane. The wisest beings with whom I have made contact in this lifetime all assure me that a soul leaves the physical plane neither a moment too early nor a moment too late. Now to us on Earth, who so strongly identify with our own bodies and personalities, this is hard to understand. Because we have usually not listened deeply enough inside ourselves to know differently, we consider duration in life as an asset. We tend to think of the earth plane as the be-all, end-all, and want to make it last as long as possible. However, once one begins to look at life from the soul's point of view, the picture is quite different.[2]

The death of the physical body immediately leads to the release of the ironclad grip of the brain circuitry that underpins our personality's stability and psychological dynamics. But it doesn't necessarily disappear completely.

During the long years of our earthly existence, our personalities take over, like a psychic skin encasing the pure heart of consciousness.

Death does not instantly dissolve decades-old habits, beliefs, and psychological dynamics. I've seen for myself in altered states of consciousness how resistant they are.

The psychospiritual process of disidentification that begins when a change in brain activity is induced, such as during an NDE or a shamanic experience, is identical to what takes place when brain activity stops altogether at the moment of death. *The Tibetan Book of the Dead*, an essential, centuries-old text of Tibetan Buddhism and a "travel guide" to the end of life and the passage into the intermediary state that occurs after physical death, emphasizes this point.[3] In fact, identifying and freeing oneself from the personality's numbing effect on the consciousness is the essential message of this sacred text.

After death, we retain our individuality, in a way. But this individuality can no longer be reduced to the elements of the physical personality we once knew. This isn't necessarily easy for us to perceive right away. It might take a little time for the water to run clear again. *The Tibetan Book of the Dead* urges us not to cling to the earthly identity we left behind.

Even though after death we become different, emancipated, and broader, we are nonetheless naturally inclined to want to hold on to what seems stable. Once the body no longer exists, time no longer exists, and there's no kind of physical support holding us to a familiar point of attachment, the only thing that seems stable is the strength of our psychic identification with our personality.

This is the point when ADCs (after-death communications) take place. In the minutes, hours, and days following our death, our most ardent desire is to come back and tell our loved ones that everything seems to be fine after all. Nothing has changed, and yet everything is different. We're stunned, and for some this might lead to a kind of confusion, but one thing is certain: we are *not dead*, and we want to let them know.

Chögyam Trungpa writes that the reality that appears to us when we first enter death is a form of extrapolation of the human psychological states we have encountered during our lives. Only the intensity of the experience changes. "Bardo experiences are not transformations of your life; they are community," he writes.[4] "Bardo" refers to an "intermediate state," in this case that which follows physical death.

On a psychological level, then, death is a continuation of our earthly journey. Yes, we will exist *individually* after we die, but in the beginning this sensation will remain tied to the personality linked to our physical form and its acquired habits, and we will be susceptible to forces of attachment.

Yet the fact remains that the moment of our death is the beginning of a new adventure—one in which we will be able to rediscover who we *truly* are, beyond the structure of the life we've left behind.

Think about what it's like to leave the theater after being engrossed in a good movie: images linger in our heads for hours, even for days. We've projected ourselves onto a character and seen something of ourselves in them; in fact, that's exactly what we enjoyed. We love to mentally replay a scene or situation so that we can feel the thrill of that projection all over again. But then there's always a strange readjustment period afterward when emerging from the darkness of the cinema. We find ourselves wanting to hold on to the silence so that the moment of transition between the film and reality can last a little longer.

This is exactly what happens when we die.

41

Detachment

The process of gradually detaching from the illusion of our personality can take varying amounts of time. This is normal, a natural consequence of all our psychological dynamics. It is a truth echoed over and over in *The Tibetan Book of the Dead*, and I have personally experienced it time and time again, especially in the Amazon.

If we feel destabilized, it's because we're constantly oscillating between two poles: our attachment to our personality and the awakening of our soul.

Our personality is familiar and reassuring, whereas our soul seems like unknown territory. Humans don't like change, so we're more reluctant to open ourselves up to this forgotten dimension. On one hand, it's present and accessible in a way that it never was during our earthly lives, and it calls to us; on the other, the idea of moving away from familiar shores is unsettling.

Imagine a wild animal who has been locked in a cage. It will need some time to realize that the door has been open for several days, and that it is only its apprehension keeping it inside. But once it recognizes its freedom, it can finally flee.

At first, moments of expansion alternate with moments of retreat. We're swept along by forces over which we don't have much control; we're free, and this much freedom is unnerving to us; our imagination brings to life all our beliefs and desires—and our fears, too.

How this period of adaptation unfolds is directly related to our psychology. On Earth, did we tend to be adaptable when faced with twists and turns? Were we able to accept both big and little changes, all life's unforeseen events? If so, even if we weren't necessarily spiritually inclined, all will proceed smoothly.

On the other hand, if we've neglected to face and work on our whole "system of psychological dynamics," as the psychologist John Welwood puts it,[1] it will be much harder to free ourselves from it after death, even if we've cultivated spiritual openness for much of our lives.

But there's no judgment in this. No condemnation awaiting us on the other side.

During this period of adaptation, we are not alone. We are never alone. Never abandoned. From the very first fragment of a second, they—our ancestors, those who left before us—are waiting. A mother, a father, a husband or wife, a child, grandparents, and other members of our family we've never even met; guides and soulmates appearing like long slivers of light, radiating endless love. They're there to welcome us, to accompany us as we awaken, to help us gradually distance ourselves from our personality. To help rebirth our souls.

As Ram Dass says:

> Death is change, just another one. If you're identified with your soul, death is a snap . . . Death does not have to be treated as an enemy for you to delight in life. Keeping death present in your consciousness as one of the greatest mysteries and as the moment of incredible transformation, imbues this moment

with added richness and energy that otherwise is used up in denial. Death is not an error. It is not a failure. It is taking off a tight shoe.[2]

During this time-outside-time, our psychological and attachment dynamics gradually begin to fade away. We slowly lose our reflexive tendency to identify with our personalities.

There's no set period of time for this process. The individual we were on Earth doesn't disappear once we're secure in our lucidity; it just loses its grip, allowing our fundamental self to (re) appear. The experience is one of the utmost harmony, filled with the ineffable light of the deepest, most profound kind of love.

Once this occurs, our personality must appear to our consciousness just like those strange spheres of life looked to me. We can observe it from a distance, seeing the entirety of a life, every last detail of its memories and experiences.

And we can also see that there are *other* spheres.

Other lives in which our consciousness experiences different incarnations. Not "past lives," but other reflections, set at different times in the history of the material world, both past and *future*.

Consciousness, remember, is nonlocal.

It exists outside of time. From its point of view, all these incarnations are superimposed on top of each other. Therefore, all "our" lives are taking place, from the point of view of our consciousness, *at the same time.* It's like how Earth's moon is reflected over and over in each puddle of rainwater. "Reincarnation" doesn't mean that our personality had "past lives"; it means that our consciousness is watching several films at the same time.

It can reimmerse itself in one, temporarily reentering a sphere, without risk of becoming trapped. It can reintegrate what is now no more than a four-dimensional costume, taking up an identity again not to drown in it but to use it, for example, to visit loved ones on Earth—perhaps to send a "sign" on an important date, or when those loved ones consult a medium. Perhaps these spheres are even vortexes, tunnels linking our earthly world to that of the soul.

That kind of temporary reimmersion takes effort for a soul that has once again expanded into nonlocal reality. It requires returning to time and matter, becoming subject once more to earthly constraints so that it can be perceptible to those who are incarnated. It means slipping into the wetsuit once more, even though it's tight, uncomfortable, and anesthetizing.

My shamanic experiences have helped me understand the effort it takes to return to the physical world once you've rediscovered spiritual reality.

Even communication is complex—having to go back to using words and concepts when we're coming from a place of absolute knowledge and harmony, a place in which consciousnesses are so clear to and for each other that they can communicate instantly and nonverbally.

That's one of the things that struck me most when I contacted your grandfather after his death through mediums.[3] It was indisputable to me that he was there during each séance, but I could tell—without being able to explain it—that he was *different* from the man he had been, and most of all, that it hadn't been easy for him to come. I understand much more now what it must have taken for him and Thomas to show up in my physical vicinity.

And I understand that for years, I kept asking them to come visit me, not knowing that a part of me was *already* in their world.

If our fundamental consciousness is not subject to time and space, that means it's already there, at this very moment, in the world of the "dead."

A part of us is already outside time. This means that as we live on Earth, our fundamental consciousnesses are not in a separate place. They're in the *same* place. In nonlocal space. There are no separate worlds for a consciousness; they're all in the same reality. Even in our earthly incarnations, blinded by our personalities, we're still connected to this nonlocal dimension, as well as to the rest of the world—all the other beings who inhabit it. We are all connected, like countless grains of sand on an immense beach.

Before my shamanic journeys, I was in thrall to my personality, and I considered the material world the center of my reality. I wanted my brother and my father to *come back*, to be able to see them manifesting in the material world. I didn't know that my soul was already in their presence, and that those of my father and Thomas were, paradoxically, more accessible than before—now that they were no longer prisoners of their personalities.

I clung to the image I had of them. I believed that the love that connected us was the same one that we'd experienced on Earth: love between two brothers, and love between a father and son. I thought that what bound us together couldn't go beyond what our personalities had developed and shared for decades.

I didn't know that we were connected by a much greater love.

One that is now free from the constraints of human attachment. "The soul is not limited by human attached love because it knows and is joined to others by what is sometimes called the love that surpasseth understanding. It is conscious or spiritual love," explains Ram Dass.[4] This true love is not affected by death: "That love is not vulnerable to time or changes in form. Only when your mind will be quiet enough will your heart give you the reassurance that you seek that the essence of the love is still very much with you."[5]

Paradoxically, the love that unites souls—our own with those of our disembodied loved ones—really is unconditional. A peaceful heart will be able to feel it.

Thomas's death, followed by that of my father, pushed me to grow spiritually. Year after year, this intuition grows stronger; every day, it gives me a little more strength to live, and most importantly, even more desire to let in the love I'm surrounded by. I can often feel it humming deep in my heart. The heart is the gateway to the soul, and love a bridge of energy between the material and spiritual worlds.

Life is an invitation to seek out our spiritual component, the dimension in us that *knows*. Reconnecting to our fundamental consciousness also means reconnecting with the loved ones whom we'd believed *gone*.

When the ego disappears, souls can meet. For souls, there are no borders. The billions of reflections of consciousness that appear in all the people and sentient beings in our material world—and probably in an infinite number of others—are all connected.

We can feel it, sometimes. In moments of joy, for example, when we can let go, when the ego spontaneously steps aside, when little parcels of spiritual love come to hold us in their gentle embrace.

The beauty of a landscape, a smile, a fleeting moment, a glance: anything that takes the ego by surprise, throwing it off balance, will allow our soul to reemerge.

42

Keeping an Open Connection with Our Souls

During all those long years of investigation, through countless journeys and experiences, I sought to understand death—and in the end, what turned out to be essential was life. Is that such a surprise? Death is a mirror, because it upends what we think we are. We believe ourselves to be stable individuals with well-established traits and characteristics, but as "death" shows us, that's merely a mask.

We go through life unaware of who we really are. We cling to the mirage of the character we've constructed for ourselves, terrified at the thought of it disappearing one day.

But we *are not* that character. Our identity is only a role we play.

Constructed amid urgency and fear as reactions to the countless events of our lives, these masks reflect our past and camouflage our inner divisions. By definition, they have no fundamental coherence; ultimately, they're a kind of reactive mishmash. The different parts of our identity are always fighting with each other, turning our unconscious into a war zone. It's an exhausting dynamic that consumes all our energy and keeps us in a state of confusion.

And yet this character stubbornly believes that they're in control of their life. They're convinced that they're aware of the entirety of their being, not knowing that 90 percent of what drives them eludes their grasp, and that various unconscious forces are the ones really driving the show. To compensate for our confusion, we live completely hypnotized by the noise of our thoughts, the sole aim of which is to maintain the apparent cohesion of the "role" we're playing.

We keep going around and around just like this, always asking the wrong questions. But life never answers the wrong questions.

We devote a lot of energy to feeding this illusion. We're always battling to get rid of anything that might upset the precarious balance we've patiently established.

And so we live a disconnected, exhausted life, drifting further and further away from the wisdom of our soul without understanding the root causes of this slow collapse. More and more terrified at the idea of losing control. Of dying. But death is merely the death of the mask. The end of a role.

Wouldn't it be useful to read the script before the film ends?

In order to do this, we have to begin by accepting a kind of vulnerability. To be vulnerable is to accept being unmasked. To give ourselves the possibility of deconstructing the character that we've created in response to everything that's happened in our past. To be vulnerable is to allow the illusion that our brains cling on to so resolutely to begin to fade away. Only the truth, with the lucidity that comes along with it, will set us free. Knowing who we really are. This means uncovering the sources of our beliefs, our emotions, and the reactions they elicited, all of which shaped us. Seeing them, with benevolence and detachment, for what they are—adaptive survival mechanisms—without letting them spark a chain reaction.

Knowing ourselves is the beginning of wisdom.

But how can we be vulnerable without falling apart?

The body knows. Our soul knows. Life knows. An immensely vast love: that's what life is. Our body, our soul, and life are always trying to help us. They're constantly sending us messages, but we don't know how to listen to them. So they repeat them again and again, in our body, in our existence. Everything is repetition until we finally hear the message. There's a guide inside us, all the time. Its voice is silenced by our thoughts and our will to control, by the idea that if we think hard enough we'll be able to "find the answers ourselves," when in fact we're just endlessly going over the same mental patterns.

Being vulnerable means putting ourselves in a position where we can listen to what's whispering inside us, without trying to solve anything, without exhausting ourselves in the attempt to "find a solution" by "thinking." For the more you think about a solution, the less you listen.

All the answers are within us, in a dimension of our eternal soul, our pure consciousness. It's just waiting for our attention. Not analysis, not judgment, not resistance; just listening.

The real journey begins where you are now, not where you'd like to be.

How can we be vulnerable without falling apart?

As you can see, I clearly chose the black diamond run. It could have easily landed me in a crevasse. In fact, it nearly did. I spent all these years working with psychedelics because I thought I needed to smash down the barriers of my mind, given how many secrets it hid from me and how much energy it spent trying to "protect" me.

I used psychoactive substances to "break down the doors," with all the resulting psychological destabilization; luckily, I was accompanied by guides. The substances also helped me overcome the stubborn resistance of my critical mind in order to access the expanded dimensions of consciousness, at a point in my journey when this felt essential to convincing the journalist in me that these spaces were real. Taking these powerful "sacred medicines" seemed like the only rational path to follow, so that there would be no more doubt in my mind as to the reality of my subjective encounters with the spiritual dimensions of existence.

For a long time, the question of how to emotionally integrate whatever I discovered was far less important. My quest had but one goal, and it required all my mental strength: acquiring an intellectual understanding of the reality of the spiritual dimensions of consciousness.

It took time—fifteen years—and I trust it's not over yet!

Paradoxically, the most important discovery was that our soul is *always* present within us. At every moment. Our nonlocal consciousness is veiled, but it's always there.

During those years, I increased the dosage and varied the substances in order to get through a set of doors that, in a way, existed only because I myself had kept them closed. As we've seen, there are neurological and psychological reasons for that, but nonetheless we are all able to do something about it.

I sought to enter the world of the dead for a long time, to see Thomas and then your grandfather, inducing powerfully altered states of consciousness in order to access my extrasensory abilities, without realizing something essential: they can also be the result of an inner spiritual practice.

There are other, less radical techniques we can use to pry open cracks in our cognitive shell. They require an ability to "let go" that I didn't think I had. In reality, I was blocking myself.

This ability can be cultivated through various training methods, as though it were a muscle. I'm focusing on those methods now that I've come to understand that we don't need psychoactive substances to connect to the resources of our consciousness and let our souls unfold; we can do so simply by developing our natural dispositions.

This approach is more integrative. And because it acts on all the different dimensions of our being—mental, emotional, and energetic—it also lasts longer.

Psychedelic substances lift the veil. They allow us to experience our fundamental consciousness for a few moments, but then we return. Invariably, our brain goes back to its normal patterns.

We might undergo the most transcendent experience imaginable, disconnecting from our ego completely; it will always be temporary. Even if we grow from the experience, if we're content to just repeat it over and over, then—as Welwood explains—we run the risk of inevitably returning to the same starting point. The intensity of all those spiritual experiences might barely change our personality structure and our neural networks, which will remain conditioned, systematically returning to their usual tendencies.[1]

This offers us no choice other than to start over again and again. It's like being isolated on an island, condemned to need a boat to reach other shores, without suspecting that it's also possible to learn to swim.

As I mentioned earlier: our default mode network, which solidifies the prison of our ego, can be quieted both through psychedelic substances and through meditation, both of which considerably reduce its activity.[2] Neurologist Steven Laureys confirms this: "Experienced meditators seem to have different and more reduced activity in this network."[3]

Rather than artificially modifying our neural connectivity for a few hours before it "returns to normal," a regular meditation practice helps us build new networks, enabling us to loosen the grip of the default mode network.

Meditation is a learning process that draws on neuroplasticity. Only twenty years ago we thought that the brain contained all the neurons it would ever have at birth, and that those neurons began to decrease in number at around eighteen years of age. We know now that that's not the case; our brains are constantly evolving in reaction to our experiences, and they produce neurons throughout our lives. Our brains can be trained, and we can change how they function.

Meditation creates new networks and allows others to atrophy. By training our brains to be less susceptible to the influence of survival and anticipatory brain networks, we make it possible to develop a more direct relationship with our soul, our consciousness, our spiritual essence.

Suddenly, we know how to swim.

A meditation practice enables our pure consciousness to remain more present in our day-to-day lives, rather than only during extraordinary experiences, such as when we've taken psychedelics.

It's more subtle, and requires us to be better at letting go, but isn't that ultimately the heart of a spiritual practice that *transforms* us profoundly?

Living a balanced life in our world requires us to undergo a long period of psychological and physiological adaptation, from our childhood into adulthood. The default mode network is part of this adaptation. Putting it to sleep artificially when we haven't developed other adaptative strategies in parallel is destabilizing, and reactivating it at the end of a psychedelic experience can be brutal. I experienced this for myself upon returning to France from the Amazon, as I mentioned; I felt so fragile and awkward, and I immediately wanted to flee this too-difficult world again, as if I'd become less suited for existence within it.

As Chris Bache says, sacred medicines are a path of *temporary immersion*, in contrast to what he refers to as the "path of meditation":

> Where meditation is a path of self-clarification that allows the layers of the mind to open gradually, the sacred medicine path cultivates intense but temporary surges of awareness. By amplifying our present awareness, the medicine path opens us more quickly to a deeper communion with the universe. This is a good thing, a healing thing, but it can also be a tricky thing because it's easy to overestimate the staying power of these dramatic exercises . . . and underestimate the challenge of achieving more stable *plateau experiences*.[4]

Achieving more stable experiences means allowing our soul's inner wisdom to express itself in our incarnate life, helping us to become balanced and peaceful beings in a more permanent way, even in a world that's neither.

"The Ego is merely a fragment of who we are," says the spiritual teacher Ram Dass.[5] But it's also our psychic backbone in this world.

Our personality, that "me" that's been forming since our conception through the conditioning we've received throughout our lives, shouldn't be "thrown away" on the pretext that it covers up and inhibits our essential self. It just shouldn't be so predominant.

Meditation makes this possible.

Meditation is not just an anti-stress technique, the way it's sometimes presented to us in the West. It's a gateway to higher levels of consciousness. As Tibetan master Yongey Mingyur Rinpoche says, "The essence of meditation is awareness. Joy, clarity, inner peace—these are the by-products, but they are not the essence of meditation itself, and the more we strive for them, the more the mind constricts around ideas of what *should* happen."[6] And this can lead to frustration and discouragement.

Meditation is not psychotherapy or self-help. It's a pathway to the soul. A spiritual practice by definition.

Like I mentioned before, Luna, just fifteen minutes a day is already an immense gift for you to give yourself. With fifteen minutes a day, you can open a precious little window for your soul to peer through and begin whispering things in your ear.

Beautiful, useful things.

The psychiatrist Christophe André has told me that he's often experienced this. "Fairly often during my mindfulness meditation exercises, I begin to feel as though I'm dissolving into the environment. After a while, I enter a state in which I'm very strongly connected to, almost identifying with, my surroundings—the bird singing, the breeze passing by."[7]

If there's one thing I've learned from my fifteen years of investigation and experience, Luna, it's this: our soul is *always* present within us. And there are so many paths leading to it. Meditation, yoga, shamanism . . . we have a thousand ways to unveil it. A thousand ways to dissolve the resistance that separates us from ourselves, others, and the worlds where spirits live.

I hope I've shown you by now that science and spirituality are not incompatible. Quite the opposite: these two ways of questioning the world complement and enrich each other.

Science enabled me to commit to shamanism in an enlightened way, and it gave me essential frameworks through which to integrate what I discovered. Similarly, my experiments with altered states of consciousness allowed me to experience nonlocal consciousness for myself, and understand things I never would have been able to learn otherwise.

One path draws on the brain and its immense capacities for reasoning and objectification. The other one, the path of the heart, grants us access to a form of intuitive intelligence.

Both paths have the same goal: to gain knowledge about who we really are and the profound nature of the world we live in. Combining the two allows us to transform this knowledge from an abstract intellectual understanding to a life force, a path to fulfilment that integrates all the dimensions of our being.

It's your turn now, Luna. There is an immeasurable treasure within you. A source of harmony, love, and light: your soul. It's there, right now, waiting patiently for you. It has so many things to tell you . . .

Epilogue

It's a day like any other. I'm sitting with my eyes closed. I've taken a short break from what I was doing so that I can take time for myself, immerse myself in the present moment. I breathe calmly, trying to just feel, to not grab hold of the thoughts that come and go. Just feel what's happening in my body.

I enter into myself, into those sensations. I visualize myself as a small sphere the size of a tennis ball. Then I see the ball turn to liquid and spill onto the ground, where it's absorbed. Feel, feel what's happening. I am the water entering the earth. No "wanting," no "deciding"; my consciousness is there, if I can let go. I must let go of my resistance, have trust, soothe my mind's tendency to want to control. Breathe, feel. Enter into myself. No thinking about what I have to do.

There's a feeling of heaviness in my belly.

A pressure, right around my pelvis. I go deeper into the sensation. I can feel an enormous ball in my stomach. I breathe. It turns into a kind of large mango pit. A pit that gets bigger and bigger until it's the size of my whole torso. I feel, I trust.

Then the pit changes. It superimposes itself on my body and becomes less solid, less material, like a cloud of filaments of energy that soon envelops my whole being. It grows larger and larger until it enters an ocean.

I become the ocean. I am a particle of consciousness nestled within a dark blue, infinite space.

The experience becomes more intense. I surrender myself to it, and it becomes just as strong as my high-dosage LSD sessions, though I haven't taken anything at all. I'm just sitting, and by breathing, I've managed to stay completely centered on what I'm feeling. I can't believe it's possible to have such an intense experience without any substances. Just by letting go entirely.

I breathe more and more slowly, until my breath becomes almost imperceptible. I don't want to block the experience by contracting a single muscle. The moment is magical, powerful, extraordinary. I am the ocean. I'm gliding through its endless waters. I am the water. The ocean. Then all the earth's oceans. Then the whole earth. And now I'm moving away from it at a phenomenal speed, the blue planet growing smaller and smaller. I pass through the sun, and for a second it dazzles me, a flash causing me to *actually* jump, and then I'm already on the other side. I'm getting bigger and bigger until I become the universe, the entire cosmos.

Then, amid this absolute infinity, I have the feeling that I'm taking the form of a kind of oblong, dark blue soap bubble. No face, no limbs, just a translucent membrane the size of the entire universe. I am the entire universe.

Suddenly, there are two other identical shapes. Two other universes. Two oblong shapes, translucent and dark blue. To my left, a little above me. We are three infinite, divine beings in an infinite cosmos. It's incredibly intense, and totally psychedelic.

Faceless, eyeless, shapeless.

Two other universes with me.

And all at once I'm overcome by an immense emotion. An

emotion that bursts open in my belly, to the point where I'm nearly swept away by tears. It's a staggering feeling of tenderness and love. The other universes are Papa and Thomas. Papa in front, Thomas a little behind. We're bathed in love. I feel that we could merge, and that it would be impossible to describe. That "my" divine universe and Papa's could become one. The moment is powerful. Incredible. Time has stopped, my breathing suspended. I remain silent in front of Papa and Thomas, waiting for something. My eyes closed, between two worlds, without really knowing what to do. "What to do." There goes my mind again, with its reflex of "thinking" that I have to "do something." Yet the experience is so powerful. So moving, so intense.

It's Papa, for real.

I feel an immense emotion as soon as our membranes touch. Would fusion be an indescribable explosion? A point of non-return? Too much emotion? Too much beauty, power, infinity. So all we do is brush against each other, and that alone is enormous. Extraordinary. Incredibly strong. Incredibly emotional.

I open my eyes again. Here I am, in my familiar universe, at home. I'm overwhelmed by how easy it was for this crazy, unexpected experience to sweep me away. All I did was sit down, breathe, and enter into myself without grabbing hold of any thoughts.

We don't need anything but love to open the door. We just need to stop trying to control everything.

What lives in us cannot die.

Notes

3: HOW I BEGAN TO INVESTIGATE DEATH

1. Bruce Greyson, MD, *Après* (Guy Trédaniel, 2021).
2. Steven Laureys, *Un si brillant cerveau* (Odile Jacob, 2015), 146.
3. Pim van Lommel, Ruud van Wees, Vincent Meyers, and Ingrid Elfferich, "Near-Death Experience in Survivors of Cardiac Arrest: A Prospective Study in the Netherlands," *The Lancet* 358, no. 9298 (2001): 2039–45.

4: BRAIN DEATH AND CLINICAL DEATH

1. J. W. de Vries, P. F. Bakker, G. H. Visser, J. C. Diephuis, and A. C. Van Huffelen, "Changes in Cerebral Oxygen Uptake and Cerebral Electrical Activity during Defibrillation Threshold Testing," *Anesthesia & Analgesia* 87, no. 1 (July 1998): 16–20; T. J. Losasso, D. A. Muzzi, F. B. Meyer, and F. W. Sharbrough, "Electroencephalographic Monitoring of Cerebral Function during Asystole and Successful Cardiopulmonary Resuscitation," *Anesthesia & Analgesia* 75, no. 6 (December 1992): 1021–24; H. L. Clute and W. J. Levy, "Electroencephalographic Changes during Brief Cardiac Arrest in Humans," *Anesthesiology* 73, no. 5 (November 1990): 821–25.
2. Steven Laureys, "Death, Unconsciousness and the Brain," *Nature Reviews Neuroscience* 6 (November 2005): 899–909.
3. Titus Rivas, Anny Dirven, and Rudolf Smit, *The Self Does Not Die* (IANDS Publications, 2016).

5: WHAT DO WE KNOW ABOUT CONSCIOUSNESS?

1. "125 Questions: What Don't We Know?," *Science* 309 (July 2005): 79.
2. Christoph Koch, *Consciousness: Confessions of a Romantic Reductionist* (Cambridge, MA: MIT Press, 2012), 119.
3. David Chalmers, *L'Esprit conscient* (Ithaque, 2010).
4. Bernardo Kastrup, *Why Materialism Is Baloney* (Iff Books, 2014), 17.
5. Kastrup, *Why Materialism Is Baloney*, 17.

6. J. M. Holden, "Veridical Perception in Near-Death Experiences," in J. M. Holden, B. Greyson, and D. James, eds., *The Handbook of Near-Death Experiences: Thirty Years of Investigation* (Praeger/ABC-CLIO, 2009), 185–211.
7. Stéphane Allix, *Un fantôme sur le divan* (Albin Michel, 2022).

6: IMPOSSIBLE EXPERIENCES

1. Pim van Lommel, Ruud Van Wees, Vincent Meyers, Ingrid Elfferich, "Near-Death Experience in Survivors of Cardiac Arrest: A Prospective Study in the Netherlands," *The Lancet* 358, no. 9298 (2001): 2041.
2. Pim van Lommel, *Consciousness Beyond Life* (New York: HarperOne, 2010), 20–21.
3. Titus Rivas, Anny Dirven, and Rudolf Smit, *The Self Does Not Die* (IANDS Publications, 2016); Laurin Bellg, *Near Death in the ICU* (Sloan Press, 2016).
4. Steven Laureys, *Un si brillant cerveau* (Odile Jacob, 2015), 167.
5. Edward F. Kelly and Emily Williams Kelly, *Irreducible Mind* (Rowman & Littlefield, 2007), 418.
6. George G. Ritchie and Elizabeth Sherrill, *Return from Tomorrow* (Old Tappan, NJ: F.H. Revell, 1978).
7. van Lommel, *Consciousness Beyond Life*, 156.
8. J. W. de Vries, P. F. Bakker, G. H. Visser, J. C. Diephuis, and A. C. Van Huffelen, "Changes in Cerebral Oxygen Uptake and Cerebral Electrical Activity during Defibrillation Threshold Testing," *Anesthesia & Analgesia* 87, no. 1 (July 1998): 16–20; T. J. Losasso, D. A. Muzzi, F. B. Meyer, and F. W. Sharbrough, "Electroencephalographic Monitoring of Cerebral Function during Asystole and Successful Cardiopulmonary Resuscitation," *Anesthesia & Analgesia* 75, no. 6 (December 1992): 1021–24; H. L. Clute and W. J. Levy, "Electroencephalographic Changes during Brief Cardiac Arrest in Humans," *Anesthesiology* 73, no. 5 (November 1990): 821–25.

7: DEATH IN REAL TIME

1. *Sciences et Avenir* 873 (November 2019).
2. J. P. Dreier et al., "Terminal Spreading Depolarization and Electrical Silence in Death of Human Cerebral Cortex," *Annals of Neurology* 83, no. 2 (February 2018): 295–310.
3. *Sciences et Avenir* 873 (November 2019): 37.
4. D. Lustbader et al., "Second Brain Death Examination May Negatively Affect Organ Donation," *Neurology* 76, no. 2 (January 11, 2011): 119–24.

8: CONTINUITY OF CONSCIOUSNESS

1. J. M. Holden, "Veridical Perception in Near-Death Experiences," in J. M. Holden, B. Greyson, and D. James, eds., *The Handbook of Near-Death Experiences: Thirty Years of Investigation* (Praeger/ABC-CLIO, 2009), 185–211; Kenneth Ring and Madelaine Lawrence, "Further Evidence for Veridical Perception during Near-Death Experiences," *Journal of Near-Death Studies* 11, no. 4 (June 1993): 223–29.
2. Stéphane Allix, *Un fantôme sur le divan* (Albin Michel, 2022).

3. Pim van Lommel, *Consciousness Beyond Life* (New York: HarperOne, 2010), 33.
4. Bruce Greyson, "Seeing Dead People Not Known to Have Died: 'Peak in Darien' Experiences," *Anthropology and Humanism* 35, no. 2 (2010): 159–71.

9: THE UNNERVING PHENOMENON OF "TERMINAL LUCIDITY"

1. M. Nahm, "Terminal Lucidity," article in the Psi Encyclopedia online, Society for Psychical Research, accessed 2017, http://psi-encyclopedia.spr.ac.uk/articles/terminal-lucidity; M. Nahm, "Terminale Geistesklarheit und andere Rätsel des menschlichen Bewusstseins," in A. Serwaty and J. Nicolay, eds., *Nahtoderfahrung und Bewusstseinsforschung* (Goch: Santiago, 2013), 78–134; M. Nahm and E. Haraldsson, "Geistige Klarheit von Psychisch Kranken Menschen Kurz vor dem Tod," *Tattva Viveka* 40 (2009): 70–75; M. Nahm, "Terminal Lucidity in People with Mental Illness and Other Mental Disability: An Overview and Implications for Possible Explanatory Models," *Journal of Near-Death Studies* 28 (2009): 87–106.
2. M. Nahm, B. Greyson, E. W. Kelly, and E. Haraldsson, "Terminal Lucidity: A Review and a Case Collection," *Archives of Gerontology and Geriatrics* 55 (2012): 138–42; M. Nahm and B. Greyson, "The Death of Anna Katharina Ehmer: A Case Study in Terminal Lucidity," *Omega* 68 (2013): 77–87; G. A. Mashour et al., "Paradoxical Lucidity: A Potential Paradigm Shift for the Neurobiology and Treatment of Severe Dementias," *Alzheimer's & Dementia* 15, no. 8 (August 2019): 1107–14; M. Nahm and B. Greyson, "Terminal Lucidity in Patients with Chronic Schizophrenia and Dementia: A Survey of the Literature," *Journal of Nervous and Mental Disease* 197 (2009): 942–44.
3. M. Nahm, "Terminal Lucidity in People with Mental Illness and Other Mental Disability: An Overview and Implications for Possible Explanatory Models," *Journal of Near-Death Studies* 28 (2009): 87–106.
4. M. Nahm and B. Greyson, "Terminal Lucidity in Patients with Chronic Schizophrenia and Dementia: A Survey of the Literature," *Journal of Nervous and Mental Disease* 197 (2009): 942–44.
5. S. Brayne, H. Lovelace, and P. Fenwick, "End-of-life Experiences and the Dying Process in a Gloucestershire Nursing Home as Reported by Nurses and Care Assistants," *American Journal of Hospice and Palliative Medicine* 25 (2008): 195–206.
6. M. Nahm et al., "Terminal Lucidity: A Review and a Case Collection," *Archives of Gerontology and Geriatrics* (2011), https://doi.org/10.1016/j.archger.2011.06.031.
7. M. Nahm and B. Greyson, "Terminal Lucidity in Patients with Chronic Schizophrenia and Dementia: A Survey of the Literature," *Journal of Nervous and Mental Disease*, 197 (2009): 942–44.
8. G. A. Mashour et al., "Paradoxical Lucidity: A Potential Paradigm Shift for the Neurobiology and Treatment of Severe Dementias," *Alzheimer's & Dementia*, 15, no. 8 (August 2019): 1107–14.

10: GHOSTS IN THE HOSPITAL

1. Imants Barušs and Julia Mossbridge, *Transcendent Mind* (American Psychological Association, 2017), 179.

2. Barušs and Mossbridge, *Transcendent Mind*, 179.
3. Eben Alexander, *Proof of Heaven: A Neurosurgeon's Journey into the Afterlife* (Simon & Schuster, 2012).
4. Mark Gober, *An End to Upside Down Thinking* (Waterside Productions, 2018).

11: AN UNEXPECTED VISIT

1. Evelyn Elsaesser, *Contacts spontanés avec un défunt: Une enquête scientifique atteste la réalité des VSCD* (Exergue, 2021).
2. Stéphane Allix, *Après* (Le Livre de Poche, 2020).
3. Allix, *Après.*

12: BEGINNING MY JOURNEY WITH AMAZONIAN SHAMANS

1. The subject of my first book: Stéphane Allix, *La petite cuillère de schéhérazade* (Ramsay, 1998).
2. G. Thomas, P. Lucas, N. R. Capler, K. W. Tupper, and G. Martin, "Ayahuasca-Assisted Therapy for Addiction: Results from a Preliminary Observational Study in Canada," *Current Drug Abuse Reviews* 6, no. 1 (March 2013): 30–42.

14: LEARNING TO "SEE"

1. Aldous Huxley, *The Doors of Perception* (Harper & Row, 1954).
2. William Blake, *The Marriage of Heaven and Hell*, https://www.gutenberg.org/files/45315/45315-h/45315-h.htm.
3. Matthieu Ricard and Wolf Singer, *Beyond the Self* (Cambridge, MA: MIT Press, 2017), 75.

15: HE WAS LOOKING AT ME SILENTLY . . .

1. Natacha Calestrémé, "Mon initiation au rituel de l'ayahuasca, plante magique," *Geo* 366 (August 2009).
2. Stéphane Allix, *Lorsque j'étais quelqu'un d'autre* (Le Livre de Poche, 2019).
3. Ram Dass, *Still Here* (New York: Riverhead, 2000), 50.

16: THE UNCONSCIOUS AND ITS GHOSTS

1. John Welwood, *Toward a Psychology of Awakening* (Boston: Shambhala, 2000), 207.
2. Welwood, *Toward a Psychology of Awakening*, 212.
3. Welwood, *Toward a Psychology of Awakening,* 97.

18: THE MOST IMPORTANT MAN IN MY LIFE

1. Yongey Mingyur Rinpoche with Helen Tworkov, *In Love with the World: A Monk's Journey Through the Bardos of Living and Dying* (New York: Spiegel & Grau, 2019), 205.
2. Ram Dass, *Still Here* (New York: Riverhead, 2000), 159–60.
3. Stéphane Allix, *Le test* (Le Livre de Poche, 2018).

19: MEDIUMS

1. Stéphane Allix, *Un fantôme sur le divan* (Albin Michel, 2022), 209.
2. Stéphane Allix, *La mort n'est pas une terre étrangère* (Le Livre de Poche, 2022).
3. Julie Beischel, *Médiumnité. Quand la science confirme* (Guy Trédaniel, 2021).
4. J. Beischel and G. E. Schwartz, "Anomalous Information Reception by Research Mediums Demonstrated Using a Novel Triple-Blind Protocol," *Explore* (New York) 3, no. 1 (January–February 2007): 23–27; Emily Williams Kelly, PhD, and Dianne Arcangel, MA, "An Investigation of Mediums Who Claim to Give Information About Deceased Persons," *Journal of Nervous and Mental Disease* 199, no. 1 (January 2011).
5. *INREES TV*, *Beyond*, season 6, episode 1.
6. J. Beischel, M. Boccuzzi, M. Biuso, and A. J. Rock, "Anomalous Information Reception by Research Mediums Under Blinded Conditions II: Replication and Extension," *Explore* (New York) 2 (March–April 2015): 136–42.
7. J. Beischel, C. Mosher, and M. Boccuzzi, "Quantitative and Qualitative Analyses of Mediumistic and Psychic Experiences," *Threshold: Journal of Interdisciplinary Consciousness Studies* 1, no. 2 (2017): 51–91.
8. Stéphane Allix, *Le test* (Le Livre de Poche, 2018).

22: A SOLITARY EXPERIENCE

1. Chögyam Trungpa, *The Myth of Freedom and the Way of Meditation* (Boulder, CO: Shambhala, 1976), 24.
2. Ram Dass, *Still Here* (New York: Riverhead, 2000), 134.
3. Dass, *Still Here*, 30.

23: THE PSYCHEDELIC REVOLUTION

1. Multidisciplinary Association for Psychedelic Studies (MAPS), "Our Research," https://maps.org/advancing-research/.
2. Stanislav Grof, *The Way of the Psychonaut,* vol. 1 (Multidisciplinary Association for Psychedelic Studies, 2019), 43.
3. Michael Pollan, *How to Change Your Mind* (Penguin Press, 2018), 8.
4. Grof, *The Way of the Psychonaut*, 43.
5. Grof, *The Way of the Psychonaut*, 41.
6. R. R. Griffiths, W. A. Richards, U. McCann, and R. Jesse, "Psilocybin Can Occasion Mystical-Type Experiences Having Substantial and Sustained Personal Meaning and Spiritual Significance," *Psychopharmacology* 187, no. 3 (August 2006): 268–283; discussion 284–92.
7. "Steven Laureys Discusses His Near-Death Experiment," *Sciences et Avenir*, accessed at https://www.sciencesetavenir.fr/sante/cerveau-et-psy/steven-laureys-j-ai-tente-de-vivre-moi-meme-une-experience-de-mort-imminente-107762.
8. Steven Laureys, interview with the author.
9. R. L. Carhart-Harris, D. Erritzoe, T. Williams, J. M. Stone, L. J. Reed, A. Colasanti, R. J. Tyacke, R. Leech, A. L. Malizia, K. Murphy, P. Hobden, J. Evans, A. Feilding, R. G. Wise, and D. J. Nutt, "Neural Correlates of the Psychedelic

State as Determined by fMRI Studies with Psilocybin," *Proceedings of the National Academy of Sciences of the United States of America* 109, no. 6 (February 7, 2012): 2138–43.

10. Pollan, *How to Change Your Mind*, 300–301.
11. R. L. Carhart-Harris, S. Muthukumaraswamy, L. Roseman, M. Kaelen, W. Droog, K. Murphy, E. Tagliazucchi, E. E. Schenberg, T. Nest, C. Orban, R. Leech, L. T. Williams, T. M. Williams, M. Bolstridge, B. Sessa, J. McGonigle, M. I. Sereno, D. Nichols, P. J. Hellyer, P. Hobden, J. Evans, K. D. Singh, R. G. Wise, H. V. Curran, A. Feilding, and D. J. Nutt, "Neural Correlates of the LSD Experience Revealed by Multimodal Neuroimaging," *Proceedings of the National Academy of Sciences of the United States of America* 113, no. 17 (April 26, 2016): 4853–58; R. L. Carhart-Harris et al., "Neural Correlates of the Psychedelic State as Determined by fMRI Studies with Psilocybin," 2138–43.
12. V. Bonhomme, A. Vanhaudenhuyse, A. Demertzi, M. A. Bruno, O. Jaquet, M. A. Bahri, A. Plenevaux, M. Boly, P. Boveroux, A. Soddu, J. F. Brichant, P. Maquet, and S. Laureys, "Resting-State Network-Specific Breakdown of Functional Connectivity during Ketamine Alteration of Consciousness in Volunteers," *Anesthesiology* 125, no. 5 (November 2016): 873–88; F. Palhano-Fontes, K. C. Andrade, L. F. Tofoli, A. C. Santos, J. A. Crippa, J. E. Hallak, S. Ribeiro, and D. B. de Araujo, "The Psychedelic State Induced by Ayahuasca Modulates the Activity and Connectivity of the Default Mode Network," *PLoS One* 10, no. 2 (February 18, 2015): e0118143; C. Timmermann, L. Roseman, M. Schartner, R. Milliere, L.T.J. Williams, D. Erritzoe, S. Muthukumaraswamy, M. Ashton, A. Bendrioua, O. Kaur, S. Turton, M. M. Nour, C. M. Day, R. Leech, D. J. Nutt, and R. L. Carhart-Harris, "Neural Correlates of the DMT Experience Assessed with Multivariate EEG," *Scientific Reports* 9, no. 1 (November 19, 2019): 16324.
13. Natalie Sudman, *Application of Impossible Things: A Near Death Experience in Iraq* (Ozark Mountain Publishing, 2012).
14. J. A. Brefczynski-Lewis, A. Lutz, H. S. Schaefer, D. B. Levinson, and R. J. Davidson, "Neural Correlates of Attentional Expertise in Long-Term Meditation Practitioners," *Proceedings of the National Academy of Sciences of the United States of America* 104, no. 27 (July 2007): 11483–88; K. A. Garrison, T. A. Zeffiro, D. Scheinost, R. T. Constable, and J. A. Brewer, "Meditation Leads to Reduced Default Mode Network Activity Beyond an Active Task," *Cognitive, Affective & Behavioral Neuroscience* 15, no. 3 (2015): 712–20.
15. Pollan, *How to Change Your Mind*, 390–91.

25: AN OUT-OF-BODY JOURNEY

1. Sylvie Dethiollaz and Claude Charles Fourrier, *Voyage aux confins de la conscience* (Guy Trédaniel, 2016).
2. iRiS. "iRiS, School of Intuition." https://www.iris-ic.com/.
3. Alexis Champion and Marie-Estelle Couval, *Développez votre intuition: La méthode efficace pour éclairer votre vie* (Leduc, 2018).

26: "PSYCHICS" AT THE WHITE HOUSE

1. Reuters, "Carter Says Psychic Found Lost Plane for CIA," September 20, 1995.
2. Joseph McMoneagle, *The Stargate Chronicles: Memoirs of a Psychic Spy* (Hampton Roads Publishing Company Inc., 2000), 115.
3. Mark Gober, *An End to Upside Down Thinking* (Waterside Press, 2018), 66.

27: THE STARGATE PROJECT

1. Kenneth A. Kress, "Central Intelligence Agency (CIA), McLean, VA. Parapsychology in Intelligence: A Personal Review and Conclusions," originally published in the winter 1977 issue of *Studies in Intelligence*, the CIA's classified internal publication, *Journal of Scientific Exploration* 13, no. 1 (1999): 69–85.
2. Kress, "Central Intelligence Agency," 69–85.
3. Joseph McMoneagle, *The Stargate Chronicles: Memoirs of a Psychic Spy* (Hampton Roads Publishing Company Inc., 2000), 72.
4. McMoneagle, *The Stargate Chronicles*, 93.
5. McMoneagle, *The Stargate Chronicles*, 109–113.

28: REMOTE VIEWING DISCOVERIES

1. Joseph McMoneagle, *The Stargate Chronicles: Memoirs of a Psychic Spy* (Hampton Roads Publishing Company Inc., 2000), 109–113.
2. Jessica Utts, *An Assessment of Evidence for Psychic Functioning*, CIA-RDP96-00791R000200070001-9, 2.
3. Utts, *An Assessment of Evidence for Psychic Functioning*, 2.
4. Utts, *An Assessment of Evidence for Psychic Functioning*, 1, 21.
5. Utts, *An Assessment of Evidence for Psychic Functioning*, 21.

29: INTUITION: THE SOUL'S LANGUAGE

1. Alain Rey, *Dictionnaire historique de la langue française*, vol. 1 (Le Robert, 2000), 1121.
2. Henri Bergson, *L'Énergie spirituelle* (Payot, 2012).
3. Marie-Estelle Couval, interview with the author.
4. Diane Hennacy Powell, MD, *The ESP Enigma* (Walker Publishing Company, 2009), 46.

30: SCIENCE VS. ANOMALIES

1. Guy Lyon Playfair, *Les jumeaux et le mystère de la télépathie* (InterÉditions, 2013).
2. Rupert Sheldrake, Hugo Godwin, and Simon Rockell, "A Filmed Experiment on Telephone Telepathy with the Nolan Sisters," *Journal of the Society for Psychical Research* 68 (2004): 168–72; Rupert Sheldrake and Pamela Smart, "Videotaped Experiments on Telephone Telepathy," *Journal of Parapsychology* 67 (June 2003): 187–206.
3. Diane Hennacy Powell, *The ESP Enigma: The Scientific Case for Psychic Phenomena* (Walker Books, 2008), 26.
4. Hennacy Powell, *The ESP Enigma*, 26.
5. D. J. Bem and C. Honorton, "Does Psi Exist? Replicable Evidence for an

Anomalous Process of Information Transfer," *Psychological Bulletin* 115, no. 1 (1994): 4–18.
6. Etzel Cardeña, "The Experimental Evidence for Parapsychological Phenomena: A Review," *American Psychologist* 73, no. 5 (July–August 2018): 663–77.
7. Etzel Cardeña, "A Call for an Open, Informed Study of All Aspects of Consciousness," *Frontiers in Human Neuroscience* 8 (January 2014): Article 17.

31: FIRSTHAND ACCOUNTS

1. INREES, "Écouter l'extraordinaire," https://www.inrees.com/.
2. Testimony published in *INREES Magazine*, no. 4 (Autumn 2009).
3. Testimony published in *INREES Magazine*, no. 6 (Spring 2010).
4. Testimony published in *INREES Magazine*, no. 7 (July 2010).
5. Testimony published in *INREES Magazine*, no. 7 (July 2010).
6. Testimony published in *INREES Magazine*, no. 5 (Winter 2009–2010).
7. Testimony published in *INREES Magazine*, no. 3 (Spring–Summer 2009).
8. Testimony published in *INREES Magazine*, no. 8 (September 2010).
9. Testimony published in *INREES Magazine*, no. 8 (September 2010).
10. American Psychiatric Association, *DSM-5: Manuel diagnostique et statistique des troubles mentaux*, translated by M.-A. Crocq and J.-D. Guelfi (Masson, 2015).
11. Paul Bernstein and Stéphane Allix, eds., *Expériences extraordinaires, le manuel clinique*, new ed. (InterÉditions, 2022), 20.
12. Stéphane Allix, *Un fantôme sur le divan* (Albin Michel, 2022).
13. Jeremy Narby, *Le Serpent cosmique* (Georg, 2006); Jeremy Narby and Francis Huxley, *Chamanes au fil du temps* (Albin Michel, 2002); Michael Harner, *La voie du chamane* (Mama, 2011); Michael Harner, *Caverne et Cosmos* (Mama, 2014); Kevin Turner, *Chamanes célestes* (Mama, 2017).

34: A NEW OPPORTUNITY

1. Michael Pollan, *How to Change Your Mind* (Penguin Press, 2018).
2. Lester Grinspoon and James B. Bakalar, *Psychedelic Drugs Reconsidered* (New York: Basic Books, 1979), 66.
3. Stanislav Grof, *The Way of the Psychonaut*, vol. 1 (Multidisciplinary Association for Psychedelic Studies, 2019).
4. Stéphane Allix, *Nos âmes oubliées* (Le Livre de Poche, 2022).

35: THE SHAMANS OF ANCIENT GREECE

1. R. Gordon Wasson, A. Hofmann, and C.A.P. Ruck, *The Road to Eleusis* (North Atlantic Books, 2008), 45.
2. Walter Burkert, *Ancient Mystery Cults* (Cambridge, MA: Harvard University Press, 1987), 11.
3. Burkert, *Ancient Mystery Cults*, 90.
4. Burkert, *Ancient Mystery Cults*, 90.
5. Burkert, *Ancient Mystery Cults*, 93.
6. Apuleius, *The Golden Ass* (New York: Penguin Classics, 1998), 183, https://ia801200.us.archive.org/15/items/TheGoldenAss_201509/TheGoldenAsspenguinClassics-Apuleius.pdf.

7. Plato, *Phaedo*, trans. Benjamin Jowett, https://classics.mit.edu/Plato/phaedo.html.
8. R. Gordon Wasson, A. Hofmann, and C.A.P. Ruck, *The Road to Eleusis*, 7, http://www.egodeath.com/eleusis.pdf.
9. Burkert, *Ancient Mystery Cults*, 21.
10. Burkert, *Ancient Mystery Cults*, 22.
11. Philodemus, *On Piety* (Oxford Clarendon Press, 1996), Part 1.
12. Joshua J. Mark, "The Eleusinian Mysteries: The Rites of Demeter," *World History Encyclopedia*, https://www.worldhistory.org/article/32/the-eleusinian-mysteries-the-rites-of-demeter/.
13. Paul Foucart, "Les Empereurs romains initiés aux mystères d'Éleusis," *Comptes rendus des séances de l'Académie des inscriptions et belles-lettres*, 36.6 (1892): 384, www.persee.fr/issue/crai_0065-0536_1892_num_36_6.
14. Foucart, "Les Empereurs romains initiés aux mystères d'Éleusis."
15. *De Natura Deorum (On the Nature of the Gods),* trans. Francis Brooks (London: Methuen, 1896), XLII, https://oll.libertyfund.org/titles/cicero-on-the-nature-of-the-gods.
16. Burkert, *Ancient Mystery Cults*, 69.
17. E. R. Dodds, *The Greeks and the Irrational* (Berkeley: University of California Press, 1951), 146, https://archive.org/stream/E.R.DoddsTheGreeksAndTheIrrational/E.R.Dodds_The%20Greeks%20and%20the%20Irrational_djvu.txt.
18. Karl Meuli, *Scythica* (Hermes, 1935).
19. Dodds, *The Greeks and the Irrational*, 140.
20. Wasson, Hofmann, and Ruck, *The Road to Eleusis*, 15.
21. Kevin Turner, *Chamanes célestes* (Mama, 2017); Michael Harner, *La voie du chamane* (Mama, 2011); Michael Harner, *Caverne et Cosmos* (Mama, 2014); Jeremy Narby and Francis Huxley, *Anthologie du chamanisme* (Albin Michel Poche, 2021).
22. Wasson, Hofmann, and Ruck, *The Road to Eleusis*, 13.

36: THE INITIATES

1. R. Gordon Wasson, A. Hofmann, and C.A.P. Ruck, *The Road to Eleusis*, 13, http://www.egodeath.com/eleusis.pdf.
2. Wasson, Hofmann, and Ruck, *The Road to Eleusis*, 19.
3. Albert Hofmann, *LSD: My Problem Child* (McGraw-Hill, 1980), https://maps.org/images/pdf/books/lsdmyproblemchild.pdf.
4. Hofmann, *LSD*, 12.
5. Hofmann, *LSD*, 12.
6. Hofmann, *LSD*, 13.
7. Apuleius, *The Golden Ass* (New York: Penguin Classics, 1998), 183, https://ia801200.us.archive.org/15/items/TheGoldenAss_201509/TheGoldenAsspenguinClassics-Apuleius.pdf.
8. Hofmann, *LSD*, 14.
9. Wasson, Hofmann, and Ruck, *The Road to Eleusis*, 11.
10. François Roustang, *Le Secret de Socrate pour changer la vie* (Odile Jacob, 2011), 164.
11. Plato, *Plato in Twelve Volumes, Vol. 9*, trans. Harold N. Fowler (Cambridge,

MA: Harvard University Press, 1925), https://www.perseus.tufts.edu/hopper/text?doc=urn:cts:greekLit:tlg0059.tlg012.perseus-eng1:244.
12. Plato, *Phaedo*, trans. Benjamin Jowett, https://classics.mit.edu/Plato/phaedo.html.

37: SURRENDERING OURSELVES IN ORDER TO LEARN

1. Stanislav Grof, *Realms of the Human Unconscious: Observations from LSD Research* (New York: Viking Press, 1975).
2. Christopher M. Bache, *LSD and the Mind of the Universe: Diamonds from Heaven* (Park Street Press, 2009).
3. Bache, *LSD and the Mind of the Universe*, 16.
4. Bache, *LSD and the Mind of the Universe*, 37.
5. Bache, *LSD and the Mind of the Universe*, 17.
6. Jean-Marie Jobelin, "Étude des transes et des états de conscience modifiés," DU thesis (Paris 8 University, 2022).

38: LSD

1. Christopher M. Bache, *LSD and the Mind of the Universe: Diamonds from Heaven* (Park Street Press, 2009), 38.
2. Bache, *LSD and the Mind of the Universe*, 29.
3. Bache, *LSD and the Mind of the Universe*, 37.

40: THE SOUL'S JOURNEY

1. Ram Dass with Rameshwar Das, *Being Ram Dass* (Boulder, CO: Sounds True, 2021), 358.
2. Ram Dass, "Loving & Dying," episode 176, https://beherenownetwork.com/ram-dass-here-and-now-ep-176-loving-dying/.
3. Chögyam Trungpa, *Transcending Madness: The Experience of the Six Bardos* (Boston and London: Shambhala, 1992).
4. Trungpa, *Transcending Madness*, 101.

41: DETACHMENT

1. John Welwood, *Toward a Psychology of Awakening* (Boston: Shambhala, 2000), 212.
2. *Ram Dass, Going Home*, directed by Derek Peck (Netflix, 2018).
3. Stéphane Allix, *Le Test* (Le Livre de Poche, 2018).
4. Ram Dass, "Loving & Dying," episode 176.
5. Ram Dass, "Loving & Dying," episode 176.

42: KEEPING AN OPEN CONNECTION WITH OUR SOULS

1. John Welwood, *Toward a Psychology of Awakening* (Boston: Shambhala, 2000), 194.
2. K. A. Garrison, T. A. Zeffiro, D. Scheinost, R. T. Constable, and J. A. Brewer, "Meditation Leads to Reduced Default Mode Network Activity Beyond an Active Task," *Cognitive, Affective & Behavioral Neuroscience* 15, no. 3 (2015): 712–20.

3. Steven Laureys, *La méditation, c'est bon pour le cerveau* (Odile Jacob, 2019), 79.
4. Christopher M. Bache, *LSD and the Mind of the Universe: Diamonds from Heaven* (Park Street Press, 2009), 13.
5. Ram Dass, *Still Here* (New York: Riverhead, 2000), 30.
6. Yongey Mingyur Rinpoche with Helen Tworkov, *In Love with the World: A Monk's Journey Through the Bardos of Living and Dying* (New York: Spiegel & Grau, 2019), 164.
7. Stéphane Allix, *Un fantôme sur le divan* (Albin Michel, 2022), 28.

About the Author

Stéphane Allix is a journalist who has reported from the front lines of war, particularly the Afghan war, and the boundary between life and death. He is the founder of the Institute for Research on Extraordinary Experiences (INREES) and *Inexploré* magazine, and the creator and presenter of the *Enquêtes extraordinaires* series on France's National TV channel 6. He has published several bestselling books, including *The Test* and *When I Was Someone Else*.

About the Translator

Gretchen Schmid is the translator of several novels and works of nonfiction for both children and adults from French into English, including *Kannjawou* by Lyonel Trouillot, nominated for an Albertine Prize, and *Make Me Famous* by Maud Ventura. She holds a degree in French literature from Columbia University and studied translation at New York University. She lives in New York and works in publishing, with a particular focus on literature in translation.